Today's Best Classroom Management Strategies

Paths to Positive Discipline

C. M. Charles
San Diego State University, Emeritus

Boston   New York   San Francisco
Mexico City   Montreal   Toronto   London   Madrid   Munich   Paris
Hong Kong   Singapore   Tokyo   Cape Town   Sydney

Senior Editor: Arnis E. Burvikovs
Editorial Assistant: Erin Reilly
Marketing Manager: Erica DeLuca
Editorial Production Service: Omegatype Typography, Inc.
Composition Buyer: Linda Cox
Manufacturing Buyer: Linda Morris
Electronic Composition: Omegatype Typography, Inc.
Photo Researcher: Omegatype Typography, Inc.
Cover Administrator: Elena Sidorova

For related titles and support materials, visit our online catalog at www.ablongman.com.

Between the time website information is gathered and then published, it is not unusual for some sites to have closed. Also, the transcription of URLs can result in typographical errors. The publisher would appreciate notification where these errors occur so that they may be corrected in subsequent editions.

ISBN-13: 978-0-205-51070-2   ISBN-10: 0-205-51070-1

Library of Congress Cataloging-in-Publication Data

Charles, C. M.
   Today's best classroom management strategies : Paths to positive discipline / C. M. Charles.
      p.   cm.
   Includes bibliographical references and index.
   ISBN 0-205-51070-1
   1. School discipline.   2. Classroom management.   I. Title.
   LB3012.C465   2007
   371.5—dc22
                                                                              2006050189

Printed in the United States of America

6 7 8 9 10   V0CR   16 15 14 13

Photo Credits: p. 57, Photo by Jay Van Rensselaer; p. 105, Copyright 2004 by Arthur Meyersen; p. 162, Photo by Heather Flamand.

About the Author

C. M. Charles was a public school teacher from 1953 to 1959, then moved into higher education and held professorships at the University of New Mexico, Teachers College Columbia University, Pepperdine University, Universidade Federal do Marahao (Brazil), and San Diego State University, where he is now professor emeritus. At San Diego State, Charles directed innovative programs in teacher education and five times received outstanding professor and distinguished teaching awards. He also served on several occasions as advisor in teacher education and curriculum to the governments of Peru and Brazil. Charles has authored or coauthored more than 25 books, many of which have attracted wide audiences in the United States and abroad, with translations into several foreign languages. Those dealing most directly with school discipline are *Teacher's Petit Piaget* (1972); *The Synergetic Classroom: Joyful Teaching and Gentle Discipline* (2000); *Essential Elements of Effective Discipline* (2002); *Classroom Management for Middle-Grades Teachers* (2004); *Elementary Classroom Management* (fifth edition, 2008); *Building Classroom Discipline* (ninth edition, 2008), and *Today's Best Classroom Management Strategies: Paths to Positive Discipline* (2008).

MyLabSchool

mylabschool Where the classroom comes to life! is a collection of online tools for your success in this course, on your licensure exams, and in your teaching career. Visit www.mylabschool.com to access the following:

- Video footage of real-life classrooms, with opportunities for you to reflect on the videos and offer your own thoughts and suggestions for applying theory to practice
- An extensive archive of text and multimedia cases that provide valuable perspectives on real classrooms and real teaching challenges
- Allyn & Bacon's Lesson and Portfolio Builder application, which includes an integrated state standards correlation tool
- Research paper assistance using Research Navigator™, which provides access to three exclusive databases of credible and reliable source material: EBSCO's ContentSelect Academic Journal Database, The *New York Times* Search by Subject Archive, and "Best of the Web" Link Library
- Career Center with resources for Praxis exams and licensure preparation, professional portfolio development, and job search and interview techniques

Contents

4 Strategy 4. **Establishing Trust and Civility**   **52**

Establishing and Maintaining an Atmosphere of Trust and Civility in Your Classroom

5 Strategy 5. **Intervening Positively**   **70**

Dealing with Misbehavior in a Positive and Productive Manner that Maintains Student Cooperation and Preserves Good Relationships

8

Strategy 8. Improving Relationships and Communication   127

**Working toward Positive Relationships and Effective Communication
among Teacher, Students, and Parents and Guardians**

Preface

Today most teachers face an ongoing struggle against *inappropriate student behavior*—or *misbehavior,* as it is often called—which interferes with teaching, weakens learning, and engenders negative attitudes toward school and education. This misbehavior occurs in degrees of seriousness. It may be relatively benign, as when Julian disrupts lessons by talking out or Alicia gazes out the window instead of doing her assignment as directed. Such behavior produces no trauma, but it does hinder progress. At a more serious level, Heather refuses to follow directions and talks back disrespectfully, or Tony aggressively bullies weaker members of the class. If such behavior occurs only occasionally, teachers can curtail it and keep students fairly well on track. But when it consumes significant amounts of time each day, teachers and students alike become dispirited and discontented with school.

If you are now teaching, you probably understand all too well the debilitating effects of classroom misbehavior. If you are preparing yourself for a career in teaching, you can anticipate the reality that classroom discipline is, for many teachers, the major obstacle to ongoing success. Yet it can be dealt with pleasantly and successfully, as will be shown in the chapters that follow.

PURPOSE OF THIS BOOK

The purpose of this book is to help teachers develop personalized systems of discipline that provide safe, productive, and enjoyable classrooms. It addresses two major tasks:

- Developing and putting in place a discipline framework that promotes safety, motivation, and goodwill in the classroom
- Increasing the effectiveness of the discipline framework by aligning it with students' needs, traits, and sociocultural realities

The successful completion of these two tasks produces a comprehensive, empowering system of discipline that optimizes student opportunity and personal growth. In addition, the system will be harmonious with the teacher's personality and philosophy. The resulting system, when implemented, will promote the following:

- A style of teaching and relating with students that attracts and inspires
- Tactics that prevent the occurrence of misbehavior
- Satisfaction of students' needs
- Growth in students' ability to relate in a positive manner with classmates and teachers
- Growth in students' sense of responsibility

- Growth in students' *moral intelligence,* or their awareness of universal values of goodness and the desire to live in accordance with them
- Teacher ability to stop misbehavior in a positive manner while helping students make choices that will serve them better in the future

UNDERTAKING THE TWO MAJOR TASKS

The tasks relating to basic structure and to alignment are addressed here as Task 1 and Task 2. Five chapters in the book are devoted to each task, with each chapter presenting and illuminating a major strategy in classroom discipline.

Task 1: Establishing the Basic Framework for Effective Classroom Discipline

Guidance for completing Task 1 is provided in Chapters 1 through 5. These chapters show how to install an effective discipline plan by employing the following five strategies, all of which are easy to implement and maintain:

1. *Provide a comprehensive, empowering approach to discipline that optimizes student success and personal growth.* This strategy calls for a particular vision of discipline that (1) sees discipline as a major strand of teaching whose purpose is to keep students safe while increasing their opportunities for success in school and (2) can be personalized to promote learning and satisfaction through addressing student needs, removing conditions that foster misbehavior, providing engaging teaching, and promoting civil, responsible behavior. Guidance for undertaking this effort is presented in Chapter 1.

2. *Identify steps that can be taken in advance to reduce the likelihood of misbehavior in the classroom.* This is one of the easiest yet most effective strategies available for curtailing disruptive behavior in school. Chapter 2 identifies a number of conditions that can lead to student misbehavior and explains how to eliminate them or soften their effects.

3. *Specify how students are expected to conduct themselves in the classroom along with what routines they are to follow when engaging in class activities.* The power of this strategy in preventing misbehavior is just now being recognized. When students know how to conduct themselves in various class matters and when they have practiced the associated behaviors and routines, the incidence of misbehavior drops dramatically. Chapter 3 provides a number of suggestions for implementing this strategy.

4. *Establish and maintain an atmosphere of trust and civility in the classroom.* Establishing trust and developing civility comprise a relatively new strategy in classroom discipline that aims at creating a helpful, nonthreatening class atmosphere that fosters trust and civil behavior. As explained in Chapter 4, these qualities are at the core of *social morality,* which consists of universal values of goodness and the desire to live in accordance with them.

5. *Identify and master tactics for intervening when students misbehave—tactics that (a) stop the misbehavior, (b) help students learn to behave in a responsible manner that brings success, and (c) maintain and promote positive attitudes, cooperation, and effective personal relations.* This cluster of tactics is employed when students break rules or agreements. Chapter 5 presents a number of suggestions from respected authorities concerning what teachers should say and do when students misbehave, emphasizing that the disruptions can be springboards for teaching students how to conduct themselves appropriately and make better behavior choices in the future.

Task 2: Enhancing the Basic Framework

The first five strategies yield an effective system of discipline that can be easily implemented and managed. Chapters 6 through 10 explain how to bring the discipline system into alignment with student traits and needs. This produces a highly professional system of discipline and is accomplished through the application of five additional strategies:

6. *Align instruction and discipline with students' traits, needs, interests, and social, cultural, and economic realities.* For maximal effectiveness, the school program should be organized to work in harmony with student nature and social realities. In the past, teaching and discipline too often conflicted with student needs and traits, causing students to take offense and become defiant when faced with demands they consider unreasonable or punitive. Chapter 6 presents information for making instruction more intriguing, inviting, and motivating while allowing students to expand their natural capabilities.

7. *Establish a sense of togetherness among members of the class, with attention to safety, belonging, cooperation, and mutual support.* For many years, there has been a growing belief that, in general, students behave better and learn more when taught in classes that promote consideration, cooperation, and mutual support. Chapter 7 presents suggestions for establishing classes that function as communities of learners, where cooperation and helpfulness receive more emphasis than individual learning and competition. To move in that direction, teachers should approach students as allies, help them connect with each other personally, and involve them meaningfully in the operation of the class.

8. *Take steps to increase the quality of communication and personal relationships among the teacher, students, and parents/guardians.* Discipline problems usually fade to a minimum when teachers and students relate to each other effectively and communicate in a way that engenders cooperation and confidence. Chapter 8 presents suggestions for teaching students the basic behaviors involved in effective relations and communication—behaviors that promote cooperation, a sense of dignity, enjoyment, and progress.

9. *Provide ongoing assistance to help students develop an internal sense of personal responsibility.* Some of today's most effective discipline programs are based on promoting student responsibility for their own behavior and for the class in

general. Chapter 9 presents suggestions for improving the level of responsibility in students, to the point that they conduct themselves appropriately not for rewards but because they consider it the right thing to do. This is accomplished by interacting with students in ways that cause them to reflect deeply about the kinds of people they want to be and the kinds of lives they want to lead and then helping them create plans of action that lead toward their goals.

10. *Develop and use special discipline tactics that help students with neurological-based behavior (NBB) prosper in school.* Most students in school respond well to the strategies of discipline reviewed so far. However, not all will be able to do so. It is estimated that about one in five students exhibits one or more mental health conditions that affect behavior. Usually, the condition involves differences in the way their brains work due to chemical imbalances, congenital brain differences, brain injuries, or brain diseases. The atypical behavior these students sometimes exhibit is loosely referred to as *neurological-based behavior,* or *NBB.* While students with NBB present special challenges for teachers, a good deal is known about reducing their episodes of disruptive behavior and helping them learn to behave in more advantageous ways. Suggestions based on this knowledge are presented in Chapter 10.

TACTICS WITHIN THE STRATEGIES

The 10 major strategies, in combination, constitute a high-quality personalized system of discipline. Their power, however, lies in the tactics they employ—the specific acts teachers and students perform. A review of this book's Contents section provides an overview of the tactics considered most useful within each strategy.

A BRIEF REVIEW OF ADVANCES IN MODERN CLASSROOM DISCIPLINE

Fifty years ago, practically everyone thought of discipline as what teachers did to make unruly students behave in school. It was accepted that discipline involved control tactics such as reprimands, admonishments, scoldings, and punishments that teachers and administrators would apply. Generally speaking, parents supported the use of these tactics and reinforced them at home.

Many people still think of discipline that way, although that older image is fading as new and more effective tactics appear. The new ideas emerged slowly at first but have gathered momentum and now are appearing regularly. To illustrate the progressive movement in school discipline and to identify concepts that are lasting over time, here is a review of what has happened in school discipline since the 1950s. (Citations can be found in the Bibliography at the end of the book.)

1951. *Group dynamics—the first modern approach to discipline.* In 1951, psychiatrist Fritz Redl and educational psychologist William Wattenberg explained their concept of *group dynamics,* or forces that cause students, when in groups, to behave somewhat differently than they do when by themselves. Redl and Wattenberg (1951) identified kinds of behavior teachers can expect of students in groups and suggested how teachers should react to them. Redl and Wattenberg's approach proved too cumbersome for teachers to use, but some of their ideas on group forces and roles of students and teachers have had lasting impact.

1954. *Reinforcement theory—a scientific basis for shaping desired behavior.* In 1954, psychologist B. F. Skinner described how the principles of reinforcement, clarified through experiments with laboratory animals, could be applied to teaching and the shaping of behavior. His contributions found wide acceptance among educators and provided the theory and tactics for *reinforcement* and *behavior modification,* which still play prominent roles in education and elsewhere.

1969. *Behavior as choice and classroom meetings—insights into why students behave as they do and how concerns can be addressed in class.* In 1969, psychiatrist William Glasser published his highly influential book *Schools without Failure,* which highlighted the debilitating effects of failure, introduced the concept of behavior as *conscious student choice* (rather than reflexive responses to conditions in the classroom), and promoted the use of classroom meetings, which are incorporated in most discipline systems today. Glasser's ideas are discussed in Chapters 6, 7, and 9.

1971. *Congruent communication—how to speak effectively with students.* In 1971, teacher and psychologist Haim Ginott urged teachers to use a type of communication he found to have powerful effects on student attitude and cooperation. He called his central concept *congruent communication,* a style of speaking in which teachers refrain from moralizing or lecturing students; instead, they address situations in terms of what has been done wrong and how it can be made right, without referring to the character of the students (e.g., saying "I am troubled by the way I hear people speaking to each other. We use good manners in this class," rather than saying "Jimmy, you are being very inconsiderate about Aldo's feelings."). Ginott's ideas, discussed in Chapter 8, are evident in most of today's systems of discipline.

1971. *Classroom and lesson management—tactics that prevent misbehavior.* Also in 1971, educational psychologist Jacob Kounin published his research findings on the discipline tactics used by highly successful teachers. He found that teachers' abilities to manage lessons and attend to class events simultaneously were significantly more effective than punishment or other discipline tactics in use at that time. His findings strongly influenced subsequent systems of discipline and are reflected in the suggestions provided by Harry Wong and Ronald Morrish in Chapter 3.

1972. *Students' prime need for belonging—the core requirement for proper behavior and how to address it.* In 1972, psychiatrist Rudolf Dreikurs pinpointed students' need for belonging as a prime motive in school behavior (Dreikurs and Cassel, 1995). He contended that students' misbehavior occurred in inverse proportion to students' sense of importance and belonging in the class. Dreikurs identified and described four categories of misbehavior that are likely to occur when the need for belonging is not being met—trying to gain attention, trying to exert control, trying to exact revenge, and withdrawing—all of which tend to disappear when students believe they are valued in the class. Dreikurs's approach is no longer used in its entirety, but his ideas have been incorporated into most of today's popular systems.

1976. *Assertive discipline—taking charge in the classroom.* In 1976, teachers Lee Canter and Marlene Canter published *Assertive Discipline: A Take-Charge Approach for Today's Educator.* The work provided the first carefully considered total approach to discipline. It stressed teachers' right to teach without interruption and students' right to learn in a calm, orderly environment. It held that students could behave properly when they wished, and it showed how to apply a series of increasingly uncomfortable conditions when students misbehaved and continued to do so. The book was an immediate hit, and assertive discipline became hugely popular and remained so for more than 20 years. The Canters' suggestions, based on behavioral psychology, have been supplanted by tactics more cognitive in nature that focus on student values and choices.

1986. *Control theory—using influence rather than power to achieve results with students.* In 1986, psychiatrist William Glasser initiated a movement he believed would produce significantly better behavior in school. Now referred to as *choice theory,* his approach emphasizes helping students make behavioral choices that serve them well, while attending to five needs that motivate school behavior—needs for safety, esteem and belonging, power, freedom, and fun. Glasser's suggestions attracted a very large following and led the way among approaches that challenged and surpassed assertive discipline. Glasser's ideas are described further in Chapters 6 and 7.

1987. *Body language and "working the crowd"—teacher actions that keep students involved.* In 1987, psychologist Fredric Jones introduced an approach to discipline that emphasized five clusters of tactics—the effective use of body language by the teacher, providing help efficiently, using incentives to motivate students, interacting regularly with all students, and keeping students actively engaged in the classroom. More recently, Jones has popularized a style of teaching called *Say See Do teaching,* which keeps students actively involved in lessons (Jones, 2001). Jones's ideas are featured in Chapter 6.

1988. *Dignity—the key ingredient in all discipline interactions.* In 1988, teacher educator Richard Curwin and school psychologist Allen Mendler pinpointed personal dignity as a key element in classroom discipline, asserting that any approach to discipline, in order to be effective, must allow students to maintain their personal sense of dignity, or self-respect. This tactic, which reduces student defensiveness and helps promote positive relations, is included in all systems of discipline introduced in the past two decades. Curwin and Mendler's ideas are featured in Chapter 5.

1989. *Cooperative discipline—teachers and students working together for better behavior.* In 1989, educational consultant Linda Albert published a new approach to discipline called *cooperative discipline,* which emphasizes students and teachers working together in a cooperative manner to address class concerns, including discipline (Albert, 1996). Albert provides a great number of suggestions that teachers have found helpful, most of which are related to establishing the three Cs of helping students make *connections* with others, *contribute* to the class, and see themselves as *capable.* Albert's ideas are discussed in Chapter 5.

1989. *Self-discipline—the primary goal of discipline.* A second major work to appear in 1989 was a book by psychologist Thomas Gordon called *Discipline That Works: Promoting Self-Discipline in Children.* Gordon made three important contributions to the discourse on classroom discipline: (1) the nature and use of noncontrolling influence techniques, (2) the use of no-lose conflict resolution, and (3) avoiding roadblocks to communication with students, such as lecturing, admonishing, and giving advice. He maintained that the most powerful influence teachers have over students is nonauthoritative, exerted in forms such as setting good examples, practicing attentive listening, and providing personal attention. Gordon's ideas are featured in Chapter 8.

1993. *Classroom meetings—bringing meetings into the class routine.* The concept of class meetings was first popularized by William Glasser in 1969. For a time, the meetings were called "Glasser circles." More recently, education consultants Jane Nelsen and Lynn Lott (2006) provided many details that helped make classroom meetings more effective and easier to use. Classroom meetings are now an integral part of virtually all of the newer approaches to discipline. Nelsen and Lott's suggestions on classroom meetings are featured in Chapter 7.

1994. *Inner discipline—developing an inner sense of self-control.* In 1994, educational consultant Barbara Coloroso introduced tactics for helping students develop *inner discipline,* which is manifested in self-control (Coloroso, 2002). Teachers can provide what Coloroso calls the "gift of inner discipline" by establishing a sense of trust and responsibility in the classroom and by giving students the power to make decisions about many of the problems they encounter. Students are then expected to manage the outcomes of their decisions, even when the outcomes don't turn out as expected. Coloroso's ideas are featured in Chapters 1 and 5.

1998. *Choice theory—updated advice on how best to obtain positive student behavior in school.* In 1998, psychiatrist William Glasser modified his control theory and changed its name to *choice theory,* contending that we can control no one's behavior except our own and that we cannot successfully force students to do anything they don't want to do. Glasser (1998a) teaches that student behavior is not automatically determined by external causes but rather by what goes on inside them. Accordingly, he says, the best way to improve student behavior is by helping students clarify what a quality school experience would be and then planning choices that would help them move toward that goal. This view has been incorporated into virtually all currently popular systems of discipline.

1998. *Pragmatic classroom management—it's the details that matter.* Also in 1998, teachers Harry Wong and Rosemary Wong published their book *The First Days of School: How to Be an Effective Teacher.* This book has subsequently become the biggest-selling education book of all time. The Wongs contend that the main problem in teaching is not poor discipline but poor classroom management. They show how teachers can teach classroom procedures and routines so that students follow them automatically; this simple tactic eliminates most class misbehavior. The Wongs, whose ideas are featured in Chapter 3, stress that effective teachers spend most of the first two weeks of school teaching students class expectations and routines.

2000. *Synergetic discipline—energizing the class for better learning and behavior.* In 2000, teacher educator C. M. Charles published *The Synergetic Classroom: Joyful Teaching and Gentle Discipline,* in which he explained the phenomenon of synergy and how it can be used, when desired, to energize classes. During periods of heightened synergy, student behavior becomes more purposeful and efficient. Charles's ideas on the role of synergy in discipline are presented in Chapter 2.

2000. *Real discipline—how the most effective teachers maintain good class behavior.* In 2000, behavior specialist Ronald Morrish published *With All Due Respect,* a book that describes three things that teachers can realistically do to establish good discipline in their classes: (1) train students to follow teacher directions, through presenting clear expectations and insisting that students comply with legitimate adult authority; (2) teach students the skills, attitudes, and knowledge needed for cooperation, proper behavior, and responsibility; and (3) increasingly offer students opportunities to make choices that take into account the needs and rights of others. When students misbehave, they simply redo the behavior properly. Morrish's work is featured in Chapter 3.

2001. *Moral intelligence—the internal desire to do what is right.* In 2001, educational consultant Michele Borba published *Building Moral Intelligence: The Seven Essential Virtues That Teach Kids to Do the Right Thing.* Borba describes *moral intelligence* as (1) the ability to distinguish right from wrong, (2) the establishment and maintenance of strong ethical convictions, and (3) the willingness to act on those convictions in an honorable way. She provides tactics teachers can use for building these qualities in students. Borba's work is featured in Chapter 4.

2001. *Classrooms as communities—one for all and all for one.* In 2001, educational consultant Alfie Kohn published *Beyond Discipline: From Compliance to Community,* in which he soundly criticized teaching and discipline approaches that do things *to* students without involving them as partners in the process. He believes students learn best when they work together cooperatively, support each other, and participate fully in dealing with class concerns. Doing these things helps students become more self-directing and more concerned with the welfare of others. Kohn's approach is featured in Chapter 7.

2001. *Raising responsibility—helping students to monitor and control their own behavior.* In 2001, educator and consultant Marvin Marshall published

Discipline without Stress, Punishments, or Rewards: How Teachers and Parents Promote Responsibility and Learning. In that book, he describes how to teach students without coercion to (1) understand four levels of social development and relate the levels to behavior and learning, (2) identify the level of their personal behavior at any given time, and (3) select better courses of action, when necessary, from self-perceptions or from guided choices the teacher offers if disruptions continue. Marshall's approach is featured in Chapter 9.

2001. *Hidden rules—understanding the value systems that function in various socioeconomic groups.* In her 2001 book, *A Framework for Understanding Poverty,* educational consultant Ruby Payne explains the hidden rules that each socioeconomic class follows to help it survive—rules that are seldom understood by people from other socioeconomic classes. Payne's depiction of the hidden rules of poverty greatly helps teachers understand the behavior of students from poverty and work with those students more effectively. Payne's contributions are featured in Chapter 6.

2002. *Same-side strategy—students and teachers working on the same side to achieve class goals.* In a 2002 website article entitled "What Is Win–Win Discipline?" psychologist and teacher educator Spencer Kagan introduced the same-side approach as a cornerstone of Win–Win Discipline, a new discipline system he was developing. In 2004, together with Patricia Kyle and Sally Scott, he published the book *Win–Win Discipline,* in which he explains how teachers and students can work together to help students develop long-term, self-managed responsibility. The approach emphasizes same-side, collaborative solutions and learned responsibility. Kagan, Kyle, and Scott's ideas are featured in Chapter 7.

2004. *Self-restitution theory—improving behavior by making things right within oneself.* In her 2004 book *It's All About We: Rethinking Discipline Using Restitution,* educational consultant Diane Gossen introduced *self-restitution* as an activity in which students who have behaved inappropriately are encouraged in a needs-satisfying environment to reflect on their behavior, identify the need that prompted it, and create a new way of behaving that exemplifies the responsible person they want to be. This is the first system to place emphasis on misbehaving students' learning how to make things right within themselves and improving their behavior from the process.

CONCERNING THE CONSULTANTS FEATURED IN THIS BOOK

The author has secured the thoughtful collaboration of most of the authorities who have created and popularized recent approaches to classroom discipline. This collaboration was sought as a means of ensuring that the authorities' ideas and terminology would be presented accurately. Those whose collaboration was obtained are referred to in various chapters as "Consultants," which indicates that they worked with the author and approved the content and wording used in presenting their contributions.

ACKNOWLEDGMENTS

The author gratefully acknowledges the collaboration and helpful contributions from the following people:

Consultant Discipline Authorities

Linda Albert, cooperative discipline; Michele Borba, moral intelligence; Barbara Coloroso, inner discipline, expert in countering bullying; Paula Cook, neurological-based behavior; Richard Curwin, discipline with dignity; Ed Ford, President, Responsible Thinking Process, Inc.; P. M. Forni, Director, The Civility Initiative at Johns Hopkins University; William Glasser, Institute for Reality (now called William Glasser Institute); Thomas Gordon, *Discipline That Works*; Diane Gossen, Self-Restitution Theory; Fred Jones, *Tools for Teaching*; Spencer Kagan, *Win–Win Discipline*; Alfie Kohn, *Beyond Discipline: From Compliance to Community*; Lynn Lott, *Positive Discipline in the Classroom*; Marvin Marshall, *Discipline without Stress*; Allen Mendler, *Discipline with Dignity*; Ronald Morrish, real discipline; Jane Nelsen, *Positive Discipline in the Classroom*; and Harry Wong and Rosemary Wong, *The First Days of School*

Critical Reviewers and Other Contributors

Gail Charles, Teacher, Middle School Spanish and Drama; Ruth Charles, Teacher, Elementary School; Allison Pryor, Student Teacher, Elementary School; Cynthia Roberts, Teacher, Elementary School; Gail Senter, Faculty, California State University San Marcos; Rachel Space, Student Teacher, High School Communication and Drama; Deborah Sund, Teacher, Elementary School; Eileen VanWie, Professor, New Mexico State University; and Manuel Vigil, Student Teacher, High School Biology

Reviewers for This Edition

Deborah Gartland, Towson University; Julie K. Jackson, The University of Texas at Austin; John E. Kesner, Georgia State University; Julie L. Reagan, SUNY Potsdam; and Edward Vockell, Purdue University, Calumet

Editors at Allyn & Bacon

Arnis E. Burvikovs, Senior Education Editor, and Erin Reilly, Editorial Assistant

Optimizing Student Success

Developing and Implementing a Comprehensive, Optimizing Approach to Classroom Discipline

You can organize a personal system of discipline, founded on professionalism and ethics, that addresses student needs, controls conditions that foster misbehavior, provides engaging teaching, and promotes civil, responsible behavior.

Chapter Preview

This chapter explains how teachers can organize personal systems of discipline that greatly enhance students' likelihood of success at school. Five guiding principles are provided for organizing such systems. In addition, notes on professionalism, ethics, and certain legal concerns for teachers are provided. Examples of efforts by three students preparing to become teachers and two sample discipline plans used by teachers in service are presented for reflection and further guidance.

DEVELOPING A PERSONAL SYSTEM OF DISCIPLINE

Comprehensive classroom discipline relies on a group of strategies that work together to optimize students' opportunity for success. Patrick Traynor (2005) says that effective discipline depends on (1) teachers' ability to recognize maladaptive behavior in the classroom, (2) their skill in selecting and implementing effective intervention tactics, and (3) their having a positive "can do" attitude toward any discipline procedure they try to use. One could add "prevention of misbehavior" to Traynor's list, as well. In order to work best, the discipline approach you use should be based on the best information available and made congruent with your personality and philosophy and the social realities your students regularly experience.

The best way to obtain a personalized system of discipline for your classes is to construct it yourself, using the best information available. While excellent ready-made discipline systems are available, they cannot adequately address all the concerns that exist in your teaching situation. This book presents state-of-the-art strategies and tactics in discipline. Among them, you will find numerous excellent ideas that you can incorporate into a system that best suits your needs. Guidance for beginning that process is presented here.

FIVE GUIDING PRINCIPLES IN BUILDING A PERSONAL SYSTEM OF DISCIPLINE

Five principles for organizing a personal system of discipline are presented for your consideration. Used together, they will ensure that your discipline system meets established standards of the profession while providing the best services for your students. These principles provide a framework for constructing a high-quality system of discipline. To that framework, you can attach ideas from today's most influential authorities in classroom discipline, as presented in this book.

Principle 1: Present yourself, conduct yourself, and interact with students and others in a professional manner. Make sure you know and put into practice the following:
- Standards of professionalism
- Ethical considerations
- Legal requirements

Principle 2: Clarify how you want your students to behave, now and in the future. You may identify attitudes and behaviors such as these:
- Show a positive attitude.
- Behave considerately toward others.
- Take initiative.
- Show self-direction.
- Make a strong effort to learn.
- Assume personal responsibility for behavior.

Principle 3: Establish and maintain classroom conditions that help students enjoy and profit from their educational experience. You may wish to give attention to these factors:
- Good environment for learning
- Compatibility with students' nature, needs, interests, and preferences

- Sense of community
- Positive attention
- Good communication
- Consideration for others
- Attention to special needs
- Trust
- Interesting activities
- Student knowledge of expectations
- Continual helpfulness
- Preservation of dignity
- Minimizing causes of misbehavior
- Teacher charisma
- Student involvement in planning the program

Principle 4. Help students learn to conduct themselves responsibly. Consider the following:
- Identify and reduce the known causes of misbehavior.
- Build a sense of community in your classroom that emphasizes collaboration, joint decision making, responsibility, and consideration for others.
- Communicate clearly and effectively with students. Keep them fully informed.
- Speak with students in ways that build dignity and invite cooperation.
- Work in a collaborative way with students, and allow them to help make class decisions.
- Reach a set of agreements about how the class is to function and how you and the students will conduct yourselves.
- Build group spirit and otherwise energize the class.
- Bring parents and guardians into a meaningful partnership with your class and program.
- Use activities that increase student self-direction and responsibility.
- Resolve class problems effectively and fairly while maintaining good personal relationships.

Principle 5. Intervene supportively and productively when common disruptions, neurological-based behavior, and/or serious actions occur in the classroom.
- Understand the nature of helpful interventions, and devise approaches that are suited to you and your students.
- Develop a repertoire of helpful things to say and do when students misbehave.
- Identify tactics and words you want to avoid using.
- Establish a clear procedure for dealing with misbehavior. Involve students in developing the procedure, and then follow the procedure consistently.
- Help students accept responsibility for their behavior and commit to better behavior in the future.

NOTES ON PROFESSIONALISM, ETHICS, AND LEGALITIES

Many teachers, especially those just beginning, do not have a clear understanding of how they are expected to conduct themselves in school. The following material is provided to help you—and your discipline system—comply with professional, ethical, and legal expectations and requirements.

Professional standards for teachers have been set forth by the National Education Association (NEA, 1975) and various other groups (see Goorian and Brown, 2002). The following list of requirements and expectations is representative but not exhaustive. Some relate to ethical or professional concerns, while others indicate legal requirements and safeguards.

- Do not intentionally expose students to embarrassment or disparagement. (ethics)
- Use appropriate language for the educational setting, following correct speech patterns and completely avoiding obscenities. (professionalism and ethics)
- Treat everyone in the school setting with courtesy and respect. (professionalism and ethics)
- Dress professionally as an adult in a professional situation. (professional consideration)
- Do not disclose information about students obtained in the course of professional service unless disclosure serves a compelling professional purpose or is required by law. (legal requirement)
- Exercise reasonable care to protect students from harm. (legal requirement)
- Be vigilant for signs that students might harm themselves. Pay attention to what they do, say, and write. Observe them for changes in behavior. Speak to the school counselor or administrator if you have concerns. (legal requirement)
- Report it if you suspect that one of your students is being abused. You should also know state law for mandated reporters, not just school policy. Follow the school guidelines to familiarize yourself with signs of abuse. If you are suspicious, report your concerns to the school counselor or administrator. (legal requirement)
- Don't allow yourself to be alone in the classroom with a student unless you are in plain sight of others. If you are male, refrain from touching students other than on the hands or arms or with pats to the head or shoulder. (professional safeguard)
- If students frustrate or anger you, never respond by touching or grabbing them. Never throw anything, no matter how strongly you are provoked. (professional safeguard)

You should carefully and sincerely explain the following to your classes, adjusting the language to their development level:

One of our main goals in this class is to help you take positive charge of your life. School is for your benefit as a human being, and I will do all I can to make it valuable for you. That is my desire and my responsibility as a teacher. But you have responsibilities to live up to, as well, and as you do so, you will find that school becomes more interesting, you enjoy it more, and it brings you greater satisfaction. Your primary responsibilities are to do your best, respect the rights of others in the class, and be helpful to others when you can. If you do these things, you will enjoy success and pleasure. If you should happen, at times, to behave in a way that is not beneficial to you and the class, I will help you see what you have done wrong and show you a better way of behaving. No punishment will be involved. As we spend more time together, we will look for ways for you to assume more responsibility. As we work together, I will never do anything to embarrass or insult you. My goal is for all members of this class to develop self-control and the desire to do what is right. Those two things will make it easier for you to deal with problems you encounter. If at any time, you have difficulty in this class, I will do my best to help you.

ONGOING ATTENTION TO THE FIVE PRINCIPLES

As you move forward in organizing a personal discipline system, you will find it helpful to keep in mind the following guidelines and criteria:

1. *Use discipline that is optimizing.* This means identifying discipline tactics that open up opportunities for students, promote learning, develop responsible behavior, and increase enjoyment. Think of misbehavior as *mistakes* that are correctible. Find ways to prevent such mistakes. When they occur, address them in ways that maintain students' dignity while promoting their ability to make better behavior choices in the future.

2. *Look for ways to prevent misbehavior.* Preventing misbehavior is much easier than having to deal with it after it occurs. As will be explained in later chapters, prevention involves these tasks:
   - Addressing conditions that foster misbehavior
   - Teaching in ways that are harmonious with student needs and preferences
   - Obtaining same-side cooperation from students in deciding on and working through many matters of class life
   - Teaching students how to relate with others, behave ethically, and show responsibility

3. *Clarify and communicate the goals of your approach to discipline.* Work with students and help them understand the goals and procedures of discipline that optimize opportunity. Students become more cooperative when they know you are working for their benefit and understand how you are going about it. You might mention outcomes of good discipline (with examples, as needed), such as willing student involvement, friendliness, cooperation, effort, good manners, enjoyable relationships, and responsible conduct—all of which make life in school more rewarding and enjoyable. Ask students if they understand the goals and will work together with you in achieving them.

4. Align your discipline and instructional programs with student needs, traits, and preferences. Identify student needs (explained in Chapter 2) and discuss as a class how they impact the educational process. Make it clear that you will provide a program that is compatible with student needs and will, to the extent possible, feature topics, activities, and ways of working that your students prefer. Point out that teachers also have needs and preferences that affect their performance. For most teachers, those needs and preferences are for a class that is orderly, has a cooperative attitude, shows courtesy and good manners, is persistent, and tries to do quality work.

5. Explain how you will intervene when misbehavior occurs. Make clear what you will do to encourage students to participate, cooperate, be productive, achieve excellence, and conduct themselves responsibly. Explain how you will emphasize positivity and concern for the well-being of all students. Indicate types of teacher misbehavior you will eliminate, such as failing to listen to students, acting disrespectfully, and allowing classes to be boring. Explain and demonstrate what you will do when students misbehave, emphasizing misbehavior as mistakes students make and explaining how these mistakes can be used to help students learn and conduct themselves in more productive ways.

THREE CONTRIBUTIONS FROM PRESERVICE TEACHERS

The following quotations present initial thoughts about teaching and discipline from three New Mexico State University students preparing to become teachers. These quotes are offered for your reflection and comparison with your thoughts at this stage. The selections were provided by Professor Eileen VanWie and are included with the students' permission.

Manuel Vigil on Conducting Himself as a Professional

I will be a professional role model. I will show dignity, class, and respect for my colleagues and students. At the same time, I will challenge my students to excel, intellectually and behaviorally. I will display a charismatic personality with good humor, as I want students to find our class fun and enjoyable.

Overall, I will model the sort of personal behavior I want to see in my students. I am intent on helping them learn to show respect and courtesy for one another. If I see students disrespecting each other, I will interrupt the behavior and explain why it is wrong and how a person should treat another individual. I will try to get the students to make amends for serious misbehavior and truly desire to be more respectful. I would hope they embrace and welcome differences among class members.

I also want my students to develop a love for learning. I will try to help them realize they already know a great deal and that there are amazingly interesting things to be learned. I want to build on their existing skills and knowledge and help them pursue their passions. I will find out what the students are interested in and try to tie the subject matter to those interests the best I can. I want them to get the feel of *learning* and of *understanding* a new idea, so they will want to continue experiencing those feelings.

I envision my future classrooms as warm and welcoming, where all students respect each other. In developing a climate of trust, I will involve students in class decisions. I will take my students seriously, encourage them to speak their minds, and understand that people have different points of view. Although I will be teaching biology, I want to have discussions on current events, especially those related to the biological sciences. I will do my best to make the curriculum relate to students' lives as much as I can.

Also, I want to encourage responsibility by raising awareness that young people do have choices and can make decisions that can be either beneficial or harmful to their education. I hope this awareness will help them to make decisions that will be positive to their lives. I will also involve parents and guardians in my plan to build discipline through warmth and responsibility. I want them to understand the important role they play in their children's education.

I want to keep the class atmosphere positive. I will be energizing, cheerful, and encouraging. When misbehavior occurs, I will ask questions such as "What is the problem?" or "What can I do to make this lesson more interesting?" For more serious infractions, I will first remind the students of the guidelines and expectations that we *all* established and agreed upon. I will also ask the students what I can do to help with the problem. I will let the students know that I understand that there may be other problems influencing their behavior at the time but also ask that in the future they talk with me or somebody else to get some assistance, rather than behaving inappropriately. I believe in treating students with respect, and I expect them to show me and others that same respect in return.

Alison K. Pryor on Developing Respect in the Classroom

The Pryor R-E-S-P-E-C-T Plan for Classroom Management is aimed at two main goals— first, a short-term goal of making the classroom run smoothly so teaching and learning can occur effectively, and second, a long-term goal of developing positive character traits that enable students to function more effectively individually and as members of society in future years. Each letter in R-E-S-P-E-C-T (Responsibility, Excellence, Self-control, Participation, Encouragement, Civility, and Trust) represents a key element that leads toward trust and productivity.

The schoolyear will begin with a discussion of the character attribute of *respect*. Students will participate in classroom discussions and formulate behavior guidelines for our class. Discussions will bring to light that respect involves esteem for or sense of worth of a person's qualities. It projects patience, open-mindedness, and fair treatment. To show respect for others, we show them consideration and at times honor them.

The theme of respect and respectful behavior will be acknowledged daily in the classroom and incorporated into every class meeting and every weekly newsletter. It will permeate interactions within the classroom, on the schoolgrounds, and with auxiliary school personnel, and when possible, it will be woven into the standard curriculum. It will guide all social interactions and will include the proper way to handle inanimate objects as well. When students show respectful behavior, they will be acknowledged for doing so. When discipline is required to correct improper behavior choices, I will help them identify positive alternatives in a respectful manner.

The classroom will display posters or items that draw attention to and encourage respectful behavior. The students will always see me model respectfulness in my interactions with them and others.

Rachel Space on Relating to and Connecting with Students

In my Theatre 101 class, I've been trying to create a more democratic classroom community as the semester goes on by involving students more closely in class matters. We have been doing a great deal of group work. The class together created a rubric for their theatre review and helped me develop a new theatre terms sheet that included their interpretations, making it easier for everyone to understand. I explain the grades I assign for their work, and if they can present evidence that shows I have made a misjudgment, I amend their grade. I also obtain student input concerning a fair way to discipline students who might be consistently late to class, might talk incessantly, or don't do the assigned reading and therefore cannot contribute to class activities.

My students love being a part of this decision-making process. They feel it shows I value their opinions, which helps me connect with them even more. Students who break the class rules know the consequences have been decided on by their peers and themselves. To help me better understand each of my students, I conduct two one-on-one meetings with each student during the semester. In those meetings, we explore two things—the student's plan for his or her final project and how the student is feeling about the class in general. This makes students feel more a part of things, and it gives me a better understanding of their progress. I am looking for additional ways to involve students in class decisions and other matters. I think we are making good progress in that regard.

For the future, I intend to develop class rules jointly with students, beginning on the first day. I will involve them in deciding what should be done when students violate the rules. We will create a specific list of unacceptable behaviors, such as abuse and bullying, and ways of stopping those acts immediately. When students misbehave, I will try to tactfully uncover their reason for doing so and follow up with an activity that helps them learn proper behavior. I will keep their parents and guardians informed and working together with us. We will emphasize that everyone has something to learn and something to teach others.

I want all of the students to become real learners, who make connections between what is being studied and what is happening in their life. I will emphasize to my students that we cannot allow anything to destroy a safe, respectful classroom. I consider it very important for students to be truly engaged and interested in their learning activities so that they really care about their education. I am willing to take suggestions from the students as to what assignments did not interest them and how I can better present their lives or cultures in the curriculum.

Finally, here are principles I will follow in teaching: I will behave professionally, follow all of the rules the students must follow, treat everyone with respect, and never be a hypocrite. I will encourage students to help maintain a safe, orderly classroom and continue their good behavior outside the class as well. I will do what I can to help each and every student have a good educational experience that brings achievement and fulfillment. I know the process requires that I be understanding of my students' needs and life experiences.

TWO SAMPLE PLANS FROM TEACHERS IN SERVICE

You are entitled and urged to devise a plan of discipline that you consider best for you and your students. The following examples are but two of many possibilities. They are not presented as exemplary models for you to emulate but merely to show how two experienced teachers organized procedures that suited their situations. You may find them useful as you plan a system for yourself. The first emphasizes rules of behavior, supported by positive and negative consequences. The second emphasizes student–teacher cooperation and focuses on preventing misbehavior.

Sample 1: An Approach That Emphasizes Rules and Consequences

Many teachers use discipline plans that feature rules and consequences. Teachers who use such plans believe the teacher should be firmly yet sensitively in control and see that everyone behaves as expected in the classroom. They feel their approach cuts down on disruptions and allows students to learn in an environment free from worry. Discipline plans of this type usually contain the following:

- *Rules.* A set of rules indicates what students are allowed and not allowed to do in class. The teacher is responsible for establishing the rules but discusses them carefully to make sure students understand their rationale and the procedures for enforcing them.
- *Consequences.* Consequences are attached to the rules and made plain to students. *Positive consequences* are pleasant experiences that students enjoy when they follow the rules. *Negative consequences* are unpleasant conditions that students experience when they break the rules.
- *Implementation and maintenance.* Students are taught how they are expected to behave, and a series of steps is established for applying the consequences. Parents and guardians are informed about the rationale, expectations, rules, consequences, and procedures of enforcement. Teachers change aspects of their programs when the need to do so becomes evident.

This approach has served hundreds of thousands of teachers for a great many years and is still widely used, although it is not as popular as it once was. To see how a present-day teacher uses the rules–consequences–procedure protocol and adjusts it to her needs, examine the following program developed by third-grade teacher Deborah Sund.

Deborah Sund's Third-Grade Discipline Program.   Deborah Sund had been teaching for two years when she devised the foundations of the following program. She wanted to provide a clear structure for behavior expectations while also meeting everyone's needs. Ms. Sund clarifies her students' needs, her own needs, and her special dislikes and then builds her discipline system so all are taken into account.

My Students' Needs

- To learn interesting and useful information, especially that which promotes skills in reading, math, and language
- To have a learning environment that is attractive, stimulating, free from threat, and conducive to productive work
- To have a teacher who is helpful, attentive, and kind
- To be given the opportunity to interact and work cooperatively with other students
- To be accepted and feel part of the group
- To learn how to relate to others humanely and helpfully
- To have the opportunity to excel

My Own Needs

- To have an orderly classroom appearance, good room arrangement, neatly stored materials, and interesting, well-thought-out displays
- To maintain structure and routines: a set schedule that provides security but also allows flexibility and improvisation when needed
- To ensure attention and participation, such that students pay attention to directions and speakers and participate willingly in all instructional activities
- To encourage situationally appropriate behaviors: quiet attention during instruction and considerate interaction during group activities
- To generate enthusiasm from me and my students
- To promote warmth, as reflected in mutual regard among all members of the class
- To maintain a positive, relaxed classroom environment reflecting self-control, mutual helpfulness, and assumption of responsibility

My Dislikes

- Inattention to a speaker, teacher, other adult, or class member
- Excessive noise: loud voices, inappropriate talking and laughing
- Distractions: toys, unnecessary movement, poking, teasing, and so on
- Abuse of property: misusing, wasting, or destroying instructional materials
- Unkind and rude conduct: ridicule, sarcasm, bad manners, and physical abuse

Class Rules

When I first meet my students, I explain that it is very important for us to have a class where everyone feels safe and is not worried about how others will treat them—where they can be happy and enjoy what we learn. I explain that to make that possible, I have prepared a list of rules for how we are to act. I explain the rules and give examples of what students do when they follow the rules and what they might do when they break the rules. I involve them in the discussion and have them practice correct ways of conducting themselves. I also tell them about some things I don't want them to do, and I show them examples to make sure they understand. I also demonstrate the prompts, cues, hints, and other assistance I will give students to help them abide by the following rules:

1. Be considerate of others at all times. (Speak kindly. Be helpful. Don't bother others.)
2. Do your best work. (Get as much done as possible. Do work neatly and be proud of it. Don't waste time.)
3. Use quiet voices in the classroom. (Use a regular speaking voice during class discussions. Speak quietly during cooperative work. Whisper at other times.)
4. Use signals to request permission or receive help. (I explain the signal systems for requesting assistance, movement, and restroom pass.)

Positive Consequences

I emphasize that I will always try to show I am pleased when students follow the rules we have agreed to:

- Mostly, I will give them smiles, winks, nods, and pats when they are behaving well.
- Sometimes, I will say out loud how pleased I am with the way they are working or behaving toward each other.
- Once in a while, when the whole class has behaved especially well, I will give them a special privilege (go early to recess, do one of their favorite activities, see a video).
- From time to time, I will send a complimentary note to their parents or guardians or call their parents and comment on how well they are doing.

Negative Consequences

When discussing the class rules, I ask students what they think should happen when someone breaks a rule. They usually suggest punishment. I tell them that because I want them always to be as happy as possible, I don't want to punish them. I say that instead of punishment, I will do the following:

- Give them "pirate eyes," or a stern glance with a disappointed or puzzled expression.
- Remind them when a rule is being broken: "I hear noise" or "Some people are not listening."
- When necessary, tell them exactly what they are doing wrong: "Gordon, you did not use the signal. Please use the signal."
- When necessary, separate them from the group until they can conduct themselves properly.
- As a last resort, contact their parents for help.

To Prevent Misbehavior

I discuss with my students a number of things I will do to help them want to behave properly:

- Show respect, for each student is entitled to the best education I can provide.
- Look for the positive and enjoyable qualities in each student.
- Take time to know each student better on a personal level.
- Each day, assess students' feelings and discuss them if necessary.
- Talk with students in ways that imply their own competence, such as "Okay, you know what to do next."
- Involve them in clarifying rules and assuming responsibility for proper behavior.
- Keep a good room environment to prevent their feeling strained, tired, or inconvenienced (proper lighting, temperature, traffic patterns, attractiveness).
- Emphasize, model, and hold practice sessions on good manners, courtesy, and responsibility.
- Provide a varied, active curriculum with opportunities for physical movement, singing, interaction, and quiet times.
- Communicate with parents and guardians in the following ways:
  1. Post messages on our Internet site outlining expectations and the discipline system.
  2. Occasionally make short, positive phone calls to parents or guardians.
  3. Send home with children notes concerning good work and behavior.
- End each day on a positive note, with a fond good-bye and hope for a happy and productive tomorrow.

Intervening When Students Misbehave

When students begin to misbehave, I do the following:

- Move close to the student.
- Show close attention to the student's work.
- Modify the lesson or activity if it seems to be causing difficulty.
- Invoke the negative consequences that we have agreed to.

Sample 2: An Approach That Emphasizes Prevention and Teacher–Student Cooperation

This second approach emphasizes preventing misbehavior through meeting student needs and building personal relationships. The rationale for this approach is that it promotes a greater sense of satisfaction and enjoyment in the class while eliminating student resentment and reluctance to cooperate. Plans of this sort emphasize the following:

- Attending continually to students' needs for security, hope, acceptance, dignity, power, enjoyment, and competence
- Communicating effectively and regularly with students and their parents or guardians

- Making sure to give all students attention, encouragement, and support
- Making class activities consistently enjoyable and worthwhile
- Ensuring that all students accept responsibility and experience success
- Establishing agreements about how everyone will interact and behave
- Discussing and practicing manners, courtesy, and responsibility
- Involving all students meaningfully in the operation of the class
- Dealing with misbehavior by attending to its causes

Teachers who employ this discipline approach feel it allows them to relate with students in a way that builds positive relationships with relatively little stress. Gail Charles uses a discipline plan that incorporates many of these qualities.

Gail Charles's Discipline Plan for Eighth-Grade English.   The following narration is in Gail Charles's words:

I have been teaching for 25 years. For many of those years, my students misbehaved much more than I thought they should, and I tried to control their misbehavior with scowls, reprimands, lectures, threats, and detentions. My students grudgingly behaved well enough to learn most of what I intended, but I'm sure they felt under siege. I know I did, and the effort it required left me continually frustrated and exhausted.

A few years ago, I began to understand that I am more effective and enjoy my work more when I organize the curriculum to accommodate and embrace the needs of my adolescent students and work cooperatively with them. While I still provide a challenging curriculum, I have switched from a coercive to a collaborative way of teaching. I now try to guide, encourage, and support students' efforts rather than endlessly push and prod. The result has been fewer power struggles, more success, and happier students and teacher.

Winning My Students Over
My students want to feel part of the group. They want to feel accepted and valued by each other and especially by me. They want to feel safe, so I forbid all ridicule and sarcasm. I've never ridiculed a student, but sorry to say, I have spoken sarcastically many times when struggling against students who defied my rules. I no longer use sarcasm or allow students to belittle each other in any way.

I give my students a voice in class matters and listen to them sincerely. I allow them to make decisions about where they sit and with whom they wish to work. I do this as part of trying to make learning enjoyable. They like to work with each other, participate, talk, and cooperate.

Meeting My Needs
We discuss the importance of making classwork enjoyable, and I tell my students that the class needs to be enjoyable for me, too. I tell them up front that I want the tone in the class to be positive, with everyone showing patience, tolerance, good manners, and mutual respect. I tell them that I want them to be enthusiastic and do the best work they can. I say that I need their attention and that I want them to help care for

materials and keep the room clean. I promise to treat them with respect, and they usually reciprocate.

Rules and Student Input

I have learned to request and make use of student input concerning expectations, operating procedures, and codes of conduct. When I meet a new class, I discuss their needs and mine and focus on how we can meet those needs and make our class productive. I give students power to make many decisions, and I respect what they say.

Together we write a plan for how we will work and behave in the class. Because I want students to make thoughtful suggestions, I ask them, for their first homework assignment, to think back on previous years in school and write brief responses to the following:

1. When have you felt most successful in school?
2. What did the teacher do to help you feel successful?
3. What kinds of class activities have you found most helpful and enjoyable?
4. What suggestions do you have for creating a classroom in which all can work, learn, and do their best?

The next day, I organize students into small groups to share and discuss what they have written. Volunteers present each group's responses, which I list using the overhead projector. Occasionally, I may add a suggestion of my own. We then streamline, combine, reword, and sometimes negotiate until we reach a set of agreements we think will serve us best. Before the next class, I type up the agreements and ask each student and his or her parent to sign, indicating their support. I do this for each of my five classes.

Prevention

In all my class activities, I try to interact personally with every student. It is not easy to forge relationships with 160-plus students, but I try to do so in order to show I see and like them. At the beginning of the year, I write a letter to my students introducing myself and telling a bit about my family, hobbies, interests, and goals. I ask them to do the same so I can know them better. I keep a birthday calendar to remember student birthdays. I try to comment on new hairstyles, new outfits, or how great a now-braces-free set of teeth looks. I chaperone field trips and dances, supervise the computer writing lab after school, and make myself available for conversation before and after school. These little things mean a lot to students.

For their part, many students like to involve themselves in the workings of the classroom. I provide them tasks such as classroom librarian, bulletin board designer, plant caretaker, and class secretary. Their involvement makes them feel important and useful.

Interventions

With the collaborative plan in place, I have few discipline problems and little difficulty dealing with those that occur. Most often, a simple reminder is all that is needed to get students back on track. For the occasional student who repeatedly misbehaves, despite our agreements, I ask the counselor to set up a meeting with the student's parents and sometimes with other teachers. We discuss the problem and explore how it can be resolved. Very occasionally, a student may behave in a dangerous manner or prevent my teaching. When that happens, I call the vice-principal for assistance.

Consultant

BARBARA COLOROSO ON THE PURPOSE AND PRACTICE OF DISCIPLINE

Barbara Coloroso has been a Franciscan nun, parent, teacher, workshop leader, author, and university instructor. She has expressed her ideas on discipline and childrearing in a number of books, articles, and conference presentations. In recent years, she has concentrated on working with troubled students, dealing with bullying, and assisting students with special needs and talents. Her ideas for helping students develop self-control, or *inner discipline,* are explained in her book *Kids Are Worth It! Giving Your Child the Gift of Inner Discipline* (2002), in which she indicates how teachers can develop systems of discipline that create trust, respect, and success in school. For more information, see Coloroso's website: www.kidsareworthit.com.

The Purpose of Discipline

Discipline should be thought of as a means of teaching students to take positive charge of their lives. Students have the right to be in school, but they also have the responsibility to respect the rights of those around them. Good discipline shows students what they have done wrong, has them assume ownership of the problem that has resulted, and teaches them ways to solve the problem, all the while leaving their personal dignity intact. This approach can lead to inner discipline that helps students manage problems they encounter. They learn to think for themselves and believe they are able to solve most problems they encounter.

Coloroso maintains that classrooms are ideal places to learn the process of responsible decision making but that teachers and students must work closely together in order to achieve that end. Fundamentally, teachers must treat students as they, themselves, like to be treated. When students encounter difficulty, teachers should help by asking how they plan to solve the problem, thus requiring students to take responsibility for resolving any problem they encounter.

Why Punishment Is Counterproductive

Punishment—treatment that is physically or psychologically harmful to students—is to be removed from the discipline process. Fear of punishment causes students to respond with one or more of the three Fs—freezing, fighting back, or fleeing.

Students who are afraid of punishment are reluctant to try new things for fear of making mistakes, which removes vital opportunities for them to learn integrity, wisdom, compassion, and mercy, all of which contribute to inner discipline.

Dealing with Misbehavior

When students misbehave, teachers should do four things that lead to positive behavior: (1) Help students see what they have done wrong; (2) give students ownership of the problem involved; (3) guide students in developing strategies for solving the problems; and (4) make sure that, in the entire process, students are never denigrated.

Coloroso describes class misbehavior as falling into three categories—mistakes, mischief, and mayhem—which are addressed in different ways. *Mistakes* are simple errors that provide opportunity for learning better choices. *Mischief,* although not necessarily serious, is intentional misbehavior. It provides an opportunity to help students learn to correct what they did wrong and avoid doing it again. *Mayhem,* which is willfully serious misbehavior, calls for application of the three Rs—restitution, resolution, and reconciliation.

Restitution is doing what is necessary to repair personal relations or physical damage that has occurred. *Resolution* is identifying and correcting the conditions that caused the misbehavior so it won't happen again. *Reconciliation* is healing relationships with people who were hurt by the misbehavior.

The best way to help students who misbehave is to allow them to make decisions and grow from the results, whatever those results may be. Teachers must make sure, however, that student decisions do not lead to situations that are physically dangerous, morally threatening, or unhealthy. Otherwise, teachers should bring students to situations that require decisions and, without making judgments, let them proceed through the process.

All this builds toward the ultimate purpose of discipline, which is to enable students to make intelligent decisions, accept the consequences of their decisions, and use the consequences to make better decisions in the future. Teachers who feel they must control their students turn to bribes, rewards, threats, and punishments to restrict and coerce behavior. In contrast, inner discipline helps students recognize the relationship between decisions and consequences. This recognition helps them see they have control over their lives, a requisite for the development of inner discipline. This is the process by which teachers empower students.

Of course, when given this opportunity, students do not always make the best choices. For that reason, they must be provided a safe, nurturing environment in which they can learn how to deal with consequences. Teachers should allow and respect student decisions, including those that are clearly in error, and let students experience the consequences that follow. Even when the consequences are unpleasant, students learn from them, and at the same time, they learn that they have control over their lives through the decisions they make. Once teachers understand the value of this process, they realize it is counterproductive to nag, warn, and constantly remind students of what they ought to be doing.

This process may seem inefficient, but it produces rapid growth in ability to solve problems. Mistakes and poor choices become the students' responsibility. If they experience discomfort, they have the power to behave more responsibly in the future. Teachers should never rescue students by solving problems for them. Doing so sends the message that students don't have power in their lives and that another person must take care of them. When students make mistakes, as they will, teachers should not lecture them. What students need is opportunity to correct the situation they have created. The teacher says, "You have a problem. What is your plan for dealing with it?" When students are given ownership of problems and situations, they know it is up to them to make matters better. Teachers are there to offer advice and support, not provide solutions.

IN SUMMARY

Teachers are more likely to have effective systems of behavior management if they construct those systems themselves, using the best information available, and make sure student and teacher needs are met. They should identify behavior they approve of as well as that which is unacceptable, understand class needs and typical interests of students they teach, and determine what they will do both to prevent misbehavior and to deal with it productively when it occurs.

REFERENCES

Coloroso, B. 2002. *Kids are worth it! Giving your child the gift of inner discipline* (2nd edition). New York: Quill.

Goorian, B., and Brown, K. 2002. *Trends and issues: School law.* ERIC Clearinghouse on Educational Management. http://eric.uoregon.edu/trends_issues/law/index.html

National Education Association. 1975. *Code of ethics of the education profession.* www .nea.org/aboutnea/code.html

Traynor, P. 2005. *Got discipline? Research-based practices for managing student behavior.* Mansfield, OH: Bookmasters.

2

Preventing Misbehavior

Taking Proactive Steps to Prevent the Occurrence of Misbehavior in the Classroom

You can take steps to address conditions that are known to foster inappropriate behavior. You can neutralize most of those factors fairly easily and minimize the effects of the others. These preventive measures are very effective in reducing misbehavior in your classes.

Chapter Preview

This chapter presents tactics for preventing the occurrence of misbehavior in the classroom. Definitions of *misbehavior* are provided. Twenty-six sets of conditions are identified as causes of misbehavior, and suggestions are provided for minimizing their effects. It is also recognized that teachers misbehave in certain ways, and suggestions are made for avoiding those misbehaviors as well. Finally, attention is given to the positive effects of *classroom synergy*, a mutually energizing phenomenon that can occur among members of the class. One of the effects of synergy is a reduction in misbehavior.

DEFINITIONS OF MISBEHAVIOR

Some educators object to the term *misbehavior* on the grounds it is prejudicial and dependent on teacher idiosyncrasies. They prefer terms such as *inappropriate behavior, disruptive behavior*, and *maladaptive behavior*. Because teacher judgment is always involved in this question and because *misbehavior* is a widely understood and accepted term, it is used in this book to refer to classroom behavior that interferes with the educational process.

Authorities have defined *misbehavior* in different ways. Which of the following do you consider most accurate or helpful?

• Thomas Gordon, renowned psychologist and author of *T.E.T.: Teacher Effectiveness Training* (1987) and *Discipline That Works* (1989), defines *misbehavior* as "an adult concept in which a specific action of the child is seen as producing an undesirable consequence for the adult" (p. 107). To paraphrase Gordon, we might say that misbehavior is anything students do that teachers don't like.

• Linda Albert, author of *A Teacher's Guide to Cooperative Discipline* (2003), defines *misbehavior* as inappropriate acts associated with students' pursuit of mistaken goals, which are attention seeking ("Look at me"), power seeking ("You can't make me"), revenge seeking ("I'll get even"), or withdrawal (dropping out). Such misbehavior appears when students fail to achieve their prime goal of acceptance in the classroom. Albert bases her definition on work done earlier by psychiatrist and child development expert Rudolf Dreikurs (with P. Cassell, 1995).

• Barbara Coloroso (2002), featured in Chapter 1, advocates an approach based on inner discipline. She categorizes *misbehavior* as mistakes (accidental or uninformed), mischief (intentional but benign), and mayhem (intentional and more serious).

• Spencer Kagan, psychologist and author of *Win–Win Discipline* (with P. Kyle and S. Scott, 2004), describes *misbehavior* as disruptions that can be categorized into four types—aggression, breaking rules, confrontations, and disengagement (ABCD). These disruptions, he says, almost always spring from one of seven student positions—attention seeking, avoiding failure, angry, control seeking, energetic, bored, or uninformed.

• William Glasser (1998), psychiatrist and prolific writer and consultant in teaching, curriculum, and discipline, defines *misbehavior* as unacceptable acts students perform in an attempt to meet one or more of five prime needs—safety, love and belonging, fun, freedom, and power. He believes misbehavior is minimized to the extent student are able to satisfy those needs in the classroom.

• C. M. Charles (2008) describes *misbehavior* as any action that, through intent or thoughtlessness, interferes with teaching or learning, threatens or intimidates others, or oversteps society's standards of moral, ethical, or legal behavior.

TYPES OF MISBEHAVIOR

Thirteen types of misbehavior are likely to occur in your classes—some frequently, some rarely. It is often helpful to talk with your students about these kinds of misbehavior, at least those that affect your class most often. This helps students understand the undesirable effects of such behavior and encourages the class to think of ways in which self-defeating behaviors can be avoided. The thirteen types are as follows:

1. *Inattention*—daydreaming, doodling, looking out the window, thinking about things irrelevant to the lesson
2. *Apathy*—a general disinclination to participate, as demonstrated by sulking, not caring, being afraid of failure, not wanting to try or do well
3. *Needless talk*—chatting during instructional time about matters unrelated to the lesson
4. *Moving about the room*—getting up and moving around without permission, congregating in parts of the room
5. *Annoying others*—provoking, teasing, picking at, calling names
6. *Disruption*—shouting out during instruction, talking and laughing inappropriately, having confrontations with others, causing "accidents"
7. *Lying*—falsifying to avoid accepting responsibility or admitting wrongdoing or to get others in trouble
8. *Stealing*—taking things that belong to others
9. *Cheating*—making false representations or wrongly taking advantage of others for personal benefit
10. *Sexual harassment*—making others uncomfortable through touching, sex-related language, or sexual innuendo
11. *Aggression and fighting*—showing hostility toward others, threatening them, shoving, pinching, wrestling, hitting, bullying
12. *Malicious mischief*—doing intentional damage to school property or the belongings of others
13. *Defiance of authority*—talking back to the teacher, hostilely refusing to do as the teacher requests

CAUSES OF MISBEHAVIOR AND WHAT TO DO ABOUT THEM

It is well known that certain classroom conditions seem to foment misbehavior. Here, those conditions are called *causes* of misbehavior, a label that is useful but not entirely correct because these conditions do not always promote misbehavior. However, the term *cause* is retained for ease of use.

Twenty-six sets of conditions can be identified that often lead to misbehavior. Preventive discipline acts to remove the conditions where possible and to limit their influence if they cannot be removed entirely. To have a well-behaved, stress-free class, you must attend to these causative conditions, which are grouped here in accordance with where they seem to reside.

Causes of Misbehavior That Reside in Individual Students

Ten causes of misbehavior seem to reside within individual students: unmet needs, thwarted desires, expediency, urge to transgress, temptation, inappropriate habits, poor behavior choices, avoidance, egocentric personality, and neurological-based behavior (NBB). The following are suggestions for addressing these ten causes.

1. *Unmet needs.* In the classroom, students continually try to meet needs related to security, belonging, hope, dignity, power, enjoyment, and competence. When any of these needs is not being satisfied, students become unsettled, distracted, and more prone to misbehave.

Teacher action: By observing students and talking with them, you can identify most student needs and help students meet them in an acceptable manner.

2. *Thwarted desires.* When students fail to get something they want badly, they may complain, become destructive, sulk, pout, or act out.

Teacher action: Tell students you can see they are troubled or distracted. Ask if there is anything you can do to help. Be sympathetic, but don't dwell on the problem. Try to get them interested in something else.

3. *Expediency.* Students always look for ways to make their lives easier and more enjoyable. They take shortcuts, conveniently forget what they are supposed to do, look for ways to get out of work, and intentionally break rules.

Teacher action: Expedient behavior is seldom a problem in classes that are interesting and enjoyable, but it appears often in classes students consider dull and boring. Hold discussions about expediency and its troublesome effects. Ask students why they sometimes take the easy way, such as reading a book summary or review rather than the assigned book, rushing through a writing assignment, or copying others' ideas. If students are comfortable enough to answer honestly, they will probably say they do so because they don't like the work, don't see the point in it, or don't want to spend time on it. Ask them what would encourage them to give their best effort. Listen to their suggestions, and make use of them if you can.

4. *Urge to transgress.* All of us feel the urge to transgress rules and regulations and often do so knowing there is a chance we will get caught or even harm ourselves or others. Students succumb to this urge frequently, especially when class activities are not appealing; they also cheat, take shortcuts, tell lies, break class rules, and annoy others, seemingly for little benefit.

Teacher action: Discuss this urge, its effects, and how it can be controlled sensibly. Discuss the reasons for rules, including how they reduce potential harm, equalize opportunity, and help us live together harmoniously. If students are old enough, ask if they understand what the terms *ethics, ethical conduct,* and *personal character* mean. Ask why they think ethical people are so widely admired.

5. *Temptation.* Students regularly encounter objects, situations, behaviors, and people they find powerfully attractive. This phenomenon is evident in association with music and lyrics, desirable objects, ways of speaking, styles of clothing, lifestyles, personal grooming, and cheating on tests and assignments. Although the pursuit of these temptations can result in mild or severe misbehavior, students nevertheless find them so attractive they will occasionally do, adopt, mimic, acquire, or associate with them, even when forbidden to do so.

Teacher action: Conduct discussions with your students where together you analyze temptation and seek to understand why certain objects, styles, and opportunities are so seductive. Help students foresee the undesirable consequences of following disapproved styles and manners. Help them clarify the lines that separate the approved from the disapproved, and reinforce their resolve to resist factors that are likely to harm them or others.

6. *Inappropriate habits.* Inappropriate habits are ingrained ways of behaving that violate established standards and expectations. Jason uses profanity at school. Maria is discourteous and calls others names. Larry shirks his assignments. Some of these habits are learned in school, but most become established in the home or community.

Teacher action: Bring inappropriate habits to students' attention without pointing a finger at anyone. Discuss their harmful effects, and if necessary, have students practice desirable alternatives to habits such as name-calling, teasing, verbal putdowns, cheating, lying, and disregarding the feelings of others.

7. *Poor behavior choices.* The behaviors students exhibit in attempting to meet their needs are sometimes acceptable, sometimes not. Levels of acceptability may not be clear to students. Alicia, when seeking attention, annoys others so much they avoid her. Alan, seeking an increased sense of power, refuses to do what his teacher requests.

Teacher action: Alicia and Alan need to understand that their behavior choices are detrimental to themselves and others. To help students such as Alicia and Alan, ask questions like these in class: What are some of the things you have seen students do to (get attention, be acknowledged, get better grades than they deserve, get out of work, become members of groups, etc.)? Does their behavior usually get them what they want? What could those students do that would probably bring better results?

8. *Avoidance.* None of us likes to face failure, intimidation, ridicule, or other unpleasant situations and treatment; hence, we are inclined to avoid situations where they might occur. But in school, we can't always do that. Consider Norona, who refuses to participate in a group assignment. Her refusal seems to show disrespect for the teacher, but her real reason is that she is intimidated by her peers and doesn't want them to think she is stupid.

Teacher action: To help students such as Norona behave advantageously in circumstances they dislike, show them how to face unpleasant situations and work through them. Rather than single out Norona, ask the following in a group discussion: Are there things you try to avoid in school, such as people, events, or activities you find frightening or embarrassing? Which of those things could best be dealt with through avoidance (e.g., a clique that is maligning other students)? Which of those things cannot be dealt with through avoidance (e.g., giving an oral report in front of the class)? What is the worst thing that can happen in class if we make a mistake? Can mistakes help us learn? What could a person do to reduce the fear of mistakes or unpleasant situations? (Consider exploring these ideas in pairs, then small groups, and then large groups.)

9. *Egocentric personality.* Students with egocentric personalities focus primarily on themselves, believe they are superior to others, and think they do little wrong. Most classes contain one or more such students.

> *Teacher action:* To help these students behave more appropriately, ask questions such as the following in class discussions: Are the needs and interests of all students important, or do only certain students deserve attention? Is one person often entirely right and everyone else entirely wrong? Is everyone entitled to an equal opportunity in the class? How should you and I react to a person who always wants to dominate, be first, be right, or quarrel with those who don't agree? (Make sure the proffered suggestions are positive in nature, not negative.)

10. *Neurological-based behavior (NBB).* A few students behave undesirably not through intent or thoughtlessness but because their brains function in ways that lead to behavior that is largely outside their control. These students do not respond well, or at all, to normal discipline tactics. NBB involves a number of different diagnoses, such as learning disabilities, attention-deficit hyperactivity disorder (ADHD), sensory-processing disorder, fetal alcohol spectrum disorder, and autism spectrum disorder.

> *Teacher action:* Teachers who have students with NBB need help from specialists, who are usually provided by the school. Behavior of students with NBB can often be improved by removing extraneous stimulation from the classroom environment. A number of other tactics are also helpful. Mel Levine (2002) says that from the moment students get out of bed in the morning until they are back in bed at night, they have one mission that overrides all others—to avoid humiliation at all costs. He also says that we need to demystify NBB for affected students and peers. He says to explain plainly to the class and others that some people function (are "wired up," if you prefer) in such a way that they lose control at times and more often than others do. Students need to be reassured that teachers can help them avoid getting into trouble and will partner with them because they care. We need to think of NBB students separately from their behavior. We should always model the calm, soothing behavior we want them to display and make sure they feel loved and respected as human beings. Other helpful suggestions are (1) to be careful with eye contact, which stimulates upper-cortex activity and is often interpreted as a challenge or threat; (2) to react to situations calmly (a raised voice tends to make students with NBB raise their voices in return); and (3) to provide additional structure to unstructured activities, which are especially difficult for students with NBB.

Causes of Misbehavior That Reside in Class Peers and Groups

Two significant causes of misbehavior reside in class peers and groups: provocation and contagious group behavior. Here are suggestions for dealing with them.

1. *Provocation.* A great amount of school misbehavior occurs from students' provoking each other through petty annoyance, putdowns, sarcastic remarks, and aggression

or bullying. Heather is trying to study, but Art's incessant chatter frustrates her to the bursting point. Marty calls Jerry a name, and Jerry responds hotly. Randall is trying to pay attention but can't because Larry keeps poking him in the back with a pencil.

> *Teacher action:* Provocation often produces strong emotions that reduce self-control and increase combativeness. Discuss this phenomenon with your class. Ask questions such as these: Can you name some things people say or do that upset you so much you want to retaliate? How do you feel when this happens? If you retaliate, is it likely to improve the situation or make it worse? What might you do that would resolve the incident peacefully? Is provoking others or bullying them consistent with the class character we are trying to build? Would you provoke or bully others if the teacher were standing beside you?

2. *Contagious group behavior.* Students often succumb to peer pressure or get caught up in group emotion and, as a result, misbehave in ways that would be out of character if they were by themselves. It is difficult for students to disregard peer pressure, easy to get swept up in group energy and emotion, and easy to justify one's misbehavior as "only what others were doing." Because Kerry and Lee want to look cool to their peers, Kerry defaces school property and Lee bullies a weaker member of the class. Neither would do these things if by himself or herself.

> *Teacher action:* Discuss this phenomenon with your class. Tell the class about some event in which a friend of yours—let's say Sarah—behaved badly just because others were doing so. Indicate that Sarah is now very embarrassed about her behavior and wishes no one knew about it. Ask your students if they know any stories like Sarah's they can share, without mentioning names the class might recognize. (Tell them they must not mention family matters or members. Doing so is a sure way to get parents upset at you.) If students share stories, guide the class in analyzing one or two of them. If they don't contribute a story, have a fictional one ready for their consideration. After hearing or recounting the story, ask questions such as the following:

- Is the behavior something the person will be proud of later?
- Why do you suppose the person behaved that way? (perhaps to have fun, show comradeship, test limits, be seen as clever or cool)
- What do you think the long-term results will be for the person? (perhaps an unpleasant story to remember, regret, guilt, getting caught, being found out, worry, disappointing one's family, possible punishment, living with knowing you did the wrong thing)
- How do you think the possible benefits compare with the probable harmful effects?
- Once you do something you are ashamed of, how can you make amends?
- How can you stay away from or keep out of group activities that are unlawful, unethical, or against the rules?

Causes of Misbehavior That Reside in Instructional Environments

Four causes of misbehavior reside in instructional environments, and all can be easily corrected. They are physical discomfort, tedium, meaninglessness, and lack of stimulation.

1. *Physical discomfort.* Students often become restless when made uncomfortable by inappropriate noise, temperature, lighting, seating, or workspaces.

Teacher action: Attend to comfort factors in advance, and ask students about them. Make corrections as necessary.

2. *Tedium.* Students begin to fidget after a time when an instructional activity requires continued close attention, especially if the topic is not appealing.

Teacher action: Add something that increases the interest level, or break the work into shorter segments.

3. *Meaninglessness.* Students grow restless when required to work at topics they do not comprehend or for which they see no purpose.

Teacher action: Make sure the topic is meaningful to students—that they understand it and see its relevance and importance in their lives.

4. *Lack of stimulation.* The topic and learning environment provide little that is attractive or otherwise stimulating. Students take no interest in the lesson.

Teacher action: Select topics and activities in which students have natural interest. When that is not possible, introduce elements students are known to enjoy, such as novelty, mystery, movement, competition, group work, and role-playing.

Causes of Misbehavior That Reside in Teachers and Other School Personnel

We must honestly acknowledge that teachers sometimes misbehave in the classroom. Other adults at school do so as well, including administrators, librarians, clerical staff, health personnel, cafeteria personnel, custodial personnel, and family members working in the school. Ten factors are occasionally evident in school personnel that can lead to student misbehavior.

1. *Poor habits.* Personnel in the schools have sometimes unknowingly acquired counterproductive ways of speaking, dealing with, or relating to students, and they may have become set in those ways.

Teacher action: Watch closely to see how students react to you and other school personnel. Toward any given school person, do they seem friendly? Wary? Eager to cooperate? Reticent? If they are reticent, fearful, uncooperative, or unfriendly, analyze the situations you observe and see if you can determine the problem. Correct your own behavior, should that be necessary, but be careful about approaching colleagues with criticism. If you need to do so, casually say to the teacher (as appropriate to the situation), "I've been getting along with Tony and other students much better since I've begun asking their opinions on matters, rather than just telling them what to do."

2. *Unfamiliarity with better techniques.* Some educators have not had occasion to learn some of the newer, more effective ways of teaching and relating with today's students.

> *Teacher action:* If you feel you might be less than well informed, ask students about things school people do that they really like. Notice what effective teachers at your school do, and don't be reluctant to request ideas from them. Your school may keep a library of professional books and journals, and through the Internet, you can access dozens of sites that present outstanding ideas and suggestions for working enjoyably and productively with students.

3. *Presenting poor models of behavior.* At times, all of us are inconsistent, irresponsible, and short on self-control, and we sometimes treat students with discourtesy or disregard. We can't expect to be perfect, but we must realize that when we behave unprofessionally or treat students poorly—which is to say, in ways we would not want to be treated—we not only damage relationships but also encourage students to imitate our poor behavior.

> *Teacher action:* Always be the best model you can for your students, who watch you very closely and often pattern their behavior after yours (especially when you misbehave). If you do anything you realize is inappropriate, call attention to it, explain why it was wrong, and apologize if doing so seems necessary.

4. *Showing little interest in or appreciation for students.* We sometimes fail to show interest in students or appreciation for them as individuals, despite knowing they want our attention. If we disregard them repeatedly, students become hesitant toward us or may seek our attention in disruptive ways.

> *Teacher action:* Give all students as much personal attention as possible. Greet them personally, exchange a friendly word, show you are aware of them and their difficulties, try to help them feel at ease, and acknowledge their progress.

5. *Succumbing to personal frustration.* Some educators are worn down from continually having to deal with misbehavior, inconsiderate parents, and other stressful conditions. They become dispirited, which makes it difficult to work with students in a kind, helpful manner.

> *Teacher action:* Educators often experience intense frustration from trying unsuccessfully to get students to comply with expectations. If you are trying to use force, replace it with encouragement and enticement, and you will see your students become more cooperative, willing to learn, and considerate. Go out of your way to communicate with parents and show appreciation for their children.

6. *Succumbing to provocation.* Students may do and say things intentionally to annoy you, hoping to see you become upset and befuddled and perhaps lose self-control.

> *Teacher action:* Do not allow students to provoke you. When they try to do so, disregard their comments and actions and proceed as if nothing has happened. If you feel it necessary to respond, say only, "Something is causing violations of our agreement about being considerate of others. I don't understand why. Is there something we can do to fix the problem?"

7. *Providing ineffective guidance and feedback.* In the absence of helpful guidance and feedback, students sometimes do not understand what is expected of them, how much progress they have made, or how they can improve.

> *Teacher action:* Make sure students understand clearly what they are supposed to do and how they should go about it. During and after assigned activities, tell students what they have done well or poorly and indicate how they can improve. Ask them to give their opinions about the activity and their efforts.

8. *Using ineffective personal communication.* Some educators are not adept at communicating with students on a personal level. This shortcoming may cause students to become uneasy and reticent.

> *Teacher action:* Speak regularly with students in a friendly way. Students want you to know their names and exchange pleasantries with them. They sometimes want to know your views on various matters and want to tell you theirs, which can provide them with a measure of personal validation. However, you should avoid comments that hurt feelings or dampen enthusiasm. Rather, say things that increase optimism and bolster confidence. Build students up when you can, but do so honestly.

9. *Failure to plan proactively.* Many educators do not plan ahead sufficiently to foresee potential problems. Then, when unexpected events occur, they are not prepared to respond effectively.

> *Teacher action:* Think carefully about problems that might arise in class and about possible student reactions to topics, lessons, requests, and unexpected events. By anticipating potential difficulties, you can avoid most problems and prepare yourself to deal with whatever might happen. Think through what you will do when people are injured or become suddenly ill, grow defiant, or get into fights. Decide what you will do and say if an unauthorized visitor approaches you, if a parent berates you, if the class moans when you make an assignment, and so forth. Determine how you can respond decisively to such eventualities yet maintain positive relationships.

10. *Using coercion, threat, and punishment.* Students don't like to be forced to do anything, and they don't like to be threatened. If you treat them abrasively, they will keep a watchful eye on you, fearful of being scolded, embarrassed, or demeaned, and will very likely develop negative attitudes toward you and school.

Teacher action: Give up coercion and threat, and replace them with considerate helpfulness, personal attention, and good communication.

RECOGNIZING AND CORRECTING TEACHER MISBEHAVIOR

As mentioned, we should frankly acknowledge that we teachers also misbehave at times. Despite our dedication and concern for students, we sometimes do or say things that provoke antagonism, inhibit student progress, or leave the class dispirited. Five types of teacher misbehavior should be addressed and eliminated: inducing fearfulness, denigrating students, being demanding and abrasive, presenting poor models of behavior, and not making classes interesting and worthwhile. When we misbehave in any of these ways, it is usually because we are either fearful of losing control or simply don't know how to use positive tactics that work well.

Do what you can to avoid such misbehavior. Think back at the end of each day and judge yourself against the types of teacher misbehavior just listed. If you see a need for improvement, work on the behaviors one by one until you get satisfactory results. Tell your students what you are doing, and ask for their feedback.

Consultant

C. M. CHARLES ON PREVENTING MISBEHAVIOR THROUGH SYNERGETIC TEACHING

C. M. Charles was for many years Professor of Teacher Education at San Diego State University, where he is now Professor Emeritus. He directed innovative programs in teacher education and five times received outstanding professor and distinguished teaching awards. He also served on many occasions as advisor in teacher education and curriculum to the governments of Peru and Brazil. Charles is author of a number of books that have attracted wide audiences in the United States and abroad, with translations into several foreign languages.

One of those books, *The Synergetic Classroom: Joyful Teaching and Gentle Discipline* (2000), explains how to energize classes, when desired, to maximize student achievement, enjoyment, and satisfaction, which in turn reduces the likelihood of discipline problems. Here are some of Charles's comments related to synergetic teaching. For more information, see Charles's website: www.teacherweb.com/ca/sdsu/charles.

Many teachers today are unhappy or frustrated in their work. Most who feel this way insist they very much want to teach and help students but find their students distressingly unmotivated, uncooperative, difficult to teach, and hard to handle. Teachers' daily struggle under these conditions, with little to show for their effort, erodes class morale and saps energy and initiative, allowing classes to decline into dull daily grinds. These teachers are not enjoying school, and they know their students are not enjoying it either.

Yet many teachers in schools everywhere are notably successful. Their students learn, enjoy themselves, and appreciate the educational experience. These results are not produced by expensive instructional materials or costly facilities. They occur because of what the teacher does to relate to students, teach effectively, and make sure students enjoy the experience. For instance, they know how to rally students to their side. They know how to build trust. They know how to strengthen and capitalize on student dignity and enhance personal relations in their classes. They know how to communicate well and help students resolve problems and conflicts. They know how to make lessons consistently interesting and worthwhile. And they add sparkle to daily classroom life with their personal charisma. By doing these things, teachers feed energy to their students who, in turn, feed energy back to the teacher. This mutually energizing phenomenon, referred to as *synergy,* is at the heart of synergetic teaching and discipline.

If you are able to teach in ways that increase class synergy, you can be sure your students will like and respect you. They will willingly, even eagerly immerse themselves in the educational activities you provide. As they do so, they will begin to show more responsibility, self-direction, and self-discipline. Discipline problems will be few and far between, and a high level of camaraderie will be present. All these things contribute to a sense of exhilaration that teachers and students prize in school but only occasionally experience.

Virtually all teachers can learn to teach in a synergetic manner. The first step is to understand students' nature and needs. You can see that all too often, our curriculum, activities, and discipline methods are not in harmony with students' needs and natures but rather work contrarily to them. Many of us expect students, even when bored to death, to pay attention, show interest, and do as they are directed. When students are slow to comply, we get upset and sometimes try to force them to do so, not realizing that coercion produces an array of student emotions that interfere with learning. Teachers err most seriously when they say and do things that damage trust and student dignity, thus promoting student dislike for teacher and school.

Synergetic teaching helps avoids those pitfalls. It provides teachers the tools they need for student enjoyment and success. It is based on working *with* students. By capitalizing on needs and desires, it makes activities enjoyable. By using effective communication and personal attention, it promotes trust and desire to cooperate. As these conditions increase in class, discipline problems fade to a minimum, and those that do occur can be dealt with easily and productively.

All teachers have two great dreams—to work with students who try to learn and to escape from the constant struggle against student lethargy and misbehavior. Synergetic teaching enables you to achieve both dreams. Students conduct themselves more appropriately because the major conditions that lead to misbehavior are removed. At the same time, your enjoyment in working with students increases. You can look forward to each day and go home at night pleasantly tired, rather than raggedly frustrated.

Students will be pleased to see you each day and you them. Teaching will increasingly become what you always hoped it would be—joyful and satisfying.

The following sections indicate what you can do to increase synergy in your classes.

Clarify Student Needs and the Kinds of Attention Those Needs Should Receive

Briefly discuss with your class the predominant needs we all share. Go through the following list, and reassure students you will take these needs fully into account in the class. (Of course, you should adjust the discussion to your students' developmental level.)

- *Security,* feeling safe without worry
- *Sense of hope,* feeling that school is worthwhile and success is possible
- *Personal dignity,* feeling respected and worthwhile
- *Belonging,* feeling a part of things, being valued, having a place in the class
- *Sense of power,* having some control of and input into events in the class
- *Enjoyment,* participating in activities that are pleasurable or rewarding
- *Sense of competence,* being able to do many things well, including the expected school work

Point out to your students that you know they become uncomfortable when these needs are not being met at school and that discomfort reduces enjoyment, learning, and willingness to try. Explain that the same is true for teachers. Reassure your students, therefore, that you will reduce or eliminate topics and activities they clearly do not like or that affect them adversely and that you will not permit anything in the class to damage their sense of safety and security, feeling of belonging, and sense of hope.

Emphasize Class Conditions and Activities Students Are Known to Like

Tell your students you will strive for the following qualities in the classroom and that you need their help making sure they occur:

- A teacher who is friendly, interesting, helpful, and supportive
- Camaraderie—enjoyable associations among classmates
- Interesting topics to learn about that are intriguing and worthwhile
- Students' awareness of the importance of what they are asked to learn
- Enjoyable instructional activities
- Opportunity for and likelihood of success and accomplishment
- Attention drawn tactfully to student accomplishments

As well, discuss with students some of the things they normally dislike in school, as listed below. Indicate you will guard against them. Note, however, that some students do not object to all of these activities or conditions. You might wish to ask their opinions about them. Also ask if they can see situations in which some of these conditions might be necessary.

- Sitting still for long periods
- Keeping quiet for long periods
- Working alone
- Not knowing why something is being taught or learned
- Memorizing facts for tests
- Completing lengthy reading and writing assignments
- Doing repetitive work
- Engaging in individual competition where there is little or no chance of winning
- Having little or no choice in activities, assignments, or assessment

Work to Develop Class Ethics and Trust

The term *ethics* refers to doing what one believes to be the honorable thing in all situations. Ethical student behavior should be a prime goal of education, and ethical teacher behavior is essential for building trust in the class. Students see teachers as ethical and trustworthy when they are unfailingly kind, considerate, helpful, fair, and tactfully honest. Trust is essential in synergetic discipline, as it enables teachers and students to count on each other for support and fair treatment.

Emphasize and Use Your Personal Charisma

Charisma is an aspect of personality that attracts others. Students greatly enjoy charismatic teachers and flock to them. Charisma seems to emerge from a blend of talent, experience, knowledge, and understanding of others, and it is made evident in how people react to each other. We can all increase our level of charisma and display it through personal charm, friendliness, enthusiasm, and helpfulness.

Improve the Quality of Communication in Your Classroom

Except for trust, no element of synergy is more important than *communication*. The type of communication that contributes most to synergy is verbal give-and-take between teacher and students. It involves listening sensitively, showing genuine interest, and speaking encouragingly rather than arguing, moralizing, or giving unsolicited advice.

Make Use of Coopetition

Coopetition, pronounced "co-opetition," refers to members of groups cooperating together in order to compete against other groups. Coopetition is not given a great deal of attention in teaching, but it contributes powerfully to synergy. In school, it is exemplified in team athletic events and other performances and competitions. Coopetition can be incorporated into almost all areas of the curriculum. Generally speaking, students respond to it more enthusiastically than to any other activity.

Resolve Class Problems and Conflicts Amicably and Productively

A class *problem* is a situation or condition that affects the class seriously enough to require attention, while a class *conflict* is a strong disagreement between students or between teacher and student.

How to Address Problems.   Suppose students in a high school geometry class are troubled by a heavy load of homework, or suppose a middle school teacher is greatly embarrassed when the principal visits and makes a comment about the room being untidy. When such situations hinder teaching or learning for any reason, they should be addressed immediately. The teacher, sensing the problem, might say, "Class, something is going on that I think we need to talk about." The problem should then be clarified, possible solutions should be sought, and a solution should be selected and tried.

How to Address Conflicts.   *Conflicts* are interpersonal situations characterized by strong disagreements, which may or may not include misbehavior. If the individuals involved do not know how to find a peaceful solution, they tend to fight each other verbally and sometimes physically. Conflict threatens personal dignity, which is strongly defended. Examples of conflict situations include disputes over who won a contest, who is entitled to play with a toy, whether work was turned in on time, and whether work has met the standards expected. Conflict is best resolved through a win–win approach, in which both sides are made to feel most of their concerns have been adequately addressed.

To resolve conflicts effectively in your class, follow these guidelines:

- Make sure all individuals involved have the opportunity to express their concerns.
- Insist that all comments, observations, and suggestions be presented in a courteous manner.
- Encourage both sides to be open and honest but tactful.
- Encourage each person to try to see things from the other's point of view.
- Try to focus attention on the areas of agreement between the disputants.
- Help disputants formulate solutions as joint agreements.
- Don't allow students to argue back and forth, defend themselves, or debate.

IN SUMMARY

Misbehavior can be defined in many ways. One of the most useful definitions is "any action that, through intent or thoughtlessness, interferes with teaching or learning, threatens or intimidates others, or oversteps society's standards of moral, ethical, or legal behavior." Thirteen types of classroom misbehavior were described, and suggestions were presented for dealing with them. Prevention—the easiest and most time-effective strategy for improving classroom behavior—calls on teachers to understand and recognize the causes of misbehavior and take steps to eliminate, soften, or circumvent them. Twenty-six causes of misbehavior were listed in the chapter. One of the main causes is incompatibility between school activities and student needs. Given this, teachers are urged to align class expectations, topics, and activities with predominant student needs, such as security, belonging, hope, dignity, power, enjoyment, and competence. Synergetic teaching was presented as one style of teaching that reduces misbehavior.

REFERENCES

Albert, L. 2003. *A teacher's guide to cooperative discipline.* Circle Pines, MN: American Guidance Service.

Charles, C. 2000. *The synergetic classroom: Joyful teaching and gentle discipline.* Boston: Allyn & Bacon.

Charles, C. 2008. *Building classroom discipline* (9th edition). Boston: Allyn & Bacon.

Coloroso, B. 2002. *Kids are worth it! Giving your child the gift of inner discipline.* New York: Quill, 2002.

Dreikurs, R., and Cassell, P. 1995. *Discipline without tears* (2nd edition). New York: Penguin.

Glasser, W. 1998. *The quality school: Managing students without coercion.* New York: HarperCollins.

Gordon, T. 1987. *T.E.T.: Teacher effectiveness training* (2nd edition). New York: David McKay.

Gordon, T. 1989. *Discipline that works: Promoting self-discipline in children.* New York: Random House.

Kagan, S., Kyle, P., and Scott, S. 2004. *Win–win discipline.* San Clemente, CA: Kagan.

Levine, M. 2002. *A mind at a time.* New York: Simon & Schuster.

STRATEGY

3

Clarifying Expectations

Explicitly Teaching Students How They Are Expected to Conduct Themselves in the Classroom

You can accomplish this strategy by making your expectations clear and having students practice the behaviors associated with those expectations until they become routine. Doing so will minimize the conditions that frequently lead to disruptive behavior. Do not assume your students know how to behave properly; teach them what is expected.

Chapter Preview

This chapter explains why many authorities believe it is necessary actually to teach students how to behave appropriately in the classroom, and it presents suggestions for doing so. The chapter first presents two somewhat different approaches to establishing and clarifying expectations, both of which are effective—the teacher/student cooperative approach and the teacher-structured approach. Ronald Morrish's suggestions for establishing and teaching class expectations are then presented, followed by a feature presentation on the ideas of Harry K. Wong, who was named by *Instructor Magazine* in 2006 as one of education's superstars.

CLARIFYING BEHAVIOR EXPECTATIONS FOR YOUR CLASS

When teachers first began using lists of rules for class behavior, which came into vogue in the 1970s, they established the rules themselves and went over them briefly with students. At first, the rules were mostly directives and prohibitions, such as these:

- No fighting or swearing in this class.
- No food or gum chewing.
- Raise your hand before speaking.
- Keep your hands and feet to yourself.

Students were expected to comply with these rules, and if they did not, the teacher reacted with disapproval or light punishment, such as detention or extra homework.

In recent years, approaches to establishing class expectations have changed considerably. They still indicate how students are to conduct themselves but differ from earlier rules in three important ways. First, rules are more positive in nature:

- Show courtesy toward all members of the class.
- Conduct yourself responsibly.
- Do the best work you can.

Second, rules are often formulated with significant input from students. Such involvement usually makes students more willing to comply with the rules. And third, rules are more akin to goals to be achieved on a continual basis, rather than discrete laws to be observed. Nowadays, when students violate a rule or agreement, they are not punished; instead, they are helped to find a better alternative behavior and encouraged or taught how to behave in the more appropriate manner.

Here, we explore two somewhat different procedures for establishing class rules, which are more appropriately called *expectations*. Both procedures work well, and you should use whichever you feel is best in your situation.

In the first approach—*teacher/student cooperation*—the teacher directs a sequence of group discussions that lead to a set of expectations for class behavior. Student input is sought from the beginning. This approach in emphasized in the teachings of authorities such as William Glasser (1998), Thomas Gordon (1989), C. M. Charles (2008), and Alfie Kohn (2001).

The second approach, the *teacher-structured method,* is efficient and easily established. The teacher, as the trained professional, specifies behaviors that will enable the class to function best. Teachers and students, although cooperative, are not depicted as working side by side toward a common end. Rather, they are assigned separate sets of duties, which they discharge for the overall benefit of the class. This approach is emphasized in the teachings of Lee Canter (1976), Ronald Morrish (2000), and Harry and Rosemary Wong (2002).

Each of these approaches has advantages and shortcomings. The teacher/student method obtains a great deal of student input and is believed by many to promote greater student buy-in and increased willingness to respect the agreements. The process takes time, however, and teachers must be willing to listen seriously to student suggestions. In the teacher-structured approach, the teacher formulates the expectations. Then he or she carefully explains them to students and conducts discussions to make sure students understand the expectations and find them fair and appropriate. In the following sections, we see in greater detail how each of these approaches works.

THE TEACHER/STUDENT COOPERATIVE APPROACH

C. M. Charles (2008) describes a multisession procedure for establishing a teacher/student cooperative approach to establishing class expectations.

Session 1

On the first day of class, arrange for students to sit in a circle, if possible. If your classroom, lab, hall, or gymnasium doesn't provide flexible seating, make the best arrangement you can for students to have eye contact with each other. Smile at the students as they arrive. Look at their faces. Say hello and tell them you are glad to see them and are looking forward to working with them. Begin by greeting the students and telling them you would like everyone to get acquainted quickly. If the students are old enough, ask them to pair up and take five minutes to learn each other's names and something memorable that will help others remember their names and faces. Have the pairs take turns introducing each other. As they do so, use your class list to check students' names. Repeat the names aloud, and ask if you have pronounced them correctly, if there is any doubt. Try to fix students' names in your mind.

When students have finished their introductions, briefly tell a bit about yourself. Let your personality show, but don't act silly. Mention your family, if appropriate, as well as a favorite hobby and another item or two of interest. Keep things quite brief at this point, but over time, add bits of information about your background, travels, special skills, unusual experiences, favorite foods, favorite books, and so forth. At some point during the first day or two, tell why you became a teacher and what you have liked most about it. Also, fairly early in the course, let students know your point of view on matters such as the following:

- *Education*—its value and what it can give people who take advantage of it
- *Students*—how you consider them all important and capable of learning and how the best part of teaching is doing what you can to help them
- *Teaching*—how teachers best help students learn by getting them interested, rather than bossing or scolding them
- *Life in general*—the enormous privilege of being alive, the great adventures life brings, the challenges it poses, and the opportunities it gives us to make something good of ourselves

When introductions have been completed, tell students you are convinced learning occurs better for everyone when teachers and students work together cooperatively. Cooperation involves everyone making some decisions together, assuming a certain duty that benefits the class, and working together to maintain an optimal learning environment. Depending on the level and subject you teach, you can mention the need for students to serve as class recorder (to document class activities and progress), equipment managers, materials managers, media managers, substitute teacher and visitor assistants, plant and animal managers (if such are in the classroom), and the like.

Later you can assign duties to students; you will have to teach them what they must do and how to do it. Don't force everyone to take on a duty at first, but as time passes, involve all students in this way. At times, ask individuals if they will assume special tasks, such as helping keep the class area neat, working together with another student, putting up displays, and investigating certain topics on the Internet.

When introductions have been completed, present a preview of the course or year, highlighting certain topics, activities, special events, and other preliminary matters.

Session 2

Later in the day or when you again see the students, ask for volunteers to assume responsibility for some of the class tasks discussed previously. Tell each volunteer briefly, so the class can hear, what the duty involves and what the student must do. Ask for comments and suggestions from the class. Tell the selected students you will help them learn how to perform their duties. If they are old enough, assign a class recorder at this point to take notes about class activities. (These notes should be organized and kept as a chronology of class activities and achievements.) If the students are too young for this, keep notes yourself for use in reviewing student activities and progress.

Next, assure students that you want their educational experience in the class to be as enjoyable and satisfying as possible and that, toward that end, you would like to hear their views on certain matters. Using a chart or transparency projector, proceed with questions such as these:

1. *What are some of the things you like best about school?* Students will probably say they like sports, being with friends, playing, doing art and music. Some may mention performing in plays, concerts, and athletics. A few may mention learning, good teachers, computers, laboratories, and library. Down the left side of your chart or transparency, make notes about what they say.
2. *What do you like specifically about each of the things we have written on the list?* Write their comments on the right side of your chart.
3. *Which of the things we have mentioned might be possible to do in this class?* Circle the things they indicate.

Thank the students for their contributions. Tell them you will review their suggestions overnight and give them feedback the next day.

Session 3

Before this session, redo the chart of student suggestions. When the students arrive, indicate which of the suggestions you believe could be put into practice for the class. Ask if they have other thoughts or suggestions. Turn to a new transparency or fresh page on the chart, and ask for students' comments about the kind of teachers they prefer:

1. Ask if they have had a teacher they really enjoyed and respected. Ask them not to mention names but to indicate what that teacher did that made such a good impression. (Students will probably say the teacher was nice, interesting, helpful, fair, or had a sense of humor. They may mention activities they liked or special talents the teacher had.) Write the traits down the left side of your chart.
2. Review the traits with the class. Where needed, ask for elaboration, such as "What does a nice teacher do? What does a helpful teacher do? What does 'we really had fun' mean?" Make notes on the right side of the chart.
3. Tell students you would like to be the kind of teacher they prefer, as much as you are able. Tell them you want time to study the notes you have made and will give them feedback at the next session. Thank them for their thoughtfulness.

Session 4

To prepare for this session, make a clean copy of students' comments concerning traits they like in teachers. Display the copy and indicate this is what you understood students to say they liked in teachers. Ask if they have corrections or further suggestions. If they have made suggestions you can't comply with, tell them why. Now draw students out regarding how they like their classmates to behave in school:

1. Ask students to think of classmates who have behaved in ways they admired or appreciated. Without naming names, let them tell what each classmate was like. List the traits they mention down the left side of your chart.
2. When several behaviors have been listed, go back and ask why those behaviors are appreciated. List the comments on the right side of the chart.
3. Move further by asking students how they like fellow members of classes to treat them. Make notes on the left side; then go back and again ask why.
4. Now ask what kind of behavior they most appreciate from other students when they are working together on assignments. Make notes and ask why.

Just before the end of the session, ask if there is agreement on the behaviors and reasons you have listed. Then ask the students if they think it would be possible to have those kinds of behaviors in this classroom.

Thank students for their input. Tell them that by the next session, you will have their ideas written out for review.

Session 5

For this session, prepare a clean chart or transparency that shows the behaviors students said they most liked in their classmates. Show students the chart, and ask if it correctly reflects their comments. Make changes as needed. Now ask for their input concerning the kind of behavior they dislike in their classmates.

1. On the left side of the chart, make a list of the disliked behaviors students mention. Ask students why they dislike them. Makes notes concerning their reasons on the right side of the page.

2. Next, ask if they have ideas about how to keep those unwanted behaviors from occurring in the class. Tell them you are interested in how to prevent the behaviors, rather than having to deal with them after they have occurred. Students may have some trouble with this question. If so, ask them if they are able to decide how they will behave or if they have no control over what they say or do. Ask them also if things in the classroom—such as noise, clutter, the lighting, and the temperature—are all right for them. Students will probably agree they can control their behavior, and they might make comments about the physical environment.

3. Ask students what makes them decide to behave either properly or improperly. Ask if there is anything you and the class can do to help them want to behave properly. Take notes. If students get stuck, ask directly about the "golden rule," making friends, caring about others, and having interesting things to do.

4. Once they have identified what might make them want to behave properly, review their suggestions.

5. Next, say the following: "Suppose despite everything we do, someone in the class decides to misbehave, to do something that we as a class do not approve of. What should we do then?" Students typically suggest punishment of some sort. If they do,

6. Now say, "I would want to help that person understand that his or her behavior is hurtful to the class. I wouldn't want to punish him or her. I don't want to be unpleasant or fight against any of you because that doesn't do any good. What I would like to do, if possible, is change whatever is causing the person to misbehave. That is how I would like to deal with the situation. What do you think of that? Put yourself in that person's place. Would you rather be punished or have conditions changed so you wouldn't feel like misbehaving any more?"

Thank the students for taking this matter seriously. Tell them you will think about their suggestions and see if you can have a plan for class behavior ready for them to consider at the next meeting.

Session 6

In advance, prepare a chart that shows the following: (1) things students have said they like best in school; (2) traits students have said they like best in teachers; (3) behaviors students have said they like in classmates; (4) behaviors students say they dislike in classmates; and (5) how students might be encouraged to want to behave properly.

1. Review the first four items. Ask students if they reflect accurately what the students said.

2. When that is settled, review your plan for dealing with misbehavior, including the following:

- Making school interesting, providing help, taking care of distractions, and treating everyone considerately so students will have little reason to misbehave
- How students can resolve most of their problems or disputes in a friendly, productive manner
- How you will work with students who misbehave to try to correct whatever is causing their misbehavior and to teach them how to behave appropriately

Ask the class to comment on the plan and make suggestions. End the session by thanking them and saying that at the next session, you hope the class can formulate some agreements about what the teacher and students can do to make the class enjoyable and worthwhile.

Session 7

Bring back the chart used in the previous session. Put it to the side but in view. Using a blank chart, tell the students you now hope they can finalize agreements that will guide the class. Ask students to help compose a succinct statement about each of the following:

1. Class activities that are valuable and enjoyable
2. The teacher's way of teaching and treating students
3. The students' ways of treating each other and the teacher
4. How students will work at assigned tasks

When satisfactory statements have been made, tell the class that you feel sure that you can, with their help, provide their preferred activities and ways of interacting. Ask individual students if they feel they will be able to abide by the agreements they have reached. Ask the group as a whole if anyone thinks they might not be able to do so. When that is done, tell the class you will print out the agreements, display them in the room, and send copies home to parents (or publish them on the school Internet site).

Following Days and Weeks

Before long, your ethical and charismatic behavior will have drawn students to you in a trusting manner. As time passes, however, some students will misbehave, occasionally seriously. At those times, remember that you have determined to do the best you can for each of your students, so try the following when speaking with students about their misbehavior:

1. Mention something positive about the student, and comment on that quality as a means of starting the communication.
2. Identify the problematic behavior, and ask what might be done so the student won't feel like repeating the behavior. Doing this may or may not take care of the problem.

3. If it does not, look for further positive qualities and draw attention to them. Ask again if there is something you can do to help the student avoid self-damaging behavior.

Your personal attention and appreciation for positive qualities will soon make inroads, and the unattractive behavior will begin to change. Show appreciation for the improvement. There is a good chance that over time, you will enjoy success with that student.

For a lesson plan with activities similar to what has been described, view a contribution from Renee Goularte (2006), in which she takes her students through activities beginning with the questions "Why are we here?" and "What do we need to be successful?" Her material is presented on the following website: www.readwritethink.org/lessons/lesson_view.asp?id=136.

Consultant
RONALD MORRISH ON THE TEACHER-STRUCTURED APPROACH

Ronald Morrish, who has developed a discipline approach he calls *Real Discipline,* explains how teachers can establish and teach behavior expectations for the classroom. Morrish was a teacher and behavior specialist for 26 years before becoming an independent consultant in 1997. He now devotes his efforts to writing, delivering conference presentations, creating professional development programs and courses for teachers, and working with parent groups and child care providers around the world. His ideas and suggestions are set forth in his books *Secrets of Discipline* (1997) and *With All Due Respect* (2000). For more information about Morrish and his work, go to his website: www.realdiscipline.com.

Morrish reminds us that students do not enter school knowing how to behave responsibly, nor do they learn self-discipline from experience alone. To acquire these advanced skills, students need supportive guidance from enlightened, caring teachers, as emphasized in his approach to behavior management. Morrish explains that Real Discipline is not a new theory but an organized set of techniques that outstanding teachers and parents have used for generations to teach children to be respectful, responsible, and cooperative. Careful teacher guidance is used to ensure children learn how conduct themselves appropriately. As Morrish (1997) puts it:

> Real Discipline is a lot more than simply giving choices to children and then dealing with the aftermath. We have to teach them right and wrong. We have to teach them to respect legitimate authority. We have to teach them the lessons that have been learned by others and by ourselves. Then, and only then, will we enjoy watching them develop into adults. (p. 33)

Morrish explains that these provisions are necessary because children, in their early years, are impulsive and self-centered. In order to develop into contributing members of society, they must learn to cooperate, behave responsibly, and show consideration for others. Sometimes, they have parents and role models who teach them these things. But too often these days, they do not. Children who are overindulged and never called to account for their behavior remain self-centered. They grow up concerned only with their own needs, without regard for the needs of others. They want things their way, cooperate in school only when they feel like it, and are seldom considerate of teachers and fellow students. For many, abusive language and bullying are the rule of the day.

This situation has come about in part because we live in a society that stresses individual rights and freedoms. We hold those rights and freedoms dear, but somehow we have lost sight of personal responsibility, without which rights and freedoms mean little. Personal responsibility is too important to leave to chance. We must live in accordance with requirements that put constraints on individual freedom. We do this in exchange for a life that is more safe, secure, and orderly.

Morrish believes students should be given choices at school but only when they are sufficiently experienced and mature to deal with them. Otherwise, having choices is more often detrimental than beneficial. Students do not know innately how to make responsible choices. Before they can do so, they must develop a degree of compliance and respect for authority. Yet many of today's discipline programs immediately give students a strong voice in deciding on class rules and personal conduct. That does little to help students learn to live by rules; rather, it permits them to do as they please as long as they are willing to accept the consequences.

In 2003, Morrish published a small spiral-bound book called *FlipTips,* containing comments and maxims from his various publications and presentations. These tips are interesting and helpful, and they reveal the mindset toward discipline Morrish would like teachers to acquire. Here are a few of the tips that illustrate that mindset (wording is slightly changed in some cases, but not the meaning):

- Discipline is a process, not an event.
- Discipline is about giving students the structure they need, not the consequences they appear to deserve.
- *Discipline* comes from the word *disciple,* not the word *ogre.* It's about teaching and learning, not scolding and punishing.
- Discipline isn't what you do when students misbehave. It's what you do so they won't.
- Discipline isn't about letting students make their own choices. It's about preparing them for the choices they will be making. Don't let students make choices that are not theirs to make.
- Train students to comply with your directions. Compliance precedes cooperation. If you bargain for compliance now, you'll have to beg for it later.
- Always work from more structure to less structure, not the other way around.
- To prevent major behavior problems, deal with all minor behavior problems.

- Students learn far more from being shown how to behave appropriately than from being punished.
- The best time to teach a behavior is when it isn't needed, so it will be there when it is needed.
- If you teach students to be part of the solution, they're less likely to be part of the problem.
- When dealing with adolescents, act more like a coach and less like a boss.
- A single minute practicing courtesy has more impact than a one-hour lecture on the importance of it.
- To stop fights, stop put-downs. Verbal hits usually precede physical hits.
- Discipline should end with the correct behavior, not with a punishment.
- Today's practice is tomorrow's performance.
- Rapport is the magical ingredient that changes a student's reluctance to be controlled into a willingness to be guided.

Rather than approaching discipline as dependent on student choice, Morrish asks teachers to guide students through three progressive phases—training, teaching, and management. Each phase is aimed at a particular goal and relies on a certain set of strategies.

Phase 1: Training for Compliance

The first phase is organized to train students to accept adult authority and comply with it automatically. Basic compliance should be taught initially as a nonthinking activity—as a habit you don't have to reflect on or make choices about, such as stopping at a red light or saying thank-you when people do something nice for you. Students should be carefully trained in how to pay attention, follow directions, and speak respectfully, to the point that they do these things automatically, or habitually.

Compliant classroom behavior is taught through direct instruction and close supervision. If you want students to raise their hands before speaking, tell them what you expect and show them how to do it. Have them replicate the act and practice it until it becomes habitual. When students make mistakes, show them again how to do the act properly and once again have them practice it. Morrish says to start small. You will see a general attitude of compliance grow out of many small compliances.

Compliance is extremely important, yet it receives virtually no attention in other popular programs of discipline. Compliance helps students conduct themselves properly and provides the basis for later decision making. It is based on the fundamental recognition that there are effective ways of behaving in civilized society that put limits on what people do.

Therefore, in compliance training, teachers should address all misbehavior. They should not overlook small misbehaviors, as they are advised to do in many discipline programs. Overlooking small misbehaviors is necessary in those programs, Morrish says, because of the excessive time requirement for explaining, negotiating, and tending to consequences. As a result, teachers are advised to "Pick your battles" and "Don't sweat the small stuff." Accordingly, teachers may allow students to slouch over their desks during opening routines, talk during announcements, throw their jackets in the corner instead of hanging them up, and wander around the room instead of getting ready to work.

Such behaviors may seem unimportant but should never be overlooked. A few poor habits can easily expand to poor behavior overall. If you walk by students who are doing something wrong and you say nothing, they will interpret that as meaning you don't care, and the next thing you know, they will be engaged in even more disruptive misbehavior. Don't get the idea you can't manage such behavior, but do understand it is not corrected by scolding or doling out consequences. Instead, the best approach is to tell students what you want them to do and then to insist they do it properly. When they do something wrong, have them do it right. That is how you establish good practices and habits in your classes. Students will get the picture quickly.

Morrish asks teachers to train their students to comply with three things—rules, limits, and authority. *Rules* indicate how students are to behave. An example of a rule might be "Show courtesy and respect for others at all times." *Limits* specify behavior that will not be allowed. An example of a limit would be "No name-calling in this room." *Authority* refers to power that has been assigned to certain individuals. Teachers are given, by custom and law, legitimate authority to control and direct students in school. They should use this authority to set and maintain standards of conduct.

Phase 2: Teaching the Skills

The second phase in Real Discipline focuses on teaching students the skills, attitudes, and knowledge they need for cooperation, proper behavior, and increased responsibility. The teacher sets the class rules and quickly teaches them through explanation, demonstration, practice, and corrective feedback. Students understand the need for rules, and they will comply with them if they accept the teacher's authority. This process teaches students to be courteous, work and play harmoniously together, resolve conflicts, set personal goals, organize tasks, and manage time.

Most teachers erroneously think students will somehow learn these skills from experience. You can't wait for experience to teach them these things, even if it could. Today's students must be taught what to do, if you are to have order and acceptable behavior in your classes. When students fail to comply with expectations, don't scold or punish them. Simply have them redo the behavior in an acceptable manner and continue to practice it.

Phase 3: Managing Choices

The third phase of Real Discipline helps students move toward greater independence by offering them more and more choices, as they show capability for handling them. A basic requirement in choice making is that students must take into account the needs and rights of others. You will need to make sure students do so. Although today's popular discipline approaches place heavy emphasis on this component, they do little to establish compliance and set limits that prepare students for effective choice making.

Morrish explains that choice management also requires specification of who has the right or duty to make a particular choice. Teachers must make certain choices, while students can be allowed to make others. As a rule, if students don't care about the outcome of a particular goal, they should not be allowed to have choices about it.

To illustrate, most people assume that students who do poor work in class should receive low marks that will make them aware of the problem and want to do better in the future. This may work for some highly motivated students, but it does nothing for those who don't care and are perfectly willing to accept low grades. If students indicate they don't care about their performance in important class matters, you should reply, "That's okay, Mary, because I do care and that's why this is my choice. Someday, when you care about it as much as I do, it will become your choice" (Morrish, 1997, p. 101). Suppose Mary has handed in poor work. You say the following: "Mary, your work is disorganized and incomplete. I'm not accepting it. Take it back, please, and fix it up. I'll mark it when it is done properly" (Morrish, 1997, p. 105).

Teachers must make decisions for students like Mary until they begin to care about quality and completeness. The teacher should never suggest that Mary can choose to do poor work if she wants to. Morrish says this is one area where we truly need to get "back to basics," meaning we should expect students to do quality work and accept nothing less. As Morrish puts it, "Schools are not democracies. Teachers must be willing to make the decisions that are theirs to make" (1997, p. 106).

HARRY K. WONG ON CLASSROOM PROCEDURES

Harry K. Wong, now an educational speaker and consultant, for many years taught middle school and high school classes in science. Named by *Instructor Magazine* in 2006 as one of education's superstars, Wong has received numerous teaching awards, including the Outstanding Secondary Teacher Award, the Science Teacher Achievement Recognition Award, the Outstanding Biology Teacher Award, and the Valley Forge Teacher's Medal. At the time of this writing, Wong's book *The First Days of School* (2004b), which he co-authored with his wife Rosemary, had sold over 2.7 million copies, making it the  best-selling education book of all time. The Wongs have produced a video series entitled *The Effective Teacher,* which won the Gold Award in the International Film and Video Festival and the Telly Award as the best educational staff development video. They also have an online course called *Classroom Management with Harry and Rosemary Wong,* which can be accessed at www.ClassroomManagement.com. Harry writes a monthly column that is posted on www.Teachers.Net. His website is www.EffectiveTeaching.com.

Wong insists that most students will behave acceptably in school if they are taught the procedures that lead to learning and responsible behavior. As these procedures are taught and used, they become routines that students follow habitually. Wong also asserts that student achievement increases as teachers establish good, workable classroom procedures, beginning the very first day. He concludes that students not only accept but appreciate uniform procedures that provide security and minimize confusion. When such procedures are not in place, however, students are likely to behave undesirably and develop poor work habits that are difficult to correct.

A Sample of Wong's Advice

Wong stresses that teachers should set high expectations on the first day and plan the entire day right down to the minute. Specific attention should be given to an opening assignment for students, establishing routines, and learning students' names. Wong says that during the first week, the most important thing you can do is provide the security of consistency (Wong and Wong, 2004b). He is quite explicit in his suggestions for setting the scene for learning and good behavior.

For example, he says if the furniture is movable, align all the desks on the first day facing the teacher, and keep them that way until you have a good reason to change. Provide a well-organized, uncluttered, attractive classroom. Have the room ready and inviting when students arrive on the first day. On a bulletin board or elsewhere, post schedules, rules, procedures, and a preview of what is to come. Also post information about yourself, including a picture and a sign that welcomes students to the class. Wear neat clothing, because first impressions will affect how students relate to you. Stand when you speak and use short, clear sentences and phrases. Use a firm but soft voice. When emphasizing, do not point your finger, as it presents an accusatory image. If you have very young students, place their names on their coat hooks, desks, and cubbyholes and tell them to use the coat hook, desk, or cubbyhole every day. For students of all ages, set up a seating plan beforehand, as this will help you to get to know your students quickly. Address your students by name as soon as possible.

On the first day, go to school early and take time to double-check everything. Have your first "bellwork" assignment ready (a short assignment that students begin working on when they first arrive in the room). Make it interesting but fairly easy so students will have an initial sense of accomplishment. Students who experience early failures tend to create problems in the classroom. Before class begins, tell yourself the following:

1. I will establish classroom management procedures from the beginning.
2. I will convey that this class will be businesslike, with a firm, competent, and warm teacher.
3. I will establish work habits in my students first and worry about content later.

Position yourself outside the classroom door to greet students as they arrive. This establishes authority and shows you consider the students important. If young children are to line up before entering, insist on a straight line. If you pick up your class from another area, don't say "Follow me" or "Come on." Rather, introduce yourself and then teach the procedure you want students to follow as they walk to your room.

The First Five Minutes Are Critical

Wong says you should have an assignment—the bellwork mentioned earlier—for the students to begin working on when they walk into the room (Wong and Wong, 2000a). He contends this eliminates 90 percent of discipline problems that otherwise arise. The first few minutes are crucial to setting the tone in your class. Students must know what they are expected to do. When they come in, remind them of the materials they need that day and to have pencils sharpened and paper ready.

When the bell rings, turn on the overhead projector and have it display a warm-up activity—perhaps important information or a brief review of something learned the previous year or term. As students work, take roll while you walk around and observe. For the next activity, students might be asked to write a reaction to a quote or newspaper article, copy a timeline, brainstorm emotions felt in response to a piece of music, or (later) complete a quiz on the previous night's reading assignment. There should be no student free time planned into the routines at first. It is better to have too much planned for the class period than too little.

How to Establish Procedures for Your Classroom

To establish good procedures, do two things: First, decide what routines are needed for the activities you provide, and second, make lists of the procedural steps students must follow in order to participate in and benefit from the activities. As you do these two things, you will find you have an astonishingly large number of procedures. But remember that every time you want students to do something, they need a procedure to follow—for example, how to enter and exit the classroom; how dismissal occurs at the end of the period or day; how to begin and finish work; how to come to attention; what to do on returning after being absent; what to do when arriving tardy; how the class is to get quiet when necessary; how the period or day is to begin; how to ask for help from the teacher or others; how to indicate when you don't understand or need help; how to move about the classroom; how papers, materials, and supplies are to be distributed and collected; how everyone is to listen to and respond to questions; how to work cooperatively with others; how groups are changed; how directions are given for each assignment and how students can find the directions; how you are to walk in the corridors; and how students are to keep personal notebooks.

Classroom Procedures Must Be Taught

Good procedures allow a great variety of activities to occur—often, several at the same time with little confusion. But you have to teach students the procedures, not just talk about them. Wong suggests a three-step method for teaching procedures:

1. *Explain:* The teacher states, explains, and demonstrates the procedure.
2. *Rehearse:* Students rehearse and practice the procedure under teacher supervision.
3. *Reinforce:* The teacher reteaches, rehearses, practices, and reinforces the classroom procedure until it becomes a habit.

The following extracted statements provide an overview of the Wongs's principal contentions (from Wong and Wong, 2000a, 2000b, 2004a, 2004b, 2005, and Glavac, 2005). Notice that the Wongs use many aphorisms that stick in the mind, such as:

- The main problem in teaching is not poor discipline, but poor classroom management.
- Procedures provide the foundation that leads to high student achievement.
- Effective teachers spend most of the first two weeks teaching students to follow classroom procedures.
- What you do on the first day of school determines your success for the rest of the year.
- Start class immediately. Do not take roll until later.
- Learning is most effective when it takes place in a supportive community of learners.
- The more students work together responsibly, the more they learn.
- Short assignments produce higher student achievement.
- Intersperse questions throughout a lesson. Ask a question after you have spoken a few sentences rather than many. By doing so, you significantly increase student learning and retention.
- Students usually learn more from an activity-question approach than from a textbook-lecture approach.
- Teachers go through four stages of development—fantasy (what they unrealistically imagine teaching will be like before they experience it), survival (getting by day-to-day), mastery (showing high level of competence), and impact (making a major difference in students' lives). Good management moves you quickly from the fantasy stage to mastery.
- You can have your achievements or you can have your excuses.
- Those who teach well never cease to learn.

About Classrooms, Teachers, and Procedures

Wong insists that the main cause of poor behavior in the classroom is not bad discipline but errors teachers make in classroom management. Unless you establish and teach clear class procedures, student behavior will never be as you want it.

Wong insists that your classroom must not be allowed to degenerate into chaos; instead, it must be established and maintained as a smoothly functioning learning environment, task oriented and predictable. Ineffective teachers begin the first day of school attempting to teach a subject. They then spend the rest of the schoolyear running after their students. Effective teachers spend most of the first two weeks teaching students to follow classroom procedures. After that, students learn better and conduct themselves better.

About Roles and Responsibilities

Wong urges teachers to help students understand both the teacher's responsibilities and the students' responsibilities in the classroom. The following, appropriate for secondary classes, appears on the cover of *The First Days of School* (2004b):

> *My Responsibilities as Your Teacher*
> 1. To treat you with respect and care as an individual
> 2. To provide you an orderly classroom environment
> 3. To provide the necessary discipline
> 4. To provide the appropriate motivation
> 5. To teach you the required content
>
> *Your Responsibilities as My Students*
> 1. To treat me with respect and care as an individual
> 2. To attend classes regularly
> 3. To be cooperative and not disruptive
> 4. To study and do your work well
> 5. To learn and master the required content

About Discipline

Wong maintains that you will have little trouble with discipline if you follow his suggestions about teaching routines. He does say that in order to maintain a safe, orderly environment, you should establish class rules that indicate the behavior you expect from students and you should enforce those rules using whatever discipline system you think appropriate. Wong explains that rules of behavior set limits, just as do rules in games, and help create a work-oriented atmosphere. Behavior associated with rules must be taught through discussion, demonstration, and practice. In addition, consequences should be attached to rules—positive consequences for compliance and negative consequences for noncompliance. Wong would have you explain your discipline plan—including expectations, rules, and consequences—the first day of school.

More about the First Day

- Have your classroom ready for instruction, and make it inviting.
- Organize your classroom in accordance with a script that you follow.
- Stand at the door and greet students as they enter.
- Give each student a seating assignment and a seating chart.
- Position yourself in the room near the students. Problems will be proportional to distance between you and them.
- Post an assignment in a consistent location for students to begin when they enter the room.
- Display your diploma and credentials with pride. Dress in a professional manner that models success and shows you expect achievement.

About the First Week of Teaching

- The three most important things you must teach the first week of school are discipline, procedures, and routines.
- Explain your discipline plan to students, and put it in effect immediately.
- State your procedures and rehearse them until they become routines.

Finally, Wong says that all these matters should be planned out in detail before the first day of teaching and then discussed systematically with students. If you do that, he says, you will feel secure in teaching and will present yourself as a knowledgeable professional.

IN SUMMARY

For the most part, students behave appropriately in the classroom if they first know what is expected of them and then practice the associated behaviors until they become routine. Two approaches were described for helping students understand how they are to conduct themselves. The first was a teacher/student cooperative approach, which involves significant student input and a mindset of teacher and students working together toward the same end. The second was a teacher-directed approach, in which the teacher establishes class expectations and procedures, explains them fully, and teaches them to students through modeling and direct practice until the associated behaviors become routine.

REFERENCES

Canter, L. (1976). *Assertive discipline: A take-charge approach for today's educator.* Seal Beach, CA: Lee Canter and Associates.

Charles, C. M. 2008. *Building classroom discipline* (9th edition). Boston: Allyn & Bacon.

Glasser, W. 1998. *Choice theory in the classroom.* New York: HarperCollins.

Glavac, M. 2005. Summary of Major Concepts Covered by Harry K. Wong. *Busy Educator's Newsletter.* www.glavac.com.

Gordon, T. 1989. *Discipline that works: Promoting self-discipline in children.* New York: Random House.

Goularte, R. 2006. Creating Class Rules: A Beginning to Creating Community. www .readwritethink.org/lessons/lesson_view.asp?id=136.

Kohn, A. 2001. *Beyond discipline: From compliance to community.* Upper Saddle River, NJ: Merrill/Prentice-Hall.

Morrish, R. 1997. *Secrets of discipline: Twelve keys for raising responsible children.* Fonthill, Ontario, Canada: Woodstream.

Morrish, R. 2000. *With all due respect: Keys for building effective school discipline.* Fonthill, Ontario, Canada: Woodstream.

Morrish, R. 2003. *Flip Tips.* Fonthill, Ontario, Canada: Woodstream.

Wong, H. 2001. Selection of tips for teachers. www.glavac.com/harrywong.htm.

Wong, H., and Wong, R. 2000a. The First Five Minutes Are Critical. *Gazette* article. Teachers.net. http://teachers.net/gazette/NOV00/wong.html.

Wong, H., and Wong, R. 2000b. The Problem Is Not Discipline. *Gazette* article. Teachers.net. http://teachers.net/gazette/SEP00/wong.html.

Wong, H., and Wong, R. 2000c. Your First Day. *Gazette* article. Teachers.net. http://teachers .net/gazette/JUN00/covera.html.

Wong, H., and Wong, R. 2002. How to Start School Successfully. *Gazette* article. Teachers. net. http://teachers.net/gazette/AUG02/wong.html.

Wong, H., and Wong, R. 2004a. A Well-Oiled Learning Machine. *Gazette* article. Teachers.net. http://teachers.net/wong/MAR04.

Wong, H., and Wong, R. 2004b. *The first days of school: How to be an effective teacher.* Mountain View, CA: Harry K. Wong.

Wong, H., and Wong, R. 2005. The First Ten Days of School. *Gazette* article. Teachers.net. http://teachers.net/wong/JAN05.

4

Establishing Trust and Civility

Establishing and Maintaining an Atmosphere of Trust and Civility in Your Classroom

This strategy can be accomplished through providing a helpful, nonthreatening class atmosphere in which the core of social morality is emphasized. This core consists of universal values of goodness and the desire to live in accordance with them.

Chapter Preview

This chapter explains how classroom behavior is affected by trust, civility, and social morality. Tactics are suggested for helping students conduct themselves—and treat others—in accordance with universal values of goodness. Ethical principles are presented that foster trust. The importance of civility (now in decline in most cultures) is explored, and tactics are presented for establishing a class climate where civility predominates. Highlighted are P. M. Forni's suggestions concerning civility and Michele Borba's views on developing moral intelligence.

THE MEANING AND IMPORTANCE OF TRUST IN THE CLASSROOM

For a classroom to function as a civil, cooperative community, a reasonably high level of trust must be established and maintained among members of the class. To *trust* someone means you feel you can count on him or her to support you and never harm you. When you trust people with whom you associate, you can work with them harmoniously and productively. Trust grows within a climate of ethics, civility, and socially moral behavior, but it cannot survive in a climate where unethical or threatening behavior is a continual concern.

Ethical Principles That Promote Trust

Teachers who consistently display certain ethical principles provide a climate that fosters trust in the classroom. The following ethical qualities are especially powerful— kindness, consideration, faith in students' potential, helpfulness, fairness, honesty, and patience. These principles should be discussed fully with students and drawn to their attention regularly. Teachers should exemplify the principles, and students should practice behaviors that reflect them. It is helpful to post reminders in the classroom.

Violations of the principles, whether by teacher or students, should be addressed immediately, either privately or with full class involvement, according to the situation. Student behavior that reflects the ethical qualities should be noted and acknowledged in appropriate ways without causing embarrassment. The following are brief explanations of the nature and role of each quality.

Kindness. This quality involves treating others with understanding, attention, courtesy, and respect. Teachers display kindness when they acknowledge students, chat with them on a personal level, and treat them gently with a smile. Students very much appreciate being shown respect, politely and courteously. They certainly do not want to be scolded or spoken to sarcastically or intimidated in any way. Teachers should help students understand that kind treatment is a two-way street: Those who desire kind treatment must give it to others as well.

Consideration. Consideration in the classroom is shown in accepting others as they are and being aware of their concerns. It involves adapting to or making accommodations for others' needs. Everyone has a strong desire to belong, to be accepted as a valued member of the group. Everyone, including the teacher, wants to talk, laugh, and have fun. And of course, every student and teacher wants to maintain a sense of personal dignity. Threatening dignity is a sure way to kill trust.

Faith in Potential. Many students today feel school holds nothing for them. Although forced to attend, they often go through the motions half-heartedly, decline to participate in activities, do little of the assigned work, and behave insolently or disruptively.

Many of these students can be brought back into active learning by being shown that we believe in their capabilities and see them as worthwhile in their own right. They respond well when they believe teachers see them as significant human beings, and they enjoy having their accomplishments mentioned. By showing faith in students' potential, teachers can do much to help them see that school does have something worthwhile for them.

Helpfulness. Helpfulness is powerful in building trust. Students in school sense helpfulness in small acts teachers perform, such as helping the kindergartner get a jacket on, helping the fourth-grader find a misplaced book, getting another pencil for the seventh-grader who has broken hers, or patiently showing the ninth-grader for the third time how to sequence paragraphs to make compositions flow. Students especially sense it when they find themselves in worrisome situations and the teacher says to them something like this:

- "Justin, I know you didn't intentionally break the window. I'll take care of that with the principal."
- "Desiree, I know the assignment you turned in was difficult for you. I'm guessing you felt you couldn't do it all on your own. Let me show you a couple of things that will help you do work you are proud of."
- "Sara, I know Alicia and Connie hurt your feelings. Sometimes people do that without thinking. By the way, I was wondering: Could you stay for a few minutes and water these plants for me? I could use the help."

Fairness.   The young have a strong concern about fairness and want it to prevail. Students repeatedly call attention to class situations they perceive as unfair. Of course, teachers quickly tire of students' whining "That's not *fair*." Hearing that makes teachers want to say (and they sometimes do), "The world is not a fair place." Unfortunately, this clever retort does nothing to reassure students.

Student comments about unfairness present good opportunities for discussing questions such as What does being fair mean? What makes a situation fair? What does a fair person do? As students explore those questions, even the younger ones will come to understand that fairness does not mean treating everyone exactly the same but depends on circumstances. That is a point Richard Curwin and Allen Mendler emphasize in *Discipline with Dignity* (1999). They say the fairest way to treat students is in accordance with their particular needs. Stephen R. Covey, author of *The Seven Habits of Highly Effective People* (2004) takes a similar view. He writes that when dealing with others, we should try to understand them deeply as individuals, the way we would want to be understood, and then treat them in terms of that understanding.

Teachers should get the following message across to students:

I will always try to treat you fairly and will help and encourage you to treat each other the same. Sometimes I will treat one of you differently from another. When that happens, it is because of differences I see in the situation or your feelings. But I will always try for fairness. When I appear to fail in that, or when anyone in the class fails, it is important that we discuss it.

Honesty.   Virtually all of us occasionally speak and behave dishonestly. At times, we may intentionally try to mislead or deceive someone. At times, we may fail to keep promises or follow through as we said we would. Frequently, we embellish our stories to make them more interesting or convincing. Most people tell so-called white lies that do not damage others; they can even be helpful at times in building relationships, as when we use them to compliment others on their appearance. Teachers, especially at the primary level, use white lies in praising and trying to motivate students: They tell students that a mediocre response is "great," that slipshod work is "super," and that a half-hearted effort shows they are "really trying."

Teachers say these things believing they will improve students' motivation and self-concept. But be wary of such statements. White lies don't damage trust between teacher and student, but they begin to ring hollow after a time. Sooner or later, students realize their poor work is not terrific.

Instead of spreading on superlatives, teachers should acknowledge student improvement and show appreciation for effort. They can say something truthful like "Last week you could only do three of these problems, and now you can do six of them. I believe you will be able to do all of them before long" or "You have worked hard on this assignment. I can see the effort you have put into it." When students are not working up to expectations, teachers needn't make them feel bad. They can tactfully say something like "We need to get these problems done in the next 10 minutes" or "I'd like to see you get this work done very neatly. I'll be right here if there is anything I can do to help you."

These are important matters for students to discuss. You might want your students to explore whether or not honesty is the best policy, given its confusing ramifications. One thing they need to know is that dishonesty destroys trust. When we make mistakes or when we fail at tasks, we should admit it. After all, making mistakes is always acceptable in life. Doing so often helps us improve.

Patience.   Patience might not seem an ethical quality in general, but it should be considered so in teaching. The best teachers are enthusiastic and motivating, but they are patient, too. They know students work and learn at different speeds, that some grasp concepts quickly while others take a while, and that some work accurately while others make many mistakes, sometimes over and over.

It is very easy to become impatient with students who continually repeat errors. In Spanish class, Michael might, for the fifth time, say *"Está listo"* when he should say *"Estoy listo"* to indicate that he is ready. Mr. Rodríguez may feel like saying "Michael, you got the verb wrong again! There is nothing hard about this. Just pay attention to what you are saying." But a considerate Mr. Rodríguez, rather than speak exasperatedly, will suggest that Michael try tapping himself on the chest to remember to say *estoy* rather than *está* when referring to himself.

THE MEANING AND IMPORTANCE OF CIVILITY IN THE CLASSROOM

Civility is behavior that shows respect and consideration of others. It is a major facilitator of trust, cooperation, and productivity. The word *civility* comes from the Latin *civitas,* which is the root word for *civilization.* It is of special importance in human life and necessary for classrooms to function well. Its opposite, *incivility,* denotes self-centeredness and lack of consideration for others. At a more serious level, it can involve insults, threats, and physical intimidation, all of which severely inhibit cooperation and the positive exchange of opinions and ideas.

Guy Burgess and Heidi Burgess (1997) add that *civility* means something more that mere politeness or "rolling over and playing dead" if someone disagrees with you. Everyone at times needs to present his or her case forcefully. In a civil classroom, well-meaning expression is valued but without insults and intimidation.

In a Public Agenda survey taken in 2003 (Raasch, 2003), 43 percent of teachers said they spend more time keeping peace in the classroom than actually teaching. (Public Agenda is a nonprofit public interest group that monitors conditions in U.S. education.) In fact, teachers have been reporting this for years, and the situation has been growing steadily worse. The survey also revealed that 70 percent of students say disrespectful behavior is common in their schools. Again, this is no surprise to teachers. What is causing this growing problem? According to the survey, 81 percent of teachers blame parents for not getting across to children that school is a place for study and proper behavior. It is hardly fair, however, to lay heavy blame on parents when they simply reflect a larger society that is ever more swamped by "me first" and "you can't make me" attitudes.

It is unfortunate that parental support for teachers has declined. Teachers have no better allies than parents who are concerned about the education and development of their children, while parents have no better allies than teachers who wholeheartedly do what they can to help students learn. It is still possible to enjoy strong parental support for your efforts, but you may have to go out of your way to establish and maintain relations with parents and guardians. The best way to do this is to communicate with them on a regular basis, ensure them you will do all you can to help their child learn, and keep them apprised of their children's progress.

Teachers and schools cannot, by themselves, cure the ills of society, but most observers believe schools can promote civility to a significant degree. Several new books provide a multitude of suggestions on promoting civility in the classroom (check booksellers on the Internet), and dozens of articles have been published recently about incivility in the classroom. The majority of these articles, interestingly, pertain to university classes, where boorish behavior is becoming increasingly evident, but the suggestions also apply well to public classrooms. One widely read and cited article is Roger Baldwin's 1998 essay, "Academic Civility Begins in the Classroom." Classes at all levels can adapt and make use of Baldwin's suggestions, which include the following:

1. Clearly communicate the meaning of civility in the classroom and how it promotes good relations and learning while reducing disruptive behavior.

2. Present students some negative scenarios of people interacting uncivilly. Ask students to critique the interactions and indicate how the incivility could be replaced with civil behavior.

3. Analyze scenarios and passages from literature or history in which people have disagreed in a destructive manner with an eye to determining how they might have worked together more effectively. Have students rewrite each scenario to reflect more civil behavior.

4. Provide instructional activities that promote the values, attitudes, and skills of civility in school. These activities can include direct teaching, modeling, role-play,

and practice and can be done in venues such as class meetings and small-group discussions. They can emphasize using I-messages to express one's opinions and feelings, converting you-messages to I-messages, and activities in which students learn to use William Glasser's (2001) "connecting habits" of listening, supporting, contributing, encouraging, trusting, and befriending as replacements for the "deadly habits" of criticizing, blaming, complaining, nagging, and threatening.

5. Use role-playing, in which students learn to interact positively through scripts they follow for speaking and acting civilly. Reverse role-playing is also useful, in which students discuss issues as strongly as they can from points of view the opposite of what they believe. This exercise will help open students' minds to other realities and possibilities.

6. Ask students to consciously speak or behave toward others, at least once every day, in a more civil way than they would otherwise have done. Ask them to make entries into log books or journals describing what they said or did, what the results were, and why it was preferable to what they would normally have done.

All the while, of course, you should continually model civil behavior and show respect and tolerance for your students' points of view.

P. M. FORNI ON CIVILITY AND CONSIDERATE BEHAVIOR

Recently, important contributions on civility have come from P. M. Forni, a professor in the Department of Romance Languages and Literatures at Johns Hopkins University. Dr. Forni co-founded the Johns Hopkins Civility Project, aimed at assessing the significance of civility, manners, and politeness in contemporary society.

The project is now called the Civility Initiative at Johns Hopkins, and it is directed by Professor Forni, who lectures and conducts workshops on the relevance of civility to the quality of life in the workplace and in society at large. He has a weekly spot, "The Civility Challenge," on the nationally syndicated radio talk show *The Satellite Sisters*. National and foreign publications have reported his work on civility, including the *New York Times, Times of London, Washington Post, Wall Street Journal, Los Angeles Times,* and *Baltimore Sun*. Professor Forni has appeared on a number of radio and television shows, including the ABC's *World News Tonight* and CBS's *Sunday Morning*. For additional information on Dr. Forni and the Civility Initiative, consult the website: www.jhu.edu/civility.

Dr. Forni reports that he decided one day that his students would profit at least as much from learning to be kind human beings as they would from grappling with the works of classical Italian writers. His thoughts, experiences, and conclusions are expressed in his book *Choosing Civility: The Twenty-Five Rules of Considerate Conduct* (2002). He says civility encompasses a wide range of values and behaviors:

respect for others and their opinions, consideration, courtesy, the "golden rule," niceness, politeness, kindness, good manners, fairness, decency, concern for others, justice, tolerance, equality, sincerity, morality, honesty, awareness, trustworthiness, moderation, compassion, friendliness, helpfulness, good citizenship, and abiding by rules.

Forni's "rules of considerate conduct" indicate what we can do to connect effectively with others. They apply in all areas of human relations. He provides examples of how to put the rules into practice to make the lives of all concerned more enjoyable, companionable, and rewarding. The following is a representative selection from Forni's list. Each rule provides a fruitful topic for class discussions and role-playing:

- Acknowledge others.
- Think the best of others.
- Listen.
- Speak kindly.
- Accept and give praise.
- Respect others' opinions.
- Respect other people's time.
- Apologize earnestly.
- Refrain from idle complaints.

Forni (2006) goes on to say that civility, politeness, and good manners are all things we do *for* other people. They show we consider their need for comfort and happiness as valid as our own needs. But at the same time, we also do these things for *our own* sake. They are good for us because they help us manage our relationships, which are crucial to our well-being and health. Conducting ourselves in a kindly manner allows us to connect meaningfully with others. We are social beings, and our happiness or unhappiness depends, in large measure, on the quality of our relationships. The more considerately we behave, the more likely we are to establish harmonious relationships that increase the quality of our lives.

Moreover, individuals who have good relational skills tend to be more successful personally and professionally. Those who have developed the capacity for empathy, in particular, have the ability to understand and respond well to others. When we know how to listen with compassion and grace, we attract others in all walks of life. Educators and managers are more successful when they have the ability to read the feelings of others, and in our personal lives, these abilities make us better friends, spouses, and parents.

We all need social support. To attract social support, we must treat others with kindness and consideration and show we value them as persons. Doing so makes them, in turn, want to remain connected to us, and as a result, we enjoy the rewards of a continuing relationship. In the past, a large amount of the support people needed came from their extended families. In today's social conditions, we turn to friends, acquaintances, and even strangers for support and care. If we are considerate, people will like and trust us; if they like and trust us, they will let us help them; and by helping them, we will help ourselves. It is a powerful truth that social skills strengthen social bonds. They are, therefore, an invaluable asset in establishing quality of life.

Forni (2002) presents a number of interesting quotations that extol the virtues of civility. Among them are the following:

- "Civility is key in learning how to live well with others." —P. M. Forni
- "A kind word is like a spring day." —Russian proverb
- "We have a choice about how we behave, and that means we have the choice to opt for civility and grace." —Dwight Currie
- "The very essence of politeness seems to be to take care that by our words and actions we make other people pleased with us as well as with themselves." —Jean De La Bruyere
- "Rudeness is the weak man's imitation of strength." —Eric Hoffer
- "Social ties are the cheapest medicine we have." —Shelley E. Taylor
- "Every action done in company, ought to be with some sign of respect to those that are present." —George Washington
- "Behave as if you were in heaven, where there are no third-class carriages, and one soul is as good as another." —George Bernard Shaw
- "I can live for two months on a good compliment." —Mark Twain
- "The idea is to attract, not to repel." —Peggy and Peter Post
- "My right to swing my fist ends at your nose. My right to make noise ought to end at your ear." —Les Blomberg
- "[Good manners] must be inspired by the good heart. There is no beautifier of complexion, or form, or behavior, like the wish to scatter joy and not pain around us." —Ralph Waldo Emerson
- "Three things in human life are important: The first is to be kind. The second is to be kind, and the third is to be kind." —Henry James

Consultant

MICHELE BORBA ON DEVELOPING MORAL INTELLIGENCE

Michele Borba has contributed strongly to the teaching of ethical and moral behavior in schools. Her work centers on the concept of *moral intelligence,* which she believes can be developed in students as a powerful competency for dealing with ethical and moral challenges in school and elsewhere. A former teacher and recipient of the National Educator Award, Dr. Borba now presents addresses and workshops on moral education and other topics throughout North America, Europe, Asia, and the South Pacific. She writes for a number of popular publications, appears regularly on TV talk shows and National Public Radio, and is author of 21 books, including *Building Moral Intelligence,* cited by *Publishers' Weekly* as "among the most noteworthy of 2001," and *Parents Do Make a Difference,* selected by Child Magazine as Outstanding Parenting Book of 1999. Her latest book is *Nobody Likes Me, Everybody Hates Me:*

The Top 25 Friendship Problems and How to Solve Them (2005). Information on her publications and seminars can be accessed through her websites: www.moral intelligence.com and www.behaviormakeovers.com.

The Nature of Moral Intelligence

Borba explains that *moral intelligence* involves (1) the ability to distinguish right from wrong, (2) the establishment and maintenance of strong ethical convictions, and (3) the willingness to act on those convictions in an honorable way. Moral intelligence, she explains, provides the foundation for what we call "good character." It grows with experience and can be taught in school. As students bring their moral intelligence to higher levels, they become more self-directing and their classroom behavior improves.

The Seven Virtues of Goodness

Borba (2001) describes moral intelligence as consisting of universally accepted virtues of goodness, seven of which strongly help students behave properly and resist pressures that often damage character—empathy, conscience, self-control, respect, kindness, tolerance, and fairness. Descriptions of the seven virtues follow, along with some of Borba's comments about them and examples of what people say and do that exemplify them.

Empathy. *Empathy* is the capacity to relate to the feelings of others. Without empathy, moral intelligence cannot develop fully. At present, a number of societal factors are working against the development of empathy in the young, such as parents who are absent or emotionally unavailable to children, an overabundance of media images of suffering that dull sensitivity, boys being discouraged from expressing their feelings, and abuse of children by peers and adults. To counteract these negative influences, Borba urges teachers to do these things:

1. Develop caring relationships with students, listen to them with empathy, help them develop stronger emotional vocabularies, and tell them stories or present scenarios that promote empathetic reaction.
2. Create a caring, prosocial learning environment.
3. Use stories and situations to enhance student sensitivity to the feelings and perspectives of others.
4. Provide meaningful activities that develop empathy for other persons' situations or points of view.
5. Use discipline techniques based on empathy for the feelings of the student.

Borba (2001, p. 19) says people who are empathetic often do the following:

- Notice when people are hurting and experience something of what they feel
- Try to console or comfort others who are in pain
- Mirror the facial expressions of people in distress

People who are empathetic often make comments such as these:

- "You look upset."
- "I think I understand how you must feel."
- "I'm happy for you."

Conscience.   *Conscience* is the ability to sense the rightness or wrongness of one's actions. Borba points to a crisis of conscience in the world today, as evident in the rise in youth violence, peer cruelty, stealing, cheating, sexual promiscuity, and substance abuse. She suggests a number of conditions and activities for the classroom that can help reverse the decline in public and individual conscience, including the following:

1. Set clear class expectations and standards based on the seven virtues.
2. Create a context for moral growth, beginning with teacher modeling.
3. Teach, cultivate, and reinforce virtues that strengthen conscience while providing a guide for behavior.
4. Help students understand how moral conscience develops, and show them how reparation (atoning for transgressions against others) can turn moral wrongs into moral rights.
5. Use meaningful moral dilemmas presented in context (e.g., historical, scientific, or literary issues, current events, peer interactions) to increase students' moral reasoning.

Borba (2001, p. 53) says people with conscience often do the following:

- Act the way they know is right
- Are not swayed by others who wish to do wrong
- Can be trusted to do what they say they will

People with a conscience make comments like these:

- "You can count on me."
- "Let's do something else. This isn't right."
- "I'm sorry. It was my fault."

Self-Control.   Borba also says there is a crisis of self-control today, evident in our undisciplined society and made worse because of overworked, stressed-out parents; early child abuse and trauma; glorification of out-of-control behavior in entertainment; and overreliance on chemical mollification in place of self-constraint. Borba suggests a number of conditions that can promote student growth in self-control:

1. Adults giving priority to and modeling self-control
2. Encouraging students to become their own internal motivators by seeking to do the right thing when met with temptation
3. Showing specific ways to control urges and think before acting, such as through anger management, self-control in stress situations, and using the three-part formula of *Think: Stop: Act Right*

4. Providing ongoing opportunities for students to practice self-control strategies and apply them to real-world situations, to the point they begin to apply them without being prompted by the teacher

Borba (2001, p. 81) says people with self-control usually do these things:

- Maintain control when angry or upset
- Behave well even when no one is watching
- Plan what they will do and follow through

People with self-control often say things such as the following:

- "I'd really like to go with you, but I have to study."
- "I need to calm down. I'm feeling upset."
- "I understand the rule and I won't break it."

Respect.   Lack of respect seems to be growing in most segments of society and is manifested in the decline in civility, rise of vulgarity, loss of the "golden rule," disrespect for authority, and low respect for children. Borba makes a number of classroom suggestions regarding respect:

1. Discuss, model, and teach the differences between *respect* and *disrespect*.
2. Act respectfully toward students, and talk regularly with them about the meaning and practice of respect.
3. Work to increase student respect for authority, and squelch rudeness. Eliminate disrespect by consistently targeting the misbehavior and specifically teaching new respectful replacement behaviors. Use signals to call attention to sassiness, back talk, whining, vulgarity, and other types of disrespect.
4. Emphasize and expect good manners and courtesy. Help students learn the basic manners that enable them to function productively in society. Teach students to say "please" and "thank-you," and otherwise increase their repertoire of respectful behaviors.
5. Involve peers in creating a respectful learning environment and reinforcing each other's prosocial, respectful behaviors.

Borba (2001, p. 131) says respectful people often do the following:

- Don't talk back, whine, or sass
- Listen without interrupting
- Are careful with someone else's belongings

Respectful people often make comments such as these:

- "Excuse me."
- "I didn't mean to interrupt."
- "I understand you feel differently."

Kindness.   The crisis of unkind behavior in today's world is being worsened by a number of factors, such as lack of good modeling by parents and adults, lack of encouragement for children to behave with kindness, influence of unkind peers, and general desensitization to kindness. To counter this crisis, Borba would like teachers to do the following:

1. Teach the meaning and value of kindness, help students understand that kindness begins with them, and explicitly teach students what kind behaviors look and sound like.
2. Establish zero tolerance for cruel, hurtful behavior at school. Put in place specific, spelled-out procedures to stop bullying.
3. Encourage kindness at school, and point out its positive effects. Ask students to behave with kindness in all situations, and point out the effect it has on others.
4. Provide meaningful activities for students to experience and practice being kind and receiving kindness, such as random acts of kindness and providing service for others.

Borba (2001, p. 163) says kind people often do these things:

- Offer to help someone in need
- Show concern when someone is treated badly
- Refuse to take part in ridiculing others

Kind people often say things such as the following:

- "How can I help you?"
- "Are you new? Would you like to join us?"
- "I really appreciate your thoughtfulness."

Tolerance.   The crisis in tolerance we are experiencing today is fueled by a lack of moral monitoring of the young, accessibility of Internet hate sites, racially charged video entertainment aimed at youth, hate music, and stereotypes displayed on television and motion pictures. To counter this crisis, Borba offers these suggestions for teachers:

1. Model and teach about tolerance.
2. Draw attention to and discourage intolerant comments and practices.
3. Instill an appreciation for diversity.

Borba (2001, p. 199) says tolerant people often do the following:

- Focus on what they have in common with others, not on their differences
- Refuse to take part in activities that make fun of people who are different
- Refuse to exclude certain students from activities

People who are tolerant may be heard to say things like the following:

- "We don't know her, so let's not make fun of her."
- "Would you like to join our team?"
- "I'd like to know more about her."

Fairness. The crisis in fairness in the treatment of others is being worsened by a breakdown of role models and an overemphasis on competition, so that winning at any cost becomes paramount. This crisis can be countered by teachers who discuss fairness with students, unfailingly demonstrate fairness, avoid making comparisons among students, help students show respect for their competitors, and limit the all-too-strong emphasis on winning.

Borba (2001, p. 235) says that fair people do these things:

- Play by the rules and don't try to change them midstream
- Keep an open mind and listen to all sides
- Compromise so everyone gets a fair share

People who are fair are often heard to say things like the following:

- "Let's find a way to make things fair."
- "Let's take turns. You go first."
- "Let's consider both sides of the story."

Why Building Moral Intelligence Is Worth the Effort

You might wonder if trying to develop moral intelligence is worth all the effort it seems to require. For Borba, there is no doubt. She insists that efforts in building students' moral intelligence can lead to the following:

1. *Good character.* The foundation to good character—or moral intelligence—consists of the virtues explained in the preceding sections. These virtues form students' character and are the principles that guide their behavior.

2. *Ability to think and act appropriately.* Character is evident in one's thoughts and actions. Borba's Moral Intelligence Program teaches the specific moral habits that help students think and conduct themselves in an ethical manner. High moral intelligence does not occur spontaneously. Teachers must intentionally model, nurture, reinforce, and teach its essential qualities. If they do not, students will be at great risk of becoming more insensitive, dishonest, aggressive, uncivil, cruel, hateful, and unjust.

3. *Protection against "toxic" influences in society.* Toxic influences such as cruelty, drugs, and self-centeredness are so entrenched in society that it is impossible to shield students from them. Moral intelligence can help students adhere to deep-seated convictions and resist influences that work against good character.

4. *Crucial life skills.* Moral intelligence incorporates skills students need for resolving conflicts, empathizing, asserting themselves, controlling anger, learning tolerance, negotiating fairly, communicating respectfully, cooperating, using self-control, sharing, and knowing right from wrong. These skills are relevant in all life arenas.

5. *Good citizens.* The most important measure of a nation is not its gross national product, its technological genius, or its military might but rather the character of its people. The seven virtues within moral intelligence provide the bedrock of good citizenship and responsible living.

6. *Resistance to temptation.* Moral intelligence enables students to resist the appeal of insidious vices such as dishonesty and gaining unfair advantage.

7. *Prevention of violence and cruelty.* The best protection against violence and cruelty is found in the core values of moral intelligence.

8. *Good behavior.* Moral intelligence incorporates the essential moral virtues that enable students to be decent, caring, and respectful. The seven virtues become a template for creating students' character, guiding their actions, and ultimately defining their reputations as good, caring human beings.

9. *Shaping moral destinies.* Moral growth is an ongoing process. Its beliefs and habits become the ethical foundations of behavior that students will use for a lifetime.

Teaching Moral Intelligence in the Schools

Borba believes the schools offer one of the last bastions of hope for developing sound character in the young. Moral intelligence grows as improvements are made in students' character traits. Schools hold the key to that improvement. There are few other places where many of the young can learn the value of responsibility, caring, respect, and cooperation or where they can observe adults displaying those traits consistently. Borba's book *Building Moral Intelligence* (2001) contains well over one thousand strategies to help students develop or deal with issues such as the following: peer pressure, bullying, anger management, disrespect, self-control, fair play, sensitivity to others, strengthening conscience, negotiation skills, peaceful confrontation, kindness, tolerance, conflict resolution, self-reliance, empathy, generosity, impulse control, responsibility, calm, group harmony, stereotypes, compromising, sharing and taking turns, decision making, motivation, respectfulness, and courtesy.

Borba also explains a five-step approach for teaching moral values that teachers can easily incorporate into the daily curriculum:

1. *Accentuate a character trait or virtue.* The first step in working to improve a character trait is to draw it strongly to students' attention over time; a different character trait can be emphasized each month. The process works best if all personnel at the school are modeling and reinforcing that particular trait. As each character trait is introduced, a student campaign committee can create banners, signs, and posters to hang up around the school. For example, students can make a poster about responsibility that says, "Responsibility: It means I'm doing what is right for myself and others and I can be counted on." Character assemblies can also be held at school. The school public address announcements can call attention to the character of the month—for example, "It's perseverance month. . . . Remember to work your hardest and not give up!" Screen savers can be written new each day about the character trait to attract attention when the computer is turned on.

2. *Explain the meaning and value of the trait.* The second step to teaching a character trait is to convey to students exactly what the trait means and why it is important and relevant to their lives. Explain the trait to your students within their realm of experience as if they have never been exposed to the trait. Borba lists ways of doing this. For example, in a story, locate an episode that exemplifies the trait.

Read it aloud and ask, "How did the main character demonstrate perseverance? How did that make the other characters feel?" Or ask students to find current news articles that describe people demonstrating the trait. To confirm the value of the trait, you might begin each day with a brief review of a real event in the world in which the trait was displayed.

Whenever you see or hear a student displaying the targeted trait, take a moment to point out specifically what the student did that demonstrated the trait: "Alex, that was respectful because you waited until I finished before you spoke." And be sure to share your beliefs about the trait. It helps students to hear why you feel the trait is important. If you are targeting respect, for example, you might tell students how strongly you believe we should avoid speaking negatively about others.

3. *Teach what the trait looks and sounds like.* There is no perfect way to teach the trait, but *showing* the behavior is always more effective than just talking about it. When you discuss a trait, model it, as well, and perhaps role-play it with a student. Borba urges teachers not to assume that students understand the actions and words associated with character traits. They may not have been exposed to them, and so the teacher must look for ways to provide examples, explicitly and implicitly.

For instance, students could identify the specific behaviors of the character trait in video clips you provide (Atticus Finch as an example of integrity in *To Kill a Mockingbird*); in literature (Julius Caesar for fortitude); in historical models (Gandhi for fairness); in scientific models (Thomas Edison for perseverance); as well as actual current events in the school, community, and world. Doing so will help students see what the trait looks and sounds like. You can also ask students to create skits involving the trait and enact them in class.

4. *Provide opportunities to practice the moral habits of the trait.* Students should be provided frequent opportunities to practice the moral habits or behaviors that comprise the character trait. Borba states that it usually takes 21 days of practice to acquire a new behavior. She makes three suggestions for reviewing progress: (1) Make or obtain character videotapes that allow students to watch demonstrations of the trait and analyze what they have seen; (2) have students keep reflection logs over the time the trait is being emphasized and write at least one action they did each day that demonstrated the trait; and (3) assign character homework that asks students to practice the skill at home with their family and record the results.

5. *Provide effective feedback.* As you teach appropriate behaviors, be sure to reinforce students as they improve: "You're on the right track; keep it up" or "Almost, but this is what to do instead." If you see students failing to demonstrate the trait, draw their attention to their behavior: "What you did was not right, but this is what you can do next time." Students benefit from immediate behavior correction, so ask them to redo any incorrect behavior immediately, if possible.

As students conduct themselves in accordance with the essential virtues of moral intelligence, they naturally display good manners and improved behavior. However, students often benefit from further instruction in prosocial behaviors and courtesy. Borba (2001, pp. 152–153) provides a list of "Eighty-Five Important Manners Kids Should Learn." Only a few examples are included here:

- *Essential polite words:* Please, thank you, excuse me, I'm sorry, may I?, pardon me, you're welcome
- *Meeting and greeting others:* Smiles and looks at the person, shakes hands, says "hello," introduces self, introduces other person
- *Conversation manners:* Starts a conversation, listens without interrupting, uses a pleasant tone of voice, knows how to begin and end a conversation
- *Sports manners:* Plays by the rules, shares equipment, provides encouragement, doesn't brag or show off, doesn't argue with referee, congratulates opponents, doesn't complain or make excuses, cooperates
- *Anywhere and anytime:* Doesn't swear, doesn't belch, doesn't gossip, covers mouth when coughing

Borba presents a number of other suggestions associated with hospitality, table manners, visiting manners, telephone manners, and manners toward older people.

The Relation of Moral Intelligence to Classroom Discipline

Borba wants teachers to understand that successful discipline depends strongly on creating a moral learning community in the classroom—an environment where students feel safe and cared about. In that environment, the teacher connects with students, shows care for them, and models the core character traits. In the absence of that environment, no approach to discipline is going to work well.

As for behavior change, teachers today simply cannot assume that students know how to behave properly. Borba emphasizes this point in her books *No More Misbehavin'* (2003) and *Don't Give Me That Attitude* (2004), explaining that if misbehavior is allowed to persist, it results in an attitude that weakens student character. The teacher must target and address the specific behaviors that damage respectful classrooms and student character, such as vulgarity, cruelty, bullying, and disrespect. Students must replace those behaviors with acceptable ones. The replacement behavior must then be practiced until it becomes internalized. Virtues must come to be exemplified in behavior. You can't successfully teach behavior only through posters or vocabulary drill. If you want students to change, you must teach them specifically how to behave.

Discipline in classes that emphasize character building calls on teachers to interact directly with students who behave inappropriately. This interaction typically calls on students to *respond, review, reflect,* and *make right.* Suppose Juan and Eddie get in a fight just outside the classroom. The teacher stops them and quickly goes through the four steps:

1. *Respond:* Stay calm and listen. Find out what happened: "Tell me what happened." "Why did you do it?" "What did you think this would accomplish?"

2. *Review:* Here you call attention to why the behavior was wrong: "Tell me what the rules are in the class." "Why do you think I called you over?" Briefly review the rules or your behavior expectations: "Fighting is not allowed in this class." "We don't solve our problems by fighting."

3. *Reflect:* Quickly go over the effects of the behavior and any impact they may have on the victim: "How do you make each other feel when you fight?" "What do you believe others think of you?" "Do you want to think of yourself as a person who tries to solve problems by fighting, or do you want to think of yourself as someone who can reason things out?" Ask questions that guide each student to empathize with or gain the perspective of the other: "How do you think your friend feels?" "If you were in her shoes, what do you think she'd like to say to you about what happened?" The student could even be required to write (or draw) the situation from the other person's point of view.

4. *Make right:* Help students atone for wrongs they have done. Encourage offending students to make reparation of some sort, something more than an apology and a promise not to do it again. Perhaps Juan and Eddie can work together on a project, such as making a chart for the class that lists alternatives to fighting.

The Patient Teacher

It will take time for the foregoing intervention process to be successful. You and the class must get used to it. Remember that you are trying to build student character, not apply quick fixes to get through the moment. You have to be patient. Borba emphasizes that patient teachers stick with students, give help over and over, and tolerate repeated mistakes. They come to students' aid repeatedly and do so pleasantly, never showing exasperation and never putting students down. Students quickly come to trust and admire such teachers.

IN SUMMARY

Many people believe incivility is reaching a level of crisis in Western society, damaging character development, hindering the effective exchange of ideas, and leading to friction in classrooms and elsewhere. Most feel that schools offer hope—some say the only hope—for reversing this trend. This chapter explained the problem of incivility, the nature of civil behavior and why it is valued, and what educators can do to increase civility as a key element in building student character. Featured were suggestions on ethical principles, P. M. Forni's rules of considerate behavior, Roger G. Baldwin's suggestions for developing civility in the classroom, and Michele Borba's work in developing moral intelligence in students.

REFERENCES

Baldwin, R. 1998. Academic civility begins in the classroom. *Essays on Teaching Excellence* 9, no. 8. Professional and Organizational Development Network in Higher Education. www.clemson.edu/OTEI/newspdf/f986.pdf.

Borba, M. 1999. *Parents do make a difference: How to raise kids with solid character, strong minds, and caring hearts.* San Francisco: Jossey-Bass.

Borba, M. 2001. *Building moral intelligence.* San Francisco: Jossey-Bass.

Borba, M. 2003. *No more misbehavin': 38 difficult behaviors and how to stop them.* San Francisco: Jossey-Bass.

Borba, M. 2004. *Don't give me that attitude! 24 rude, selfish, insensitive things kids do and how to stop them.* San Francisco: Jossey-Bass.

Borba, M. 2005. *Nobody likes me, everybody hates me: The top 25 friendship problems and how to solve them.* San Francisco: Jossey-Bass.

Burgess, G., and Burgess, H. 1997. *The meaning of civility.* Conflict Research Consortium, University of Colorado, Boulder. www.colorado.edu/conflict/civility.htm.

Covey, S. R. 2004. *The seven habits of highly effective people.* New York: Free Press.

Curwin, R., and Mendler, A. 1999. *Discipline with dignity.* Alexandria, VA: Association for Supervision and Curriculum Development.

Forni, P. M. 2002. *Choosing civility: The twenty-five rules of considerate conduct.* New York: St. Martin's Press.

Forni, P. M. 2006. The other side of civility. Dr. Forni's Civility Website. www.jhu.edu.

Glasser, W. 2001. *Every student can succeed.* Chatsworth, CA: William Glasser Incorporated.

Raasch, C. 2003. Teachers, parents, outside world are key to classroom civility. *USA Today.* www.usatoday.com/news/opinion/columnist/raasch/2003-08-25-raasch_x.htm.

5

Intervening Positively

Dealing with Misbehavior in a Positive and Productive Manner That Maintains Student Cooperation and Preserves Good Relationships

You can accomplish this strategy by using disruptions and other incidents of misbehavior as opportunities for teaching students how to conduct themselves appropriately and make behavior choices that lead to success in the classroom and elsewhere.

Chapter Preview

Teachers concerned about discipline invariably ask the question What do I do when . . . ? They end the question by specifying a type of misbehavior that is troubling them. Their questions typically concern what they should do (1) at the moment of disruption, the point when a given behavior becomes troublesome enough to require teacher intervention, or (2) when the student continues to disrupt despite the teacher's best control tactics. These two areas of concern are addressed in this chapter.

NORMAL TACTICS TO USE AT THE MOMENT OF DISRUPTION

In this section, we review suggestions from respected authorities about what teachers should do and say when students disrupt. The major discipline emphasis of each authority is shown in italics to provide a context for the suggestions.

Suggestions from Haim Ginott

Haim Ginott (1971), featured in Chapter 8, places major emphasis on congruent communication between teacher and students. Congruent communication *addresses situations rather than students' character and is in harmony with students' feelings and perceptions.* Ginott says that when teachers need to intervene in misbehavior, they should invite cooperation from students by calmly and briefly describing the situation and what needs to be done. For example, a teacher might say, "This is journal writing time. We need to be writing in our journals rather than talking."

At times, Ginott has teachers remind students of the behavior expected, and at other times, he has teachers reteach the expected behavior. He urges teachers never to ask students why they are acting in a particular manner because "why" questions—such as "Why am I having to tell you this again?"—produce feelings of guilt and defensiveness. Ginott also advises teachers never to use sarcasm when dealing with misbehavior because it is too often hurtful to students and likely to produce resentment and disinclination to cooperate.

One of Ginott's favorite tactics is asking students "What can I do to help you?" or "How can I be most useful to you now?" He urges teachers always to use I-messages (indicating the teacher's position) rather than you-messages, which refer at least obliquely to the character of the student involved. If the class is unduly noisy, for instance, he might say, "I am concerned about the noise."

Suggestions from Linda Albert

Linda Albert is developer and disseminator of *cooperative discipline* (2003). The underlying concept in cooperative discipline is that *discipline occurs best when teachers and students work together in a genuinely cooperative manner (1) to establish a classroom that is safe, orderly, and inviting; (2) to provide students with a sense of connectedness and belonging; and (3) to turn all behavior mistakes into opportunities for learning.*

Albert has structured her discipline approach to emphasize helping students connect with others, contribute to the class, and see themselves as capable. When students disrupt, Albert suggests teachers intervene as follows:

1. *Take charge of your negative emotions.* If the student has made you feel angry, frustrated, or hurt, control those emotions so you can respond calmly, objectively, and noncombatively. This reduces antagonism and helps everyone calm down.

2. *Focus on the behavior, not the student.* Describe aloud the behavior that is occurring without evaluating it. Use objective terms and avoid subjective words such as *bad, wrong,* and *stupid.* For example, you might say, "I heard some name-calling." Deal with the moment, only what is happening now, not what happened yesterday or last week. Be firm but friendly. Indicate that the behavior must stop, but at the same time, show continuing concern for the student's well-being. You might say, "We have all agreed we will not call each other names. Do we need to discuss this matter now, or can we continue without the name-calling?"

3. *Allow the student to save face.* Students know you have the ultimate power in a confrontation, so eventually, they will comply with your expectations. However, to save face with their peers and make it seem that they are not backing down completely, they often mutter, take their time complying, or repeat the misbehavior one

more time before stopping. It is best to overlook these face-saving behaviors rather than confront the student anew.

4. *If a behavior needs further attention, discuss it with the student at a later time.* The next day, when feelings have abated, is perhaps a better time. For more serious matters, Albert suggests teachers consider making a "graceful exit." Suppose a very upset student is having a real tantrum, yelling and throwing things. Making a graceful exit allows the teacher to distance himself or herself from the situation. Such an exit is made calmly, with poise, and without sarcasm.

To make a graceful exit, first acknowledge the student's power but also state your expectation: "I can't make you write this essay, but it does need to be turned in by Friday. Let me know your plan for completing the assignment." Then move away from the student and table the matter. You might say, "Let's talk about it later" or "I am not willing to talk with you about this right now." If the defiance persists, call the student's bluff and deliver a closing statement: "Let me get this straight. I asked you to complete your assignment and you are refusing. Is this correct?" Using a pencil and clipboard, write down what the student says. You may wish to say, "You've mistaken me for someone who wants to fight. I don't." If the student cannot calm down, have him or her take a time-out in the classroom or a designated room.

Suggestions from William Glasser

William Glasser, featured in Chapter 7, places *choice theory* (1998) at the center of his suggestions for working with students. *The fundamental tenet of choice theory is that we cannot force students to change behavior, but we can influence them to do so and to make choices that serve them better in school.*

Glasser believes each class should have a set of rules or agreements concerning behavior, which all members of the class are willing to support. When anyone violates an agreement, the teacher intervenes in a nonpunitive manner that stops the misbehavior and gets the student's mind back on class work. Suppose Austin has come into the room obviously upset. As the lesson begins, he swears at Michael, a violation of the class agreement on treating others with respect. Glasser suggests the teacher respond as follows:

> **Teacher:** It looks like there is a problem, Austin. How might I help you with it? [Austin frowns and looks down, still obviously upset.]
> **Teacher:** If you will calm down, I will discuss it with you in a little while. I think we can work something out.

Make it clear you are unable to help Austin unless he calms down. Indicate this without emotion. If Austin doesn't do so, there is no good way to deal with the problem. Glasser (1990) says to allow Austin 20 seconds, and if he isn't calm by then, simply acknowledge that there is no way to solve the problem at that time. Give Austin timeout from the lesson, but don't threaten or warn him. Instead, say something like this:

> **Teacher:** Austin, I want to help you work this out. I am not interested in punishing you. Whatever the problem is, let's solve it. But for now, you must go sit at the table. When you are calm, come back to your seat.

Later, at an opportune time, discuss the situation with Austin:

> **Teacher:** What were you doing when I noticed the problem? Was it against the rules? Can we work things out so it won't happen again? What could you and I do to keep it from happening?

If the problem involves hostilities between Austin and Michael, the discussion should involve both boys and proceed along these lines:

> **Teacher:** What were you doing, Austin? What were you doing, Michael? How can the three of us work things out so this won't happen anymore?

Don't place blame on Austin or Michael or spend time trying to determine whose fault it was. Remind the boys that you are only looking for a solution so the problem won't occur again. Treat Austin and Michael courteously, show you don't want to punish them, and talk to them as a problem solver.

Suggestions from Marvin Marshall

Marvin Marshall, featured in Chapter 9, has created a discipline program based on levels of responsibility, in which students are influenced to conduct themselves in ever more responsible ways. *The fundamental concepts in Marshall's approach are (1) that students will cooperate willingly in the educational program if they see a clear reason for doing so and find the experiences enjoyable and (2) that good discipline occurs as students are influenced to conduct themselves more responsibly.* Central to Marshall's approach is his *hierarchy of social development* (2001), which depicts progressive levels of responsible behavior:

> *Level A* (the lowest) is anarchy, where students do as they wish.
>
> *Level B* is bothering and bossing others.
>
> *Level C* is cooperating and conforming.
>
> *Level D* (the highest) is democracy and taking the initiative to do the right thing.

The hierarchy is referred to when students misbehave. It causes them to reflect and decide willingly to behave at a higher level of responsibility. This process increases responsible behavior not only in the classroom but in all aspects of life.

Here is how you use the hierarchy: Suppose two boys are talking audibly while another student is making a class report. The teacher quietly asks the disruptive boys, "At what level is that behavior?" They think for a moment and answer,

"Level B." Their misbehavior typically ceases at that point and they seek a more responsible level. They behave responsibly without having to be told to do so because of the internal motivation associated with the desire to do what they know is proper. Over time, they will become more likely to take the initiative to do what they know is right.

Suggestions from Barbara Coloroso

Barbara Coloroso (2002) was featured in Chapter 1. Fundamental to her approach is the conviction that *when students misbehave, they must be guided to accept ownership of their behavior and then figure out how to deal with its ramifications. Through repetition of this process, they develop self-control.* Coloroso advises teachers to do four things when students misbehave: (1) Help students see what they have done wrong; (2) give them ownership of the problem involved; (3) encourage them to develop strategies for solving the problems; and (4) follow through, making sure that in the entire process, students are never denigrated. Because students will make mistakes in how to deal with their behavior, it is best if they learn this process in a friendly classroom environment, where mistakes are accepted and used as platforms for new learning.

Coloroso identifies three categories of misbehavior—mistakes, mischief, and mayhem. Each is addressed in its own way:

1. *Mistakes* are not serious but can be disruptive. When students forget rules or do not understand how they are expected to behave, teachers can offer reminders or reteach the expected behavior.
2. *Mischief* is a bit more serious because it is intentional misbehavior. When you see students misbehaving intentionally, address the problem by asking them to correct what they did wrong. Ask them to think about how they can avoid repeating the behavior in the future.
3. *Mayhem* is willfully serious misbehavior. Teachers should address it by applying the tactics of restitution, resolution, and reconciliation.
   - *Restitution* involves doing what is necessary to repair physical damage or restore personal relations. Mark is asked to clean the desk on which he has written symbols and unsavory words. Susan is encouraged to find a way to atone for the uncomplimentary remarks she made about Margarita.
   - *Resolution* is identifying and correcting the conditions that seemed to prompt the misbehavior, so plans can be made to keep it from happening again. With the teacher's help, Juan reflects on his repeated loss of temper in ballgames and recognizes the harm it is doing. He identifies situations that cause his temper to boil over, and he makes plans for preventing that happening in the future.
   - *Reconciliation* is the process of healing relationships that were damaged by the misbehavior. Here, students are encouraged to make a plan for reconnecting positively with people they have offended. They then carry out the plan and grow from the results it brings.

Just make sure that student decisions do not lead to situations that are physically dangerous, morally threatening, or unhealthy. Otherwise, without making judgments, let the students proceed through the process. Even though they might make mistakes, working through the process will help them learn to make intelligent decisions, accept the consequences of their decisions, and use the consequences to make better decisions in the future.

Suggestions from Spencer Kagan

The central concept in Spencer Kagan's approach is that *at any given time, students occupy one of seven different* positions—*states of mind that predispose students to behave in certain ways, such as seeking attention, avoiding failure, being angry, seeking control, being overly energetic, being bored, and being uninformed. Intervention tactics are used in accordance with the position the student is in at the moment of disruption.*

The following is an intervention protocol drawn from suggestions made by Kagan and his associates (Kagan, Kyle, and Scott, 2004). When misbehavior occurs, the teacher should take these steps:

1. Give a reminder by referring to the class rules posted in the room.
2. For more serious disruptions, validate the student's position and ask the student to suggest a proper way of meeting the need of the position involved. For example, the teacher might say, "It is OK to need attention. We all do. What do you think a responsible person might do to gain attention?"
3. Verbally support the student's reply, if it is appropriate.
4. If the student repeats the disruption, use a follow-up question, such as "What might you do instead of shouting out that would help you and the class?"
5. Follow by working with the student to develop a plan for self-improvement that offers a long-term solution.

Further suggestions from Kagan concerning what teachers should do when dealing with students in various positions are as follows:

- *For attention seeking:* Use physical proximity, hand signals, I-messages, and personal attention.
- *For avoiding failure:* Encourage students to make an effort; assign partners or helpers; reorganize and present the information in smaller instructional pieces.
- *For being angry:* Ask students to identify responsible ways of handling anger; ask them to sit and cool down and think; table the matter until emotions subside.
- *For control seeking:* Acknowledge the student's power and use language of choice—a structure with which teachers provide students with choice ("You may either . . . or . . ."), or provide options for what students will do and when.
- *For students who are overly energetic:* Use periods of relaxation; remove distracting elements and objects; channel students' energy productively.
- *For students who are bored:* Restructure the learning task; involve students more actively; infuse timely energizers such as pictures, stories, skits, and the like.

- *For students who are uninformed:* Gently ask students if they know what they are supposed to do. If necessary, reteach the class rules and the behaviors that each implies; teach the class routines; ask other class members to explain or demonstrate rule compliance.

Two generic intervention tactics that Kagan suggests for all positions are (1) to ask the question "Is this how we want our class to be?" or "Is this how we want others to think of us?" and (2) to picture it right, which asks students to picture how they would like the class to be or how they would like others to see them and then verbalize what they need to do to make it that way. Kagan emphasizes that the purpose of all these activities is not to make students conform to rules but to help them internalize a process of seeking satisfactory solutions that take everyone's needs into account.

Suggestions from Ronald Morrish

Ronald Morrish, featured in Chapter 3, was for many years a teacher and school counselor. Now in private practice, he approaches discipline from the position that *students do not enter school knowing how to behave responsibly, nor do they learn self-discipline from experience alone. To acquire these advanced skills, they need supportive guidance from enlightened, caring teachers.* He explains how to provide that guidance in an approach called *Real Discipline* (1997, 2000), which is founded on techniques that outstanding teachers have used for generations to teach children to be respectful, responsible, and cooperative.

Two tactics that Morrish emphasizes strongly are "do-overs" and insistence. Morrish says that when a student fails to follow your directions or, in the heat of the moment, reverts to other inappropriate behaviors, you should intervene by having the student do the behavior over but properly this time: "Carl, you didn't ask permission in a courteous manner. Would you please ask again in a respectful way?" Most of the time, that is all you need to do. Morrish says teachers' most important and powerful tool is *insistence,* in which they convey to students they have no choice in the matter. He asserts that students who are never required to act appropriately seldom will.

If there is still no compliance after you have asked a student to repeat a behavior properly, ask him or her to wait a minute for further instructions. Then, after a short time, simply involve the student again in the lesson. By now, the student will be more inclined to behave correctly. Give him or her the opportunity to do so. Morrish says that most of the time, when we isolate students, there is no need for it. We only need to have them redo their behavior correctly.

Suggestions from C. M. Charles

C. M. Charles's ideas on *synergetic discipline* were presented in Chapter 2. You can review his background there. The basic premise of synergetic discipline is that *we can identify and correct most conditions that lead to student misbehavior, and we can teach in ways that raise the energy level in the class to provide better engagement in instructional activities.* Charles suggests teachers do these four things when students misbehave:

1. *Subtly remind students of the expected behavior.* Do this with physical proximity, eye signals, or facial expressions. If these reminders don't work, point to the chart posted in the room that refers to class agreements or aspects of responsible behavior. Say, "Class, let's please remember agreement number 3 about behaving responsibly."

2. *Identify what seems to be causing the misbehavior and correct it.* Even if you think you know the cause, check with students to make sure. Ask, "Is this too boring for you? If so, what might we do differently?" or "Boys, is there a problem I can help you with?" or "Something is causing us to be inconsiderate of others. What might be causing that? Can we fix it? What can we do that would show greater responsibility?" Then address the cause if you can. You can usually remove it easily if it is associated with activities, classroom, or teacher behavior. You can lessen its effects when it involves student needs simply by trying to provide what students are seeking. It is more difficult to limit causes that have to do with egocentric personalities. You can say privately, "Jason, something is causing you to call out and disrupt the lesson. That makes it difficult for me to teach and for other students to learn. Can you help me understand what is causing you to do that so we might make things better for you?"

3. *Ask the misbehaving student how he or she might behave in a more responsible manner.* If there is any hesitation on the student's part, make a direct suggestion, such as, "Let's keep our hands to ourselves. Will you do that for me, please?" or "Let's start again and find a more responsible way of acting. May I show you once more what is expected? Thank you."

4. *If the misbehavior involves or leads to a confrontational dispute, help those involved identify the cause of the disagreement and work together to find a solution.* If the confrontation is between students, as when Jason and Nathan are speaking angrily to each other, consider saying the following: "Boys, this is disturbing the class. Can you work the problem out between yourselves, or do you need my help?" If they say they can work it out, ask them if they can keep their dispute from affecting the class. If the boys can't resolve the matter, get together with them at a suitable time and in a nonthreatening manner. Then do the following:

- Ask each to tell you calmly what is troubling him. (Explain that you need to hear each person clearly, so there should be no interrupting or arguing while each is talking.)
- Ask Jason what he would like Nathan to do differently. Nathan should listen carefully.
- Ask Nathan what he would like Jason to do differently. Jason should listen carefully.
- Ask each of the boys if he feels he could do part or most of what the other wants.

- If they agree on a possible solution, thank them and leave it at that. If they cannot reach a solution, ask them if they would allow the class to discuss the matter as a way of learning how to settle disputes in a considerate manner.
- If they agree to that, bring up the matter at the next class meeting. If they decline, say, "Boys, it is not good for any of us in the class when bad feelings exist. How can we resolve this matter so both of you feel all right? What ideas do you have?" If they reach a settlement, thank them. If they can't, say, "I'm disappointed we can't settle this matter so both of you feel all right. But since we can't, I need to ask you to control yourselves, for the sake of the class." It is unlikely that the conflict negotiations will ever reach this point; the boys will agree to a solution earlier in the process.

If the conflict is between you and a student, remember that your efforts will seldom lead to conflict if you treat the student kindly and helpfully. Suppose Melissa has once again failed to do her homework. You ask her gently if there is a problem that is preventing her from complying with the class expectation. For some reason your question strikes a nerve and Melissa retorts, "There wouldn't be a problem if you didn't assign this stupid stuff!" At that point, consider saying "Melissa, can you help me understand why you consider the homework stupid? I'd like your opinion because I want the homework to be valuable to you. Can you suggest a way to make it better?" Melissa may apologize, say nothing, come back with another snide remark, or give a suggestion. If she says nothing or remains uncooperative, consider saying "Now is not a good time for us to discuss the matter. Let's do so later, just the two of us. Could you meet with me for two or three minutes at (name a time and place)?" When you meet, tell her you are willing to listen if she has something she needs to talk about. If she declines, assure her you are interested in her views and are always ready to help.

If Melissa apologizes or explains her feelings or talks about some other problem that is probably the real cause of her being upset, consider saying "Thank-you for informing me, Melissa. If I can make some changes in the homework or otherwise help with your situation, I'd like to do so. I'll listen to any suggestions you might have."

Suggestions from Michele Borba

Michele Borba (2001) was featured in the previous chapter. You can refer to her background presented there. Borba advocates helping students build moral intelligence and contends that as they do so, their classroom behavior improves. She describes *moral intelligence* as comprised of (1) the ability to distinguish right from wrong, (2) the establishment and maintenance of strong ethical convictions, and (3) the willingness to act on those convictions in an honorable way. The fundamental concept in her program is that *moral intelligence, which provides the foundation for good character, grows with experience and can be taught in schools. As students learn to increase their moral intelligence, they become more responsible and self-directing in the classroom and elsewhere.*

When students misbehave, Borba would like to have teachers intervene by *responding, reviewing, reflecting,* and *making right.* As shown in Chapter 4, these steps involve the following:

1. *Respond:* Stay calm and listen. Find out what happened. Say something like "Tell me what happened" or "Why did you do it?" or "What did you think this would accomplish?"
2. *Review:* Have the students involved indicate why the behavior was wrong: "Tell me what the rules are in the class" or "Why do you think I called you over?" Then remind the students of the class expectation: "We never speak to others in a way that hurts their feelings."
3. *Reflect:* Quickly explore the effects of the behavior. Ask questions such as these: "How do you feel when people call you names?" "How do you think that makes the other person feel?" "Do you want to think of yourself as a person who treats others that way?" "If you were in her shoes, what do you think she would like to say?"
4. *Make right:* Help students learn how to atone for wrongs they have done. A good way is to encourage offending students to make reparation of some sort but not an apology. The best solution is to encourage the offending student to do something nice for the other person.

As you can see from the four steps, Borba recommends that whenever you need to intervene in misbehavior, you should remind students of class expectations. Ask students if they are being the kind of people they want to be. Ask what they plan to do to improve their behavior. Keep them accountable for their behavior so they recognize they have choices over their actions and that actions have consequences. As they demonstrate more appropriate behavior, make supportive comments such as "You're on the right track. Keep it up" and "Almost, but this is what to do instead." If they do not show improvement, say, "What you did was not right. Let me show you what to do next time." Students benefit from immediate behavior correction. Ask them to redo any incorrect behavior immediately, if possible.

Suggestions from Ed Ford

Ed Ford, featured in Chapter 9, is president of Responsible Thinking Process, Inc., which is devoted to training educators and parents in using The Responsible Thinking Process to assist the young in conducting themselves effectively, relating with others, and becoming responsible people (Ford, 2003, 2006; Ford and Venetis, 2006). The basic premise of The Responsible Thinking Process is that *behavior is best understood in terms of how we perceive situations and react to them. The best way to promote good behavior in the classroom is to help students clarify what they want for themselves in life and plan the behavior that will get them what they want, without infringing on the rights of others.*

In keeping with this premise, Ford suggests that you intervene when students misbehave by asking those involved the following sequence of questions.

1. *What are you doing?* This question should be asked first but always in conjunction with question 2. When students hear this question, they look within themselves and identify their behavior. Your telling them what they are doing wrong doesn't prompt them to self-reflect, but asking them does.

2. *What are the rules?* When asked this question, students quickly review rules related to their present behavior. In so doing, they become aware of how their behavior compares to the rule. You may also ask them how their behavior affects the rights of others in the class.

3. *What happens when you break the rules?* This question prompts students to reflect on consequences that may follow when they break rules.

4. *Is this what you want to happen?* This question prompts students to look within themselves and decide how they want to see themselves as persons and how they want to live their lives.

5. *Where do you want to be?* or *What do you want to do now?* These questions help students begin to make a plan of action that will resolve the incompatibility between their behavior and the rights of others.

6. *What will happen if you disrupt again?* This question asks students to consider the consequences of repeating their misbehavior. The question should always be asked, even if students have already reflected and decided on changes they want to make.

These questions should never sound like warnings to students, because warnings imply the threat of punishment. The questions should simply lead students to think about what they are doing in relation to rules and consider, without being prompted, whether they might choose better courses of action.

TACTICS FOR USE WITH STUDENTS WHO ARE MORE DIFFICULT TO MANAGE

This section presents suggestions from three respected authorities on what teachers can and should do when they encounter misbehavior from students referred to as "difficult to manage." Suggestions are presented from Richard Curwin and Allen Mendler on working with students who are at risk of failure because of their behavior, Marvin Marshall on working with disaffected teenage students, and Barbara Coloroso on dealing with bullying.

Richard Curwin and Allen Mendler on At-Risk Students

Richard Curwin and Allen Mendler attracted national attention with their 1988 book *Discipline with Dignity,* which featured the power of personal dignity in discipline and has, for two decades, remained a very influential work. In 1992, Curwin published *Rediscovering Hope: Our Greatest Teaching Strategy,* in which he explained how to improve the behavior of difficult-to-control students who are otherwise likely to fail in school. In 1997, Curwin and Mendler published *As Tough as Necessary: Countering Violence, Aggression, and Hostility in Our Schools,* in which they provided suggestions for working with hostile, aggressive students. They followed in 1999 with *Discipline with Dignity for Challenging Youth,* designed to help teachers work productively with students with especially difficult behavioral problems.

Curwin and Mendler note that students are becoming increasingly aggressive, hostile, and violent and are doing so at an earlier age. Teenagers are 2.5 times more likely to experience violence than people over age 20. Curwin and Mendler say the increase in violence has occurred in part because society has been dealing with behavior by rewarding and punishing students in school, home, and community, rather than teaching them values—for example, that it is wrong to intimidate others, hurt them physically, or destroy their property. A large proportion of students who use violence have little sense of compassion or remorse and thus do not respond to normal discipline techniques.

Curwin and Mendler have addressed this issue in their 1997 book *As Tough As Necessary: Countering Violence, Aggression, and Hostility in Our Schools.* They point out that by the phrase "as tough as necessary," they do not mean a zero-tolerance stance but instead using "a variety of ways to help aggressive, hostile, and violent children learn alternatives to hurting others" (p. ix). They contend that "behavior change among hardened, antisocial, and angry students cannot result simply from offering more love, caring, and opportunities for decision making" (p. 16). They say that if schools are to deal with violence, they must adopt schoolwide approaches that (1) teach students how, when threatened or frustrated, to make nonviolent choices that serve them more effectively than do violent choices, (2) model for students nonhostile ways of expressing anger, frustration, and impatience, and (3) emphasize the teaching of values that relate to cooperation, safety, altruism, and remorse.

Curwin and Mendler suggest several strategies for teachers and students to use when they encounter violence. These strategies are designed to help everyone calm down, decide how to proceed, and move ahead in a positive manner. Teachers should teach the procedures to students and model them in practice. The following are a few of the many techniques suggested (1997, pp. 94–118):

1. *How I solve my problem.* Teach students to react to conditions they don't like in the following way: First, name the problem, indicating specifically what somebody has said or done. Second, say what you would like to have happen. Third, say what you believe you can do to make things as they should be. Fourth, carry out the plan. (If the plan doesn't work, use a backup plan.)

2. *Learn to have patience.* As we grow up we learn that our needs can't always be met when we'd like—that often we have to wait. If we don't learn to have patience, we will feel frustrated and angry because we are not getting what we want when we want it. Learning to be patient requires the practice of actions such as walking away from a fight, waiting in line with a smile, and remaining calm when somebody cuts in line.

3. *Wear an invisible shield.* Pretend you are wearing an invisible shield that deflects all bad thoughts and unkind words. It makes you immune to them. You cannot be hurt as long as you are wearing it.

4. *Use words that work.* Instead of being provoked into retaliation, practice doing the following, which will stop almost all attacks against you: (1) Speak politely, using words such as *please* and *thank-you,* (2) ask if you have done something that has upset the other person, and (3) apologize if you have offended the person.

5. *Plan ahead for confrontations.* Curwin and Mendler suggest that you list five situations you recall where people got into a dispute. Next to each, write down strategies you think would bring the situation calmly to a close. Have students practice what they would say and do should they find themselves in one of those situations.

Teachers who agree with these suggestions still ask the legitimate question What, specifically, do I do when . . . ? In answer to this question, Curwin and Mendler provide many concrete suggestions concerning how teachers can respond best when students misbehave (1997, p. 66):

- Use privacy, eye contact, and proximity when possible. Speak privately and quietly with the student. This preserves his or her dignity and takes away the likelihood of his or her fighting back.
- Indicate to the student politely but clearly what you want. Use the words *please* and *thank-you* (e.g., "Bill, please go to Mr. Keene's room. There's a seat there for you. Come back when you are ready to learn. I hope that doesn't take very long. Thank you, Bill.").
- Tell the student that you see a power struggle brewing that will not be good for anyone. Defer discussion to a later time (e.g., "Juan, you are angry and so is Shawn. Rather than have a dispute now, let's calm down and talk later. I'm sure we can help each other out after we cool off. Thanks a lot.").

Marvin Marshall on Working with Disaffected Teenagers

Earlier in this chapter, you saw intervention tactics suggested by Marvin Marshall in his *raise responsibility system.* He recognizes that some modifications must be made in that system if teachers are to use it effectively with disaffected teenage students—those who have concluded school has nothing to offer them, attend school only under duress, and show very little inclination to follow teacher directions or engage in lessons. Marshall has provided the following suggestions for teachers who work with such students. This material is adapted from *Promoting Responsibility & Learning: The Monthly Newsletter* by Marvin Marshall (2006):

Marshall on Realities Concerning Adolescent Students Who Are Disaffected with School

- *Regarding coercion.* These students will not tolerate coercion in any form. They react to it negatively. Doing so is their way of staying in control and exercising power.
- *Regarding trust.* These students have an ingrained distrust of teachers. It will take time for them to understand that you are truly concerned about them and their best interests.
- *Regarding reading.* Most of these students do not read for pleasure. You may discover that some of them get a headache when they read or that reading is physiologically painful to them. A simple change in *where* they read may have an effect on them—such as moving out from a standard classroom with fluorescent lights to outdoors or incandescent lighting. Some may have difficulties with visual perception. Ask each student privately if he or she finds it painful to read or gets a headache from reading. The following websites are two excellent sources of information on this topic: www.irlen.com/index_migrane.html and www.dyslexiacure.com.
- *You as students' last chance.* You may well be the last chance for these students in their formal schooling to develop a positive mindset leading to responsible and successful lives.

Marshall's Suggestions for Teachers

- *Teach procedures.* Teach a procedure for everything you want the students to do. Assume they know nothing. Even with homework assignments, have them practice in class before giving them any assignment to do on their own. When they have practiced and visualized exactly how to attack the assignment so they feel confident in completing it, the chances of their doing it significantly increase.
- *Use the hierarchy of social behavior.* When referring to the hierarchy, do not ask disaffected adolescents to identify a level. They will think you are being coercive. Instead, just drop a comment, such as "Lee, please take a moment and reflect on the level you have chosen."
- *Empower students through choices.* When giving options or choices, always give *three* of them. Giving only two options may seem coercive to adolescent students.
- *Choice–response thinking.* Refer regularly to the process of choice–response thinking and remind students of the process. First, an individual experiences a situation, stimulus, or urge; next, the individual has a choice in how to

respond; and finally, a response is made. Point out the control students have over the choices they make.

- *Emphasize and recognize success.* Since success is built on success, not failure, compliment students on their successes. This will give them hope— the most essential ingredient for success and something they have had very little of.
- *Remain continually patient.* Patience is critical with these students. Stick with them. Building relationships with them is the only way you will have success.
- *Show empathy for your students.* Always empathize with these students and then ask, "How are we going to handle the situation?" This approach will elicit a procedure that will help them to help themselves.
- *Avoid the "seven deadly habits."* Carefully guard against speaking with students in ways that suggest criticism, blaming, complaining, nagging, threatening, punishing, or rewarding/bribing to control.
- *Use caring techniques.* Use caring techniques of listening, supporting, encouraging, respecting, trusting, accepting, and negotiating.
- *Deflect student anger.* If a youngster is angry, do not take it personally. Ask, "Are you angry with me or the situation?" The anger will always come from a frustration of which you are rarely the cause.
- *Remain positive in all interactions with students.* Always remain helpful and encouraging, without showing frustration or irritation.
- *Use journal writing.* Have students write in a journal the very first thing upon entering the class each day. Assure students that you will never read what they have written, unless they ask you to and give you permission. Writing how they feel is a clarifying and cathartic exercise for these students, who constantly experience alienation and stress.
- *Be mindful of health concerns.* Periodically drop in a word (but don't teach a formal lesson unless asked) about the importance of getting a good night's sleep and exercising and the problems associated with eating too much sugar and too few fruits, vegetables, and sources of calcium.

Barbara Coloroso on Dealing with Bullying and Hate Crimes

Barbara Coloroso, featured in Chapter 1, is author of *The Bully, the Bullied, and the Bystander: How Parents and Teachers Can Break the Cycle of Violence* (2003). *Bullying* is defined as intentionally and repeatedly committing hurtful acts against others. *Hate crimes* are similar to bullying but are related to a dislike for other races, ethnic groups, and religions. Such crimes typically involve intimidation, harassment, bigoted slurs or epithets, force or threat of force, and vandalism. Bullying and hate crimes can have devastating effects on students who are victimized, and they present serious concerns for teachers.

Bullying is a daily occurrence in most schools. It may consist of physical aggression, sexual aggression, name-calling, threatening, taunting, intimidating, or shunning. Four kinds of bullying are common:

1. *Physical bullying* includes punching, poking, strangling, hair pulling, beating, biting, kicking, and excessive tickling.
2. *Verbal bullying* includes hurtful name-calling, teasing, and gossip.
3. *Emotional bullying* includes rejecting, terrorizing, extorting, defaming, humiliating, blackmailing, rating/ranking of personal characteristics (such as race, disability, ethnicity, or perceived sexual orientation), manipulating friendships, isolating, ostracizing, and exerting peer pressure.
4. *Sexual bullying* includes many of the actions just listed as well as exhibitionism, voyeurism, sexual propositioning, sexual harassment, physical contact, and sexual assault.

Among middle school students, one in four is bullied on a regular basis, while one in five admits to bullying others. About one in seven says he or she experienced a severe reaction to the abuse.

Acts of bullying usually occur away from the eyes of teachers and other responsible adults. As perpetrators go undetected, a climate of fear develops that affects victims adversely. Their grades may suffer because their attention is deflected away from learning. Fear may lead to absenteeism, truancy, or dropping out. If the problem persists, victims occasionally resort to drastic measures, such as fighting back, carrying weapons, and occasionally suicide.

Bystanders and peers of victims can suffer harmful effects as well. They may be afraid to associate with the victim for fear of lowering their own status or of receiving retribution from the bully. They may not report bullying incidents because they do not want to be called a "snitch," a "tattler," or an "informer." Some experience feelings of guilt or helplessness for not standing up to the bully on behalf of their classmate. They may feel unsafe, with loss of control and inability to take action.

The incidence and effects of bullying and hate crimes is grossly underreported. Educators, family members, and children concerned with violence prevention must be concerned with hate crimes and their linkage to other violent behaviors. Excellent suggestions for limiting and dealing with bullying and hate crimes are found in Coloroso's book and in a 1998 publication by the U.S. Department of Education, *Preventing Bullying: A Manual for Schools and Communities.* Here are a few of the many suggestions provided in those two resources:

- Closely supervise students on the grounds and in classrooms, hallways, restrooms, cafeterias, and other areas where bullying occurs. Immediately intervene in all bullying incidents and put a stop to them.
- Involve students in establishing classroom rules against bullying. Such rules may include a commitment from the teacher not to ignore incidents of bullying. Post and publicize clear behavior standards, including rules against bullying, for all students. Consistently and fairly enforce such standards.
- Schedule regular classroom meetings during which students and teachers engage in discussion, role-playing, and other activities to reduce bullying and hate crimes. Develop an action plan to ensure that students know what to do when they observe a bullying situation or are victimized by a bully.

- Don't try to have a bully and a victim try to resolve their situation. The difference in power between the two may cause the victim to feel further victimized by the process.
- Involve parents and guardians of bullies and victims of bullying and hate crimes. Listen receptively to family members who report bullying. Establish procedures whereby such reports are investigated and resolved expeditiously.
- Form friendship groups and other supports for students who are being victimized by bullying or hate crimes.
- Establish a confidential reporting system that allows children to report victimization. Keep records of all incidents.
- Provide students with opportunities to talk about bullying and hate crimes, and enlist their support in defining bullying as unacceptable behavior.

IN SUMMARY

This chapter presented suggestions from leading authorities on what teachers should say and do when students misbehave. The discussion focused first on intervention tactics that work for most students and then on tactics that are more effective with students whose behavior is considered difficult to manage. Suggestions were also provided to help teachers deal with issues of bullying and hate crimes.

REFERENCES

Albert, L. 2003. *A teacher's guide to cooperative discipline.* Circle Pines, MN: American Guidance Service.

Borba, M. 2001. *Building moral intelligence.* San Francisco: Jossey-Bass.

Coloroso, B. 2002. *Kids are worth it! Giving your child the gift of inner discipline.* New York: Quill.

Coloroso, B. 2003. *The bully, the bullied, and the bystander: How parents and teachers can break the cycle of violence.* New York: HarperCollins.

Curwin, R. 1992. *Rediscovering hope: Our greatest teaching strategy.* Bloomington, IN: National Educational Service.

Curwin, R., and Mendler, A. 1988. *Discipline with dignity.* Alexandria, VA: Association for Supervision and Curriculum Development. (Revised editions 1992, 1999, 2002)

Curwin, R., and Mendler, A. 1997. *As tough as necessary. Countering violence, aggression, and hostility in our schools.* Alexandria, VA: Association for Supervision and Curriculum Development.

Ford, E. 2003. *Discipline for home and school, book one* (3rd edition). Scottsdale, AZ: Brandt.

Ford, E. 2006. How the Responsible Thinking Program works. www.responsiblethinking.com.

Ford, E., and Venetis, G. 2006. Teaching respect using RTP. www.responsiblethinking.com.

Ginott, H. 1971. *Teacher and child.* New York: Macmillan.

Glasser, W. 1990. *The quality school: Managing students without coercion.* New York: Perennial Library.

Glasser, W. 1998. *Choice theory in the classroom.* New York: HarperCollins.

Kagan, S. 2002. What is win–win discipline? *Kagan Online Magazine* 1(15). www .KaganOnline.com.

Kagan, S., Kyle, P., and Scott, S. 2004. *Win–win discipline.* San Clemente, CA: Kagan.

Marshall, M. 2001. *Discipline without stress, punishments, or rewards: How teachers and parents promote responsibility and learning.* Los Alamitos, CA: Piper Press.

Marshall, M. June 2006. *Promoting Responsibility and Learning,* 6(6). www.Discipline WithoutStress.com.

Mendler, A., and Curwin, R. 1999. *Discipline with dignity for challenging youth.* Bloomington, IN: National Education Service.

Morrish, R. 1997. *Secrets of discipline: Twelve keys for raising responsible children.* Fonthill, Ontario, Canada: Woodstream.

Morrish, R. 2000. *With all due respect: Keys for building effective school discipline.* Fonthill, Ontario, Canada: Woodstream. (2003 edition from Colorado Springs, CO: Purposeful Design)

U.S. Department of Education. 1998. *Preventing bullying: A manual for schools and communities.* www.cde.ca.gov/spbranch/ssp/bullymanual.htm.

STRATEGY

6

Adjusting Instruction

Teaching in a Quality Manner, with the Instructional Program Aligned with Students' Traits, Needs, and Interests

In order to make sure your instructional program intrigues, invites, and motivates students, make it harmonious with their traits, needs, interests, and values. Teach in a way that attracts students and allows them to use and expand their natural capabilities.

Chapter Preview

Quality instruction—powerful in reducing the incidence of misbehavior—is accomplished through the use of certain instructional activities and the alignment of instruction with students' traits and needs. Two effective methods of teaching are described in this chapter. Notations are made of variations in student characteristics associated with ethnic origin and economic status, and suggestions are provided for enhancing the quality of instruction for all students.

PERFORMANCE GOALS FOR QUALITY INSTRUCTION

This book presents a large number of suggestions for providing a quality instructional program for your students. Here are five things you can do to help ensure quality teaching. Use these five statements as performance goals or as criteria in reflecting on your performance:

1. *Give your genuine best to the profession.* Always conduct yourself ethically and professionally. Do the best you can to help every student profit from school and experience satisfaction in doing so. Teach in a manner that provides enjoyment and success for your students. Emphasize subject matter that is worth learning and activities that

students find appealing. Help convince students of the value of what they are expected to learn, including how it increases competence and/or makes life more satisfying.

2. *Treat students civilly, respectfully, and fairly.* Treat all students as your social equals. Give each of them personal attention. Learn their names quickly, and remember important things about them. Smile and interact with them in a friendly manner. Acknowledge their accomplishments and their considerate acts toward others. Spread your attention around evenly. Do not disparage students in any way or attack their dignity. Always treat them as you would like to be treated in similar circumstances. Hold high but reasonable standards for them, and show your confidence in their ability to learn and assume responsibility.

3. *Involve students in a collaborative manner.* Invite students to work with you as allies in a common enterprise. Increase their stake in the educational program by involving them in planning and making decisions. Show consideration for their opinions, desires, and feelings. Help them assume responsibilities in the class.

4. *Communicate effectively.* Make sure students know what is expected of them. Take time to listen to their concerns and points of view. Be helpful and encouraging, but don't give much advice and don't preach to students or put them on the defensive. If they misbehave, politely ask them to help you understand why they have done so. If you can, make changes that will help them avoid inappropriate behavior in the future.

5. *Maintain a modestly charismatic demeanor.* Charisma is a quality of attractiveness that draws attention and fosters desire for association and interaction. Increase your charisma by making yourself personally interesting to students. Be open to students, upbeat, and pleasant. Avoid being overbearing; use a touch of humor when appropriate. Share some of your interests, experiences, and talents. Let students know a bit about your family life and interests outside school. Use the tactics William Glasser (1990) advocates for connecting with students—caring, listening, supporting, contributing, encouraging, trusting, and befriending.

METHODS OF TEACHING THAT PRODUCE THE RESULTS YOU WANT

Several different methods can be used to present effective instruction. (For a broad description of *models of teaching*, see Joyce, Weil, and Calhoun [2003].) Two examples are William Glasser's *lead teaching* and Fred Jones's *Say See Do teaching*. Lead teaching is especially effective for helping students develop initiative, self-direction, and perseverance. Say See Do teaching is especially effective for teaching factual information, procedures, and skills. The two methods can be alternated in the same class in accordance with the topic and goals of learning. Following are brief descriptions of these two excellent methods of teaching.

William Glasser's Lead Teaching

Lead teaching is especially well suited for cooperative learning, project development, and independent research and study. Glasser, whose suggestions for connecting with students are featured in Chapter 7, believes lead teaching has superior qualities for what we are trying to accomplish with learners today. He contrasts lead teaching with the more traditional "boss teaching." Most teachers, he laments, function as boss teachers. They organize every aspect of the learning program: They set the tasks and standards for student learning, lecture rather than demonstrate, only rarely ask for student input, grade student work without involving students in the evaluation, and use coercion to try to make students comply with expectations.

Lead teachers work differently. Recognizing that genuine motivation resides within students in the form of needs and interests, lead teachers spend most of their time organizing activities that interest students, obtaining needed materials, and providing assistance. They discuss the curriculum with the class in such a way that many topics of interest are identified, and they encourage students to identify topics they would like to explore in depth. Lead teachers discuss with students the kind of schoolwork that would produce quality learning. They explore resources that might be needed and judge the amount of time such work might require. When necessary, these teachers demonstrate how the work can be done, using samples of work that reflect quality. They make it clear that their job is to do what they can to provide good tools and a place for learning that is noncoercive and nonadversarial. Such a place has the following characteristics (Glasser, 1992, pp. 22 ff):

1. *A warm, supportive classroom climate.* Help students know and like you. Use natural occasions to tell students who you are, what you stand for, what you will and will not ask them to do, and what you will and will not do for them. Show you are always willing to help.

2. *A helpful teacher.* Encourage students and draw them out. Don't try to force information into them.

3. *Schoolwork that is useful.* Useful work leads to knowledge and skills that are valuable in students' lives. Students should not be required to memorize information beyond that essential to the skill being learned.

4. *Encouragement for students to do the best they can.* The process of doing quality work develops slowly and must be nurtured. Glasser advises teachers to discuss quality work enough so that students understand what it means. Begin with an assignment that is clearly important enough to do well. Ask students to do their best work on the assignment. Do not grade their work, because grades suggest to students that the work is finished.

5. *Evaluation and improvement of student work.* Quality usually accrues through progressive modification. When students feel they have completed a piece of work, ask them to make value judgments about it, in which they explain why the work shows high quality and how they think it might be improved further. As students try repeatedly to improve their work, quality grows naturally.

For an interesting presentation on lead teaching from a school principal's perspective, see this website: www.greatschools.net/content/principals/LTL_h.html.

Fred Jones's Say See Do Teaching

Fred Jones is author and publisher of *Tools for Teaching* (2001), in which he describes a method of instruction called *Say See Do teaching*. Jones, a clinical psychologist, has worked for many years helping teachers motivate, manage, and instruct students. For more information on Dr. Jones, go to www.fredjones.com.

Jones says that too often, ineffective teachers beyond the primary grades spend most of their time presenting information while their students remain relatively passive. It is not until near the end of the lesson that students are asked to do something with the information. Jones (2001) depicts this timeworn approach as follows:

(Teacher) input, input, input, input, input–(Student) output

Jones says this approach suffers from three major problems. First, the large amount of teacher input produces cognitive overload; students simply receive more than they can process or remember. Second, when students sit passively for a long time, their urge to do something builds up, and before long, they are behaving in an unacceptable manner. Third, because the teacher does not adequately interact with individual students, particularly in the back of the classroom, students tend to disengage from the lesson.

The most effective teachers, Jones says, put students to work from the beginning and keep them occupied. They present information and then quickly have students do something with it. This approach is *doing* oriented, with activities occurring often at short intervals, and is depicted as follows:

Teacher input–student output–teacher input–student output–teacher input–student output

In this approach, students learn one step at a time, with active involvement. As Jones (2003) puts it, students must *do* the lesson, not just listen to it. He says that once you see lessons as kinetic—as performance for both you and your students—you come to understand that your job is to coach correct performance. This involves creating a behavior that students practice, with your feedback, until it becomes easy and automatic. The principle applies equally to teaching facts, skills, and concepts. Students must do something with what is being taught. That might involve talking, writing, role-playing, or other activities you might choose. But unless students perform the lesson, they remain passive rather than active. When they are passive, you can expect your teaching to go in one ear and out the other.

In the classroom, we typically teach to three modalities of learning—verbal, visual, and physical (thus the name Say See Do teaching). Think of each modality as a different way of learning. You can integrate the three by doing them at the same time. Performance welds them together to form a single pattern in the brain (see Figure 6.1).

Why Say See Do Teaching Reduces Behavior Problems. Say See Do teaching improves learning and behavior because it corrects the problem of cognitive overload, which typically begins to occur after the teacher has spoken only a few sentences. If the

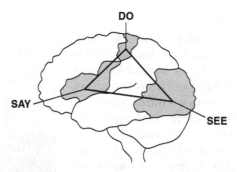

FIGURE 6.1

teacher goes on for 15 or 20 minutes or more, many of the students will have disengaged, won't remember what the teacher said, or will be passing notes, gazing out the window, whispering to neighbors, doodling, or daydreaming.

As you begin using Say See Do teaching, you will notice a change in your role. Instead of being a performer (the traditional teacher role), you will become a manager of student activities. Admittedly, this will slow lessons down somewhat. Active doing takes time, and you need to observe student performance carefully so you can provide corrective feedback. But that is how to build performance correctly from the beginning. If that is not done, students will tend to develop bad habits. Any time required in the beginning will be quickly recovered when you no longer have to correct mistakes and reteach endlessly.

Structured Practice. In order to make Say See Do teaching maximally effective, you must add one other thing—structured practice, which is tightly organized repetition that reduces student errors dramatically. Students often chafe at structured practice. They want to work quickly and raggedly, but they will do better if they slow down and get it right. Teachers must keep students going slowly at first, but later, their speed of performance will increase without an increase in errors. Jones contends that only with tight structure do we have enough control over performance to produce near-perfect practice.

If we provide adequate repetition with constant monitoring and feedback, students will develop correct patterns of thought and action. In the process, they will develop enough habit strength to move ahead to guided practice, which can then produce truly independent learning, rather than learned helplessness. The familiar "helpless hand-raising" will become a thing of the past, setting teachers free to monitor students and engage with them personally.

ALIGNING INSTRUCTION WITH STUDENT CHARACTERISTICS

General Traits of Students at Four Levels in School

The following sections present a succinct review of the typical interests of students at four levels of development. They indicate what you can expect of students, in general, and suggest curriculum topics and activities that serve students well. Keep in mind that these depictions are general and not shared by all students.

Primary Grades (Ages 5 to 8).   Children first come to school full of life and eager to learn. Most have a loving disposition. They are receptive to almost everything we introduce. They especially enjoy stories, music, and rhythmic activities. Many—especially girls, whose language capability develops quickly—give the impression of being intellectually precocious, which sometimes causes us to expect more from them than they can deliver.

Until approximately age 7, they function intellectually at what Swiss psychologist Jean Piaget (1951) called the *preoperational stage,* where they reason not on the basis of logic but on impressions they receive (see Piaget, 1951; Charles, 1974). During this developmental phase, students are poor at remembering the order of events, understanding rules, explaining relationships, comprehending number relationships, and understanding other speakers accurately, including the teacher. They get along reasonably well together, although they squabble a lot. They tire easily and get fussy, so they require frequent rest. They make little distinction between work and play.

At around age 7, on average, they begin to mature noticeably. Intellectually, they become able to consider the relationship of parts to whole and are thus able to reason logically in terms of cause and effect. Where previously they reasoned and explained on the basis of appearances or intuition (e.g., "The sun moves because the wind blows it along"), they can now understand number relationships and science concepts, such as why we have day and night. They are learning to play well together.

By second grade, they are enjoying games such as tag and hide and seek. They like puzzles, riddles, and guessing games. Although they can learn rules for games, they are poor at following them. They accept adult authority with little question. They tell fabrications routinely but seldom in a malicious way. They are highly imitative of each other. For them, misbehavior is whatever adults don't like, and guilt is getting caught.

Before leaving the primary level, students have become socialized to raising hands, standing in lines, taking turns, and waiting patiently. They continue to respond well to affection and personal attention. All the while, students at this level enjoy activities in science, especially those having to do with plants and animals.

Intermediate Grades (Ages 9 to 11).   As students move into grade four, they become increasingly independent, although they still want attention and affection from teachers. Holding hands with the teacher takes the place of hugging. Intellectually, their ability to think logically grows stronger. They use concrete language for thinking; they cannot yet think in terms of pure abstractions.

Socially, students have become highly argumentative. Many are loud and abusive, yet there is increasing evidence of reason and persuasion. They like to play group games and show an increasing bent for competition. Losing is difficult to accept; many cry and throw temper tantrums. They recognize the need for rules and rule enforcement, both in games and class behavior. No longer is teacher authority blindly accepted. Students may argue with the teacher, talk back, and be uncooperative. They show a growing awareness of honesty and its importance in relationships. They see that the more a lie intends to deceive, the worse it is.

Conscience develops along with respect for others. A growing sense of right and wrong is evident. Students are growing in respect for each other and increasingly want to share each other's company. They like group names and begin to form gangs, clubs, and cliques. Their behavior begins to reflect peer norms. Their interest in the natural world continues strongly.

Middle School Grades (Ages 12 to 14).   Behavior becomes more diverse as students move into the middle school years, and teachers require exceptional skill in order to teach well and build supportive relationships. Bodily changes worry, perplex, excite, and dismay these students. New realities of an opposite sex stir and baffle. Psychological weaning from parents leaves them feeling lost and cut off. They crave adult support, yet the emerging need for independence produces conflict with adults. Factors such as these provide serious distractions to learning.

Meanwhile, students are becoming increasingly rebellious and disposed to probing at the boundaries of rules and customs. Their awe of the teacher has waned, but it has been replaced with respect and affection for those who show understanding and helpfulness. Intellectually, these students have acquired a great new power—the ability to think abstractly. Their minds work as quickly as do those of adults, although they lack adult wisdom. Students can make use of concepts such as love, hate, honesty, loyalty, negative numbers, force, speed, time, and atomic particles. They have become able to think about thought.

High School Grades (Ages 15 to 18).   Before entering high school, students have become able to do deep thinking. They now show a proclivity for theorizing. Everything has a cause, a purpose, a place. They think about the *possible* as much as the *actual* and have acquired a strong sense of right and wrong. Their rational power produces the idealism characteristic of adolescence. Propositional thinking emerges: "If I do so and so, then so and so will result." Interest in nature and society is growing rapidly.

Lies are now seen as anything intentionally false. Punishment must take into account factors such as intent to break a law, age of the violator, and previous record of behavior. Many rules and laws are seen as unfair or irrelevant, so breaking them is no longer seen as absolutely wrong. Socially, these students can see various groups' points of view, which they like to weigh, clarify, and evaluate against each other. They can't see why everything is not ideal—politics, institutions, human relations, and so forth—which makes them overly critical of the way institutions and people actually function. Students may scathingly reject existing social arrangements and values. Their behavior, however, usually indicates adherence to existing social norms.

As they near the end of high school, students begin to settle down emotionally. They understand themselves better and have reached a truce with their bodies and feelings. They have begun to think about what they hope to do in the future. Some, lamentably, become further alienated from the educational mainstream. A new relationship with adults emerges. The love–hate attitude of earlier years fades, while respect for adults grows as students recognize their own interdependence with the community. Teachers can now treat these students as fellow adults, while students see teachers as guides and role models.

Student Needs That Affect Behavior

Educational programs that are not harmonious with basic human needs cannot achieve their intended results; thus, it is highly important that you and your program meet basic student needs, descriptions of which are presented in this chapter. When students' needs are being met, they willingly cooperate and learn and cause little disruption. Teachers who capitalize on this principle find little need to resort to demands, penalties, and struggles to get students to behave and learn. Meeting student needs is not difficult, as we will see.

Maslow's Hierarchy of Needs. Abraham Maslow (1954) is given credit for pinpointing human needs and explaining the role they play in motivation. He depicted his conclusions graphically as a hierarchy of needs (see Figure 6.2), now often referred to as *Maslow's hierarchy,* which has received worldwide attention. The meanings of the various levels in Maslow's hierarchy are evident. Needs at lower levels, especially the first four, must be met in order to provide a platform for addressing higher-level needs.

Dreikurs's Prime Need and Mistaken Goals. In 1972, Rudolf Dreikurs, a psychiatrist and family counselor, proposed that behavior problems in the classroom occur mainly when students are unable to satisfy their prime need of belonging in the class or school. If that need is not met, Dreikurs said, students turn to so-called mistaken goals in an attempt to satisfy it (Dreikurs and Cassel, 1972). Those mistaken goals are typically sought in the following sequence: First, students try for *attention.* If that fails, they try for *control.* If that fails, they seek to enact *revenge,*

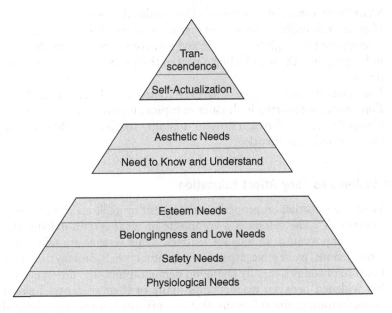

FIGURE 6.2

and failing that, they slip into *withdrawal*. Dreikurs contended that teachers must first and foremost make sure that every student gains a sense of belonging in the class. When that is accomplished, discipline problems will tend to fade away.

Glasser's Five Needs in the Classroom.   William Glasser (1998) has done more than anyone else to call educators' attention to student needs and explain why they must be met if teaching is to be successful. He has articulated five needs that all students sense and strive for:

- Students' need for *survival* is met when the school environment is kept safe and free from personal threat.
- Students sense *belonging* when they are involved in class decisions and receive positive attention from the teacher and others.
- Students sense *power* when the teacher allows them to accept responsibility for selected duties and involves them in making decisions about matters pertinent to the class.
- They experience *fun* when able to work and talk with others, engage in interesting activities, and share their accomplishments.
- And they sense *freedom* when the teacher allows them to make responsible choices concerning what they will study, how they will do so, and how they will demonstrate their accomplishments.

Charles's Seven Needs in the Classroom.   C. M. Charles (2008) expanded Glasser's list of needs to a total of seven, which he believes must be met if teachers are to have successful programs:

- *Security,* met through a sense of safety without worry
- *Hope,* met through the conviction that school is worthwhile and success is possible
- *Dignity,* met through being respected and considered worthwhile
- *Belonging,* met through feeling a part of things, being valued, having a place in the class
- *Power,* met through a degree of personal control and ability to contribute to the class
- *Enjoyment,* met through pleasure in topics and instructional activities
- *Competence,* met through growth in ability to do many things well, including the expected schoolwork

Value Systems as They Affect Education

In order to align instruction properly with student traits, it is necessary to understand value systems. A *value system* is a composite of what certain individuals or groups believe to be important in various life matters. Value systems are reflected in personal habits, interactions, work ethic, aspirations, spiritual beliefs, and myriad other activities.

    Because of today's rapidly changing demographics, the difference in value systems has widened between teachers and many of their students. To help promote better understanding, the following sections present information about the typical values and behaviors of students in various ethnic and cultural groups. The groups are listed in order of size within the overall U.S. population.

Information about Middle-Class European American Students

Most teachers, school administrators, and other educators in the United States reflect the beliefs and behaviors characteristic of white, middle-class society. This value system stems from the Judeo–Christian ethic and is influenced by a capitalistic outlook and individualistic traditions of work ethic, future orientation, enterprise, and self-sufficiency. The following are a few examples of white, middle-class values held by a large proportion of students and teachers in schools, regardless of their ethnic or racial origins. (Please remember that values can vary from person to person within any societal group.)

- *Time orientation:* Promptness is valued; orientation is toward the future.
- *Planning ahead:* Plans are made ahead of time, often for years in advance.
- *Work:* Hard work brings financial rewards but is also good in its own right. It is not good to be lazy in either the classroom or the workplace.
- *Relations with others:* A sense of equality prevails; others are to be treated with consideration and respect.
- *Personal achievement and competition:* Individuals are urged to aspire to personal achievement in all matters. It is good to compete as individuals and rise above the norm.
- *Child-to-adult relations:* Adults are shown respect but not seen as infallible.
- *Adult-to-child relations:* Children require guidance but are not to be treated subserviently.
- *Opportunity:* Potential to advance in life is available to everyone; one has only to seize the opportunity and follow through.
- *Verbal learning:* Much learning, especially in school, occurs verbally through listening, reading, and discussing.
- *Success:* Success is seen as obtaining a good job, holding responsible positions, providing a good home, and acquiring a degree of wealth.
- *Personal behavior:* We are all ultimately responsible for our own behavior; most people behave ethically; laws and regulations serve as guidelines.

Human behavior and values across all groups of people are far more similar than different. Nevertheless, certain cultural differences have a strong bearing on learning in school. In contrast to the white, middle-class values just presented, some groups frown on individual achievement and recognition. Some place great emphasis on traditions. Some see little purpose in working at school activities that do not seem useful or are not inherently interesting. Students in some groups adopt a subservient manner when interacting with teachers and are made uncomfortable by eye contact. Many do not want to voice opinions that disagree with what the teacher believes. Many do not look for educational opportunities to advance themselves, and many consider class rules and school regulations merely restrictions imposed by teachers in power. A failure to approach such differences sensitively can lead to malaise between teachers and students, promote misunderstanding, and put a strain on relationships, thus making teaching and learning more difficult than necessary.

The following sections review some of the information available in the literature concerning the values and customs typical of other ethnic and societal groups in U.S. schools—information that can help teachers better understand and work more effectively with all their students.

Information about Hispanic American Students

Hispanic: People who are of Mexican, Puerto Rican, Cuban, Central or South American, or another Spanish culture or origin, regardless of race

Hispanic American students, often called *Latinos,* are members of various ethnic groups whose native or ancestral language is Spanish. These students now comprise just over 17 percent of public school enrollment in the United States, up from 6 percent in 1972 and expected to reach 25 percent by the year 2025 (*Latinos in School: Some Facts and Findings,* 2001). Large numbers of these students have blended into the dominant society, speak English perfectly, and assume leadership roles in the broader society. However, as a group, Hispanic American students are the second most likely (after American Indian/Alaska Native students) to drop out of school. Their high school completion rate in 1999 was 63 percent, as compared with 81 percent for African Americans and 90 percent for European Americans. Hispanic American students are less likely than African American and European American students to have had early childhood education, including preschool or Head Start (*Strategies for Teaching Minorities,* 2004).

Although there are strong common characteristics across the larger Hispanic American population, the group as a whole is comprised of distinct subcultures that vary significantly in customs, values, and educational orientation (Griggs and Dunn, 1996). One characteristic common to all subgroups is family commitment, which involves loyalty, a strong support system, a belief that a child's behavior reflects on the honor of the family, a hierarchical order among siblings, and a duty to care for family members. The dignity of each individual and respect for authority figures are also strongly valued throughout Hispanic American culture.

Teachers should ensure that Hispanic cultural concerns are addressed in the curriculum. They should emphasize hands-on cooperative activities, while taking care that students' intellectual and emotional well-being is protected. Wendy Schwartz (2000) and Anne Lockwood and Walter Secada (2000) have presented several additional suggestions for improving the quality of classroom experiences for Hispanic American youth. To make the classroom safe and inviting, they advise the following:

- Personalize instruction, and give students the opportunity to assume positions of leadership and responsibility.
- Convey high expectations, provide options, and furnish resources needed for an effective education.

- Emphasize the prevention of problems, and respond to early warning signs that a student is beginning to disengage from school.
- Respect and show interest in students' native language, culture, and ethnicity.
- Provide help in reducing student anger and building trust as a means of countering attitudes produced by negative experiences with schools and adults.
- If possible, identify for each Hispanic student an adult in the school who is committed to nurturing a sense of self-worth and supporting the student's efforts to succeed. Such mentors can help students withstand the peer, economic, and societal pressures that lead to dropping out.
- Bring attention to the lives and contributions of outstanding people of Hispanic origin, and engage family members and the community in the education of their children.

As for the learning environment, a somewhat more formal design has been identified as helpful to Hispanic American elementary and middle school students (Dunn, Griggs, and Price, 1993). Hispanic American students seem to like a higher degree of structure than do European American students (Yong and Ewing, 1992). Hispanic American students also enjoy and profit from cooperative learning with peers, kinesthetic instructional resources, and a variety of activities.

Information about African American Students

African American, not of Hispanic Origin: A person having origins in any of the black racial groups of Africa

African American students comprise approximately 17 percent of the public school population in the United States. The Education Trust reported in 2003 that 61 percent of African American fourth-graders were lagging behind the established standards for reading proficiency and mathematics. Earlier, Ashcher (1991) cited evidence that low-achieving students from all groups seldom catch up with their peers but instead fall further behind over time.

The following observations and suggestions for working with African American students are adapted from a website presentation entitled Strategies for Teaching Science to African American Students (2005). This resource, which also makes many suggestions concerning avoiding bias, advises the following:

- Many African American students profit from visual, kinesthetic, and tactile learning, more than from verbal explanations from the teacher.
- These students tend to respond well to cooperative learning.
- Their preferred discussion style is simultaneous talk instead of alternating talk.
- They tend to use colorful language in verbal communication.
- Many African American students are physically active and do not adjust well to a sedentary learning environment.
- They are sensitive to and responsive to what others feel and think, and they consider how their actions may affect others.
- African American students enjoy close proximity to other students and respond well to praise, smiles, and pats on the back.

The Education Trust (2003) reports that African American students also respond well to clear public standards for what students should learn at benchmark grade levels, challenging curricula with standards, and extra instruction for students who need it. Jackie Irvine and James Fraser (1998) suggest the following for teachers of African American students:

- Think of yourself as a surrogate parent for your students.
- Use a teaching style filled with rhythmic language and rapid intonation, with many instances of repetition, call and response, high emotional involvement, creative analogies, figurative language, gestures and body movements, symbolism, aphorisms (short sayings), and lively and often spontaneous discussions.
- Use students' everyday cultural and historical experiences as links to new knowledge, and strive to develop good personal relationships with students.

Johnnie McKinley (2003) has reported on a study involving 29 teachers in a large urban district that showed African American students responded well to culturally relevant curriculum and materials, cooperative group instruction, structured lessons, heavy use of questions, and student recitation. Other authorities (Bempechat, 2001; Diller, 1999; Foster, 1999; Ladson-Billings, 2000; McCollough, 2000; Schwartz, 2002) advise teachers to spend classroom and nonclassroom time developing personal relationships with students, frequently teasing and joking with them, and showing solidarity with them and their concerns.

Information about Asian American and Pacific Islander Students

Asian: A person having origins in any of the original peoples of East Asia, Southeast Asia, and the Indian subcontinent, including China, India, Indonesia, Japan, Korea, Vietnam, Thailand, Cambodia, and other smaller nations

Pacific Islander: A person having origins in any of the original peoples of Hawaii; the U.S. Pacific territories of Guam, American Samoa, and the Northern Marinas; the U.S. Trust Territory of Palau; the islands of Micronesia and Melanesia; and the Philippines

Jianhua Feng (1994) points out that Asian Americans comprise a variety of national, cultural, and religious groups, more than 29 of which differ in language, religion, and customs. These various groups are commonly categorized as East Asian, Southeast Asian, South Asian, and Pacific Islander. While these distinct groups often get lumped together as *Asian,* they differ considerably from each other.

Asian Americans are generally viewed as successful, conforming, and high achieving. Their school behavior is much in keeping with those perceptions, and they do not often present behavior problems for teachers. They tend to be strongly group and family oriented, which for a time may interfere with newly arrived students' adaptation to the independence, competition, and individualism emphasized in Western education.

Students from many East and Southeast Asian cultures are imbued with Confucian ideals, which value learning, respect for elders, responsibility for relatives, deferred gratification, and self-discipline (Feng, 1994). They tend to view failure as representing a lack of will. They tend to be conforming and willing to place family welfare ahead of individual wishes. They are usually self-effacing, willing to wait patiently, and seem to learn best in a well-structured, quiet environment (Baruth and Manning, 1992). Asian American students tend to dislike having public attention drawn to them as individuals. Most listen carefully, think before they speak, use a soft voice, and are modest in personal dress and grooming.

In conversations and other verbal communication, Asians seldom speak their minds as plainly as Westerners do. They often display verbal hesitancy and ambiguity to avoid giving offense, and they do not make spontaneous or critical remarks (Kim, 1985). Their body language is noticeably different from that of Westerners, too, as characterized by head nodding and lack of eye contact (Matsuda, 1989). The Japanese and Vietnamese are noted for being unwilling to use the word *no* even when they disagree with you (Coker, 1988; Wierzbicka, 1991). Seldom are Asian American students, their family members, or their teachers aware of the cultural differences that affect communication. This leads to one side or the other being misunderstood or ignored.

A sense of time unfamiliar to most teachers in Western schools can also cause difficulties. Many Asian cultures operate on what is called *polychronic time,* as distinct from the *monochronic time* familiar to Western people (Storti, 1999). Polychronic time allows different social interactions to occur at the same time, while monochronic time is linear, such that one thing is done at a time, in a fixed sequence. This difference in time orientation sometimes causes misunderstandings because Asians may not be prompt or ready to get down to business as quickly as Westerners would like. (The traditional sense of monochronic time among Western people seems to be changing somewhat among today's middle-class youth, evident in their use of technology for multitasking.)

Teachers of Asian American students should also understand that when their students show delay or hesitation, it may be because they are unsure of an answer, unfamiliar with the discourse style, or simply disengaged and lost. When they fail to stick with the topic, it may be due to insufficient knowledge, unfamiliarity with how to gain the floor, or fear and avoidance of interactions. These students often make what teachers consider inappropriate nonverbal expressions, such as avoiding eye contact with adults (doing so is a sign of respect), frowning (they do this when concentrating, as opposed to displeasure), or giggling (they do this from embarrassment or lack of understanding, not in response to something perceived as humorous).

When Asian American students make short responses, it is sometimes because their English proficiency does not permit replies in long, cohesive utterances or because they are too shy to respond. They typically use an overly soft voice, something that is typical for children in some Asian cultures. If these students show an unwillingness to take risks, it is probably from fear of being embarrassed or ridiculed. When they are reluctant to participate, it might be because volunteering information is considered overly bold. When they receive praise, they may be embarrassed because their native culture values humility and self-criticism. They may appear impolite or unfriendly by diverting their eyes downward and offering no greeting when the teacher approaches, but this can be because of either respect or fear.

Li-Rong Cheng (1996) adds that Asian students who have had school experience in their native countries are accustomed to learning through (1) listening, observing, reading, and imitating; (2) responding to teachers' questions based on lectures and textbooks; and (3) taking tests that require only the recall of factual information. These students may be left feeling ambivalent and confused by class work that involves group efforts, discussions, and creative activities.

Matsuda (1989), Baruth and Manning (1992), Trueba and Cheng (1993), Huang (1993), Feng (1994), and Cheng (1996, 1998) make a number of suggestions to help teachers work more effectively with Asian American students:

- Carefully observe and understand students' sense of communication and time, and adjust your interactions accordingly.
- Learn at least a few words of the students' native languages. Ask students to teach them to you.
- Help students understand that while at school, they may offer their opinions and challenge the views of others.
- Explain to family members that parental involvement in their child's education is a tradition in the Western world. Be patient during verbal exchanges.
- Consider periods of silence as opportunities for reflection on what has been said.
- Be attentive to nonverbal cues.
- When you can, meet with students individually and communicate with them orally, rather than in writing.
- Encourage students to join student clubs to increase their exposure to language, socialization, and different types of discourse.
- Facilitate students' transition into mainstream culture through activities and discussions of culturally unique experiences and celebrations, such as birthday parties and Thanksgiving.
- Role-play, practice colloquialisms, and act out skits that involve typical verbal exchanges in English.
- Read to students to increase their vocabulary, and expose them to various narrative styles used in letters, stories, articles, biographies, and poetry.

Information about American Indian/Alaska Native Students

American Indian or Alaska Native: Persons having origins in any of the native or indigenous peoples of North America and who maintain such cultural identification through affiliation or community recognition

Susan Faircloth and John Tippeconnic reported in 2000 that there were approximately 500,000 American Indian and Alaska Native students attending kindergarten through grade twelve schools in the United States, which is just over 1 percent of the total school population. These students come from more than 500 tribal groups that have their own government and social systems and speak an estimated 200 different languages. Many of the tribes are *matrilineal,* where females hold positions of authority and are the main property owners.

Overall, the students from these various tribal groups have been experiencing below-average success in school and have the highest dropout rate of all racial/ethnic groups in the United States (National Center for Education Statistics, 2001). The reasons for these students' relative lack of success in school are not known, although possible causes include poverty, a curriculum that is unconnected to students' lives, and the feeling that success in school suggests selling out older traditions in favor of "white man's ways" (St. Germaine, 1995).

It has been suggested that American Indian/Alaska Native students may have a learning style that differs somewhat from that of students in the dominant culture (Cornett, 1983; Swisher, 1991). Many of these students have a strong capability for learning visually, perceptively, and spatially and tend to use mental images in thought processes, rather than word associations. They may learn better by seeing the entire overview of what is to be learned, rather than learning bits of information that slowly build up to the full picture. These students show an affinity for manipulatives and hands-on activities and seem to learn better in cooperative groups than individually. They show an ability to learn from experience without constant supervision and feedback. They best demonstrate their learning in contexts similar to those from which they have learned.

European American teachers usually consider American Indian/Alaska Native students to be quiet and not very talkative in the classroom. While these students may be hesitant to participate in large- and small-group recitations, they have been described as more talkative than other students when working in student-led group projects (Philips, 1983). Philips explained that American Indian/Alaska Native students seem to acquire competence best through a process of observation, careful listening, supervised participation, and individualized self-correction or testing.

A number of other sources offer information about working with these students (see Butterfield, 1994; Cajete, 1986; Cornett, 1983; Cox and Ramirez, 1981; Portland Oregon Schools, 2003; Swisher, 1991). Some examples are that American Indian/Alaska Native students become uncomfortable when asked in school to behave in ways not valued in the communities where they live. They are also more cooperative and less competitive individually than European American students, although their behavior does emphasize group achievement. Very able students often hide their academic competence to avoid appearing superior. Many do not like to make direct eye contact. When students divert their eyes, teachers should not interpret it as disobedience or disrespect. Before singling out students to talk about their culture or community, teachers should make sure that doing so will not cause embarrassment. Many of the parents of American Indian/Alaska Native students have had negative experiences in school and are hesitant to become involved in their child's educational process. They will respond and participate, however, when approached sensitively, sincerely, and respectfully.

Cornel Pewewardy and Patricia Hammer (2003) urge teachers of American Indian/Alaska Native students to do the following:

- Acquire better awareness and understanding of native culture and learning style.
- Analyze one's own attitudes and beliefs.
- Develop caring, trusting, inclusive classrooms.

- Model respect for native knowledge and ways of knowing.
- Provide a curriculum that promotes critical thinking and social justice.
- Provide a lot of helpful feedback, which should be immediate and as private as possible.
- Include art and other creative activities in lessons.
- Enrich class experiences by asking American Indian or Alaska Native speakers or performers to become involved in the class.
- Allow students to relate learning activities to their personal experiences.
- Hold and express high expectations to students.
- Evaluate progress in terms of goal attainment, behavior, and involvement.
- All the while, work to develop positive rapport with family members. Invite them to school and to the class.

Information about Recently Arrived Immigrant Students

Recently arrived immigrant students have needs not only for academic learning but also (and sometimes more importantly) for socialization and language development. Suggestions for working with these students have been put forth by several writers (see Benard, 1997; Chavkin and Gonzalez, 2000; Krovetz, 1999; Lucas, Henze, and Donato, 1990; National Coalition of Advocates for Students, 1994; Qualities of Effective Programs, 1998; and Walsh, 1991). Here is a summary of their advice:

- Use a repertoire of instructional approaches that upholds high expectations of students while affirming the acceptance of differences among students.
- Learn as much as possible about students' families, and request support from family members.
- Become familiar with English as a second language (ESL) and sheltered English instruction.
- Learn a few words of students' native languages.
- Give much personal attention to each student.
- Use a flexible approach that involves peer tutoring, mentoring by sympathetic adults, home–school liaisons, and links with community agencies.
- Work to increase student self-esteem, motivation, and willingness to accept responsibility. Emphasize prosocial skills and academic success.
- Develop personal relationships with students to increase motivation.

Information about Economically Disadvantaged Students

The term *economically disadvantaged* is used synonymously with *living in poverty,* a condition that increasingly affects students in school. *Students in poverty* are defined as students who are members of households that must spend more than one-third of their disposable income for food adequate to meet the family's nutritional needs.

Karen Pellegrino (2005) writes about the factors that make education difficult for students in poverty. She lists poverty as a leading factor that puts students at risk of failure in school. She notes that students in poverty often have single parents who are very young. The parents tend to be poorly educated and place relatively little importance on education. They often live in dangerous neighborhoods. Some are homeless. Their rate of mobility is high, and many do not stay in the same community or neighborhood long enough for the children to become established in school.

Ruby Payne (2001, 2003) has made many important contributions by describing the impact of poverty on education. She noted in 1996 that approximately one out of four individuals under the age of 18 in the United States was living in poverty. Payne says poor children are much more likely than nonpoor children to suffer developmental delay and damage, to drop out of high school, and to give birth during the teen years.

Payne also explains that each economic class has its own set of hidden rules that help it survive. The hidden rules for schools, teachers, and the majority of students reflect the values of white, middle-class society, which were summarized previously. But the hidden rules for students from *generational poverty* (meaning long-term poverty) are different from those in the mainstream. Payne urges teachers to learn those rules because they provide keys to understanding and communicating with students.

Payne (2001) illustrates her conclusions by comparing the hidden values of three different groups—those in generational poverty, those in middle-class society, and those in the society of wealth. For people from the middle class, the major driving forces are work and achievement; high value is placed on material possessions. For people of wealth, the driving forces are social, financial, and political connections; high value is placed on legacies and pedigrees. For people in poverty, the driving life forces are survival, personal relationships, and entertainment.

Students in poverty usually value relationships over achievement. Mother is the most important person in one's life, and insults against her will not be tolerated. Relatives and close friends are also defended, no matter what they have done. The world is defined in local terms. Too much education can be disquieting because the educated person might leave the community. Conflict is resolved by fighting, and respect is accorded to those who can defend themselves. School discipline is about penance and forgiveness, not about behavior change. Students often save face by laughing when they are disciplined. One's sense of personal value is tied up with the ability to entertain others. Money is to be used and spent, not managed and saved. Destiny and fate govern most matters; individuals feel they have relatively little control over their lives.

Students in poverty often use a casual, informal style of speech that contrasts with the more formal style of speech used in school. Teachers should point out the difference, help students use the appropriate language for various situations, and help them understand that a formal style is helpful in school and the workplace. Clothing is very important and is seen as an expression of personality. Noise level among people of poverty is high, with frequent displays of emotion. At home, the television is almost always turned on, and the sound mixes with participatory conversation, in which two or more people are talking at the same time. This is in contrast to the classroom, where everything is quieter and speakers take turns.

As with other groups, a first step in working with students who are economically disadvantaged is to learn about their values, customs, and lifestyles. Payne, in an interview with Diana Claitor (2003), explains that in addition to understanding their students, teachers must work to build personal relationships with them. More specific suggestions from Ruby Payne and Shirley Heath have been presented by Linda F. Hargan (2003):

- Teach and model explicitly how students should organize, prioritize, and set timelines for completion of tasks.
- Help students learn *procedural self-talk,* in which they verbalize how to break tasks down into steps and write down their conclusions.
- Teach students how to speak and write in a formal manner.
- Give students examples and modeling of acceptable behavior. Have them practice that behavior in school.

Donna Beegle (2004) further urges teachers to act as mentors for their students. Teachers are at times the only people children from poverty know that live outside poverty. Beegle says that if we treat students as competent, they will begin to behave competently.

General Suggestions for Working with Students from All Ethnic and Economic Groups

In the preceding sections, you have seen many suggestions for helping teachers understand their students and work more effectively with them. While those descriptions and suggestions were suggested to be typical of students from particular groups, teachers should not allow themselves to stereotype students. The following suggestions apply to teaching students from all cultural and economic groups:

- Learn as much as you can about the value systems of students from backgrounds different from your own, including what they consider important, how they relate to each other and to adults, and how they relate to teachers and school in general.
- Become knowledgeable about the hidden rules that regulate group and personal behavior.
- Show acceptance of your students, their families, and their lifestyles.
- Show solidarity with students, and be eager to help them learn and find success.
- Emphasize the knowledge, skills, and values needed for school success and for a healthy personal and cultural identity.
- Link curriculum content to students' out-of-school experiences.
- Attempt to mentor students; this is an especially effective tactic for improving motivation and good personal relations between student and teacher.
- Create a more hospitable environment by communicating the expectation that all students can succeed and will be helped to do so.
- Develop codes of class behavior that are culturally sensitive yet emphasize responsibility and respect.
- Keep family members informed about their child's performance and behavior, and ask them to work with you for the child's benefit.

IN SUMMARY

Both learning and discipline improve greatly when we teach in ways that increase students' desire to learn. We can increase this desire by providing activities students enjoy or find especially useful, by interacting with students sensitively, by aligning instruction with students' needs and traits, and by using methods of teaching that keep students actively involved.

REFERENCES

Ascher, C. 1991. School programs for African American males. ERIC Digests. ED334340. www.ericdigests.org.

Baruth, L., and Manning, M. 1992. *Multicultural education of children and adolescents.* Boston: Allyn & Bacon.

Beegle, D. 2004. Quoted in Breaking barriers: Poverty—The elephant in the room. www .osba.org/hotopics/gap/poverty.htm.

Bempechat, J. 2001. Fostering high achievement in African American children: Home, school, and public policy influences. ERIC Document ED348464. www.eric.ed.gov.

Benard, B. 1997. Drawing forth resilience in all our youth. *Reclaiming Children and Youth,* 6(1), 29–32.

Butterfield, R. 1994. Blueprints for Indian education: Improving mainstream schooling. ERIC Digests. ED372898. www.ericdigests.org.

Cajete, G. 1986. Science: A Native American perspective (A culturally based science education curriculum). Ph.D. dissertation, International College/William Lyon University, San Diego, CA.

Charles, C. 1974. *Teachers' petit Piaget.* Belmont, CA: Fearon.

Charles, C. 2008. *Building classroom discipline.* Boston: Allyn & Bacon.

Chavkin, N., and Gonzalez, J. 2000. Mexican immigrant youth and resiliency: Research and promising programs. ERIC Digests. ED447990. www.ericdigests.org.

Cheng, L. 1996. Enhancing communication: Toward optimal language learning for limited English proficient students. *Language, Speech and Hearing Services in Schools,* 28(2), 347–354. www.ericdigests.org.

Coker, D. 1988. Asian students in the classroom. *Education and Society,* 1(3), 19–20.

Cornett, C. 1983. What you should know about teaching and learning styles (Fastback no. 191). Bloomington, IN: Phi Delta Kappa Foundation.

Cox, B., and Ramirez, M. 1981. Cognitive styles: Implications for multiethnic education. In J. Banks (ed.), *Education in the 80s: Multiethnic education* (pp. 61–71). Washington, DC: National Education Association.

Diller, D. 1999. Opening the dialogue: Using culture as a tool in teaching young African American children. *Reading Teacher,* 52(8), 820–858.

Dreikurs, A., and Cassel, P. 1972. *Discipline without tears.* New York: Hawthorne Books.

Dunn, R., Griggs, S., and Price, G. 1993. Learning styles of Mexican-American and Anglo-American elementary-school students. *Journal of Multicultural Counseling and Development,* 21(4), 237–247.

Education Trust. 2003. African American Achievement. Washington, DC. www.edtrust.org.

Faircloth, S., and Tippeconnic, J. 2000. Issues in the education of American Indian and Alaska Native students with disabilities. ERIC Digests. EDO-RC-00-3. www .ericdigests.org.

Feng, J. 1994. Asian-American children: What teachers should know. ERIC Digests. EDO-PS-94-4. www.ericdigests.org.

Foster, M. 1999. Teaching and learning in the contexts of African American English and culture. *Education and Urban Society, 31*(2), 177ff.

Glasser, W. 1992. The quality school curriculum. *Phi Delta Kappan, 73*(9), 690–694.

Glasser, W. 1993. *The quality school teacher.* New York: Harper Perennial.

Glasser, W. 1998. *Choice theory in the classroom.* New York: HarperCollins.

Griggs, S., and Dunn, R. 1996. Hispanic-American students and learning style. ERIC Digests. www.ericdigests.org.

Hargan, L. 2003. Teaching students of poverty. NCL Brief. www.ctlonline.org/ESEA/newsletter.html.

Huang, G. 1993. Beyond culture: Communicating with Asian American children and families. ERIC Digests. ED366673. www.ericdigests.org.

Irvine, J., and Fraser, J. 1998. Warm demanders. *Education Week on the WEB.* www.edweek.org/ew/1998/35irvine.h17.

Jones, F. 2001. *Fred Jones's tools for teaching.* Santa Cruz, CA: Fredric H. Jones & Associates.

Jones, F. 2003. Weaning the helpless handraisers: Part 3. Teaching to the physical modality. *Education World.* www.educationworld.com/a_curr/columnists/jones/jones005.shtml.

Jones, F. 2004. Beyond Say, See, Do teaching: Exploiting structured practice. *Education World.* www.educationworld.com/a_curr/columnists/jones/jones006.shtml.

Joyce, B., Weil, M., and Calhoun, E. 2003. *Models of teaching* (7th edition). Boston: Allyn & Bacon.

Kim, B. (Ed.). 1985. *Literacy and languages. The second yearbook of literacy and languages in Asia.* International Reading Associations special interest group. International Conference on Literacy and Languages, Seoul, South Korea, August 12–14, 1985.

Krovetz, M. 1999. *Fostering resiliency: Expecting all students to use their minds and hearts well.* Thousand Oaks, CA: Corwin Press.

Ladson-Billings, G. 2000. Fighting for our lives: Preparing teachers to teach African American students. *Journal of Teacher Education, 51*(3), 206–214.

Latinos in School: Some facts and findings. 2001. ERIC Digests. www.ericdigests.org.

Lockwood, A., and Secada, W. 2000. Transforming education for Hispanic youth: Exemplary practices, programs, and schools. U.S. Department of Education. www.ncela.gwu.edu/pubs/resource/hispanicyouth/ch6.htm.

Lucas, T., Henze, R., and Donato, R. 1990. Promoting the success of Latino language minority students. An exploratory study of six high schools. *Harvard Educational Review, 60,* 315–340.

Maslow, A. 1954. *Motivation and personality.* New York: Harper.

Matsuda, M. 1989. Working with Asian family members: Some communication strategies. *Topics in Language Disorders, 9*(3), 45–53.

McCollough, S. 2000. Teaching African American students. *Clearing House, 74*(1), 5–6.

McKinley, J. 2003. Leveling the playing field and raising African American students' achievement in twenty-nine urban classrooms. New Horizons for Learning. www.newhorizons.org.

National Center for Education Statistics. 2001. Overview of public elementary and secondary schools and districts: School year 2001–02. http://nces.ed.gov/programs/quarterly/vol_5/5_2/q3_5.asp#top.

National Coalition of Advocates for Students. 1994. *Delivering on the promise: Positive practices for immigrant students.* Boston: Author.

Payne, R., 2001. *A framework for understanding poverty.* Highlands, TX: Aha! Process.

Payne, R. 2003. Breaking through: Interview of Ruby Payne. Quoted in Claitor, D. 2003. www.hopemag.com/issues/2003/septOct/breakingThrough.pdf.

Payne, R., 2005. Making the transition out of generational poverty. Aha! Process. www
.ahaprocess.com.

Pellegrino, K. 2005. The effects of poverty on teaching and learning. www.teach-nology
.com/tutorials/teaching/poverty.

Piaget, J. 1951. *Judgment and reasoning in the child*. London, England: Routledge & Kegan Paul.

Philips, S. 1983. *The invisible culture*. New York: Longman.

Portland Public Schools. 2003. Supporting American Indian/Alaska Native Students in
School. Title IX Indian Education Project Staff and Parent Board. http://comped
.salkeiz.k12.or.us/indian-ed/ai-an.htm.

Poverty in America. 2006. U.S. Census Bureau. www.educationcoffeehouse.com/K12/poverty.htm.

Qualities of effective programs for immigrant adolescents with limited schooling. 1998. ERIC
Digests. ED423667. www.ericdigests.org.

Schwartz, W. 2000. New trends in language education for Hispanic students. ERIC Digests.
ED442913. www.ericdigests.org.

Schwartz, W. 2002. School practices for equitable discipline of African American students.
ERIC Digests. ED455343. www.ericdigests.org.

St. Germaine, R. 1995. Drop-out rates among American Indian and Alaska Native Students:
Beyond cultural discontinuity. ERIC Digests. ED388492. www.ericdigests.org.

Storti, C. 1999. *Figuring foreigners out: A practical guide*. Yarmouth, ME: Intercultural Press.

Strategies for Teaching Minorities. 2004. www.as.wvu.edu/~equity/general.html.

Strategies for Teaching Science to African American Students. 2005. www.as.wvu.edu/
~equity/african.html.

Swisher, K. 1991. American Indian/Alaskan Native learning styles: Research and practice.
ERIC Digests. ED335175. www.ericdigests.org.

Trueba, H., and Cheng, L. 1993. *Myth or reality: Adaptive strategies of Asian Americans in
California*. Bristol, PA: Falmer Press.

Walsh, C. 1991. Literacy and school success: Considerations for programming and instruc-
tion. In C. Walsh and H. Prashker (Eds.), *Literacy development for bilingual students*.
Boston: New England Multifunctional Resource Center for Language and Culture
Education.

Wierzbicka, A. 1991. Japanese key words and core cultural values. *Language in Society*, 20(3),
333–385.

Yong, F., and Ewing, N. 1992. A comparative study of the learning-style preferences among
gifted African-American, Mexican-American and American-born Chinese middle-grade
students. *Roeper Review*, 14(3), 120–123.

7

Fostering a Sense of Togetherness

Developing a Sense of Togetherness among Members of the Class, with Emphasis on Safety, Belonging, Cooperation, and Mutual Support

It is desirable to enlist students' cooperation in developing and maintaining a positive classroom, where students feel safe and where trust, civility, and productivity are evident. You can accomplish this by approaching students as allies, helping them connect with each other personally, and involving them meaningfully in the operation of the class—leading to what is often called a sense of community in the classroom.

Chapter Preview

This chapter is presented in four parts that address four closely related topics: (1) classrooms as communities, (2) classroom meetings, (3) connecting with students, and (4) cooperative learning. Understanding each of these topics will promote learning and have a positive effect on class behavior.

PART 1. CLASSROOMS AS COMMUNITIES

Many authorities believe learning occurs best in classrooms where students are encouraged to interact with each other, cooperate, and provide mutual support. Such classrooms are often referred to as *classroom communities*. Toni Bickart, Judy Jablon, and Diane Dodge (2000) explain the strengths of such classrooms and provide these valuable suggestions for teachers who wish to maintain them:

- *Emphasize learning through interacting.* A cooperative classroom community, by nature, attends to students' needs, promotes their resilience in hardship conditions, teaches the values of respect and responsibility, and fosters social and academic competence. Because students learn morality by living it, they need to be in a safe class community where they can interact, form relationships, and work out problems. That permits them to learn firsthand about fair play, cooperation, forgiveness, and respect for the worth and dignity of every individual.

• *Help students develop personally and socially.* Students, more now than in the past, are preoccupied with questions that the class community can answer best: Do I fit in with the group? Am I accepted by others? Do I have friends? How do I measure up to others? Am I competent? Students answer these questions for themselves when they begin to acquire social and emotional competence, which grows from cooperative work with peers and contact with adults who are successful academically and socially. Students' growth is shown in their abilities to express their feelings, recognize the feelings of others, share ideas, take turns, compromise, entertain different points of view, and respect others' belongings and physical space.

• *Provide positive examples for students to emulate.* Students learn to relate positively with others when teachers model courtesy, respect, and attentive listening. If a student interrupts the teacher, rather than replying, the teacher might put his or her hand on the student's shoulder and when finished speaking, say "Now can I help you?" Teachers should frequently say "please" and "thank-you" to students, and their daily regimen should include greeting students as they arrive and interacting with them when they leave by saying something encouraging and personally meaningful, giving compliments, and commiserating with students for whom things did not go well. From time to time, teachers should also comment on something the class as a whole has done well, such as "I very much appreciate the courtesy you showed each other in today's assignment. That speaks very well for you."

• *Establish and strengthen relationships.* Students in highly interactive classrooms have abundant opportunities to establish positive relationships with others. As they do so, they develop skills in cooperating, sharing, showing empathy, expressing affection, offering ideas, helping, taking turns, and expressing enthusiasm. Students who have these skills are considered by their peers as reliable and fun to be with. Those skills can be contrasted with behaviors that tend to alienate others, such as aggression, unwillingness to cooperate, showing off, and acting in ways that annoy others. Through coaching, specific teaching, and role-playing, teachers can help students see that certain behaviors build friendships while others cause difficulties. A recommended activity is allowing students to work together as partners; this is considered especially useful when students are paired with partners they would not normally choose. A beginning activity can have each partner introduce the other to the class or relay some interesting information about him or her.

• *Dealing with conflict.* Students in highly interactive classrooms must learn to negotiate conflicts and find acceptable solutions together. Students need help in learning how to express their ideas reasonably, to explain how they feel, to listen to others' points of view, and to try to work out solutions when problems or conflicts arise. Teachers can provide practice in these matters as well as in skills of asking questions, making positive comments, offering help, and taking turns. Role-playing is one of the best activities for this purpose.

ALFIE KOHN ON CLASSROOMS AS COMMUNITIES

Alfie Kohn has done more than anyone to explain and promote the concept of classrooms as communities. Formerly a teacher, he now writes and speaks widely on human behavior, education, and parenting. He has authored 10 books and scores of articles, and he lectures widely at education conferences and universities as well as to parent groups and corporations.

Kohn has been a severe critic of many aspects of education, including virtually all of the discipline systems in use at the beginning of the twenty-first century. His criticisms of competition and rewards have been widely discussed and debated, and he has been described in *Time* magazine as "perhaps the country's most outspoken critic of education's fixation on grades [and] test scores." For more information on Kohn's background, ideas, and publications, see his website: www.alfiekohn.org.

On Classrooms as Communities

Kohn describes the classroom community as

> a place in which students feel cared about and are encouraged to care about each other. They experience a sense of being valued and respected; the children matter to one another and to the teacher. They have come to think in the plural: they feel connected to each other; they are part of an "us." And, as a result of all this, they feel safe in their classes, not only physically but emotionally. (1996, pp. 101–102)

On Teaching

Kohn's suggestions focus on helping teachers develop caring, supportive classrooms, in which students pursue in depth topics of interest and participate fully in solving class problems. He has roundly criticized teaching that that does things *to* students rather than *involve* them as partners in the process. He advises teachers to strive to make their classes places where students feel safe and are brought into making judgments, expressing their opinions, and working cooperatively toward solutions that affect them and the class. He believes the class community is well suited to purposeful learning and the best venue for developing caring, responsible students.

Kohn insists the best approach to teaching begins not with facts to be learned or disciplines to be mastered but with questions to be answered. These questions should not lead directly to correct answers but should make students pause, wonder, and reflect. Three things we should remember about student learning are: (1) students learn most avidly and have their best ideas when they get to choose which questions they want to explore, (2) all of us tend to be happiest and most effective when we have some say about what we are doing, and (3) when student choice and control over learning are not allowed, achievement drops.

On Students

Kohn contends that educators must take students seriously, involve them in decisions, and help them explore in-depth topics they consider worthwhile. Doing so helps avoid the high rate of forgetting that occurs in most classrooms, where students forget most of what they learn because the learning is superficial and of little importance, in their point of view. Teachers should honor students as individuals and seek to determine what they need and enjoy. Teachers should lead students to explore topics of interest, grapple with those topics, and make sense of them. Teachers should provide challenges and emphasize that making mistakes is an important part of learning. They should help students think by asking for examples and asking questions such as "How do we know that?"

Growth toward kindness, happiness, and self-fulfillment occurs as students work closely together with peers. Rewards and punishment are not used in an attempt to make students more compliant; they tend to remove student commitment to learning. You can expect cooperative work to lead to disagreements, which are natural occurrences as students learn to speak their minds. When concerns arise, the teacher should not impose resolutions, but should ask, "What do you think we can do to solve this problem?"

Kohn says that although it is unnerving at first to teach in the manner he advocates, it is astonishing how well students learn when they have a say in the curriculum and can decide what they will do, when, where, with whom, and toward what end.

On Discipline

Teachers who wish to avoid continual hassles with student misbehavior can do so by providing an engaging curriculum based on student interests, developing a class sense of community, and drawing students into meaningful decision making. Kohn is quite critical of most popular systems of discipline. He says that, when analyzed, those systems reveal several underlying assumptions: namely, (1) that students are naturally predisposed to disrupt learning and deal misery to teachers; (2) that learning occurs best in an atmosphere of structure, quiet, and order; and (3) that the teacher's role in discipline is to keep students obedient, compliant, and quiet. Educators must look beyond the techniques of discipline and ask the question What are we attempting to accomplish with discipline? Doing so will make it evident that most teachers are thinking in terms of making students compliant and quiet, conditions that do not develop the kinds of people we would ultimately like students to become.

Rewards and punishments should not be used to control behavior or encourage learning. They produce no commitment to learning or better behavior. Kohn says they are counterproductive; the more one uses rewards (including praise) and punishment (including logical consequences), the less responsible, generous, and interested students tend to become. The danger in formalized discipline is that "the more we 'manage' students' behavior and try to make them do what we say, the more difficult it is for them to become morally sophisticated people who think for themselves and care about others" (Kohn, 1996, p. 62). The way to help students develop initiative, self-direction, self-control, concern for others, and responsibility is to put them into situations where they are asked to display those qualities, on an ongoing basis.

ESTABLISHING BEHAVIOR STANDARDS IN COOPERATIVE CLASSROOMS

Daniel Solomon, Eric Schaps, Marilyn Watson, and Victor Battistich (1992) consider it important for students to take active roles in helping establish behavior expectations in classrooms that function as communities. Periodic group meetings can be held to discuss class concerns and promote the development of responsibility and respect for others. Specific activities can help students learn about each other and about the value of ethics, respect, and responsibility, and students should be continually asked to reflect on the importance of those values.

In the process, teachers should not try to impose those values on students or use rewards and punishments to obtain student compliance. Instead, they should try to attract student cooperation through instructional topics and activities of high interest to students. When misbehavior occurs, it should be dealt with through a teaching approach that, with consideration and dignity, shows students better ways of conducting themselves. All the while, a primary focus should be kept on the development of student autonomy and self-direction.

Certain instructional activities are considered especially useful in helping students establish a mindset regarding the treatment of others. One example (Solomon, Schaps, Watson, and Battistich, 1992) is using entertaining stories and books to promote values such as fairness and kindness. These materials can also communicate the inner lives of people from other cultures, ages, and circumstances who have faced and dealt with universal issues and concerns. Students have a high natural interest in such literature, and its use allows them to explore, together with peers, the nuances of selected events and relationships. Teachers can read many of the stories aloud so that slower readers can appreciate them and participate in discussions.

Further activities include those that cause students to interact and come to know each other better, which promotes their working together more easily in group endeavors. Suggested activities include academic games and group problem-solving exercises; establishing procedures for welcoming new students; and randomly selecting a Person of the Week and asking that person to tell others in class about himself or herself or perhaps organize a display that includes family members and special activities. Another option is to provide the opportunity for students to get to know school staff members and understand the work they do—principal, counselors, clerical staff, custodians, parent volunteers, lunchroom workers, bus drivers, and teachers of other subjects or higher or lower grades.

RESOLVING BEHAVIOR ISSUES IN COOPERATIVE CLASS COMMUNITIES

Toni Bickart, Judy Jablon, and Diane Dodge (2000) report that when teachers are asked "If you could teach only one thing, knowing that it would be learned, what would it be?" the most commonly given responses are respect for others, communication skills, and the skills for resolving interpersonal problems nonviolently. Brickart, Jablon, and Dodge comment that, given the importance of these prized outcomes, it is surprising that so little time is typically devoted to achieving them. Teachers are naturally reluctant to add additional topics to an already overcrowded curriculum, yet on reflection, teachers readily agree that anything that reduces hostile behavior in the classroom is well worth the time required to teach it.

It certainly seems clear that by teaching students alternatives to violence and hostility, we can make their lives and ours more enjoyable and productive. But how do we go about teaching these things when so many students regularly see violence in response to perceived insults, personal conflicts, and infringement into one's personal space? The answer seems to lie in teaching students two things more or less simultaneously—first, how to behave in ways that do not offend others and, second, how to respond nonviolently to offenses that are received.

The cooperative class community is an ideal venue for teaching these two skills, which can be done through modeling, direct instruction, and practice. Classroom meetings provide excellent venues for addressing these matters. In Part 2 of this chapter, you will find suggestions for organizing and using classroom meetings and you will see how they can provide for calm, fruitful discussions about interpersonal problems and their resolution. These discussions lead naturally to scenarios for analysis and role-play that help students learn ways of responding effectively to conflict. A good way to begin is to analyze a conflict reported in the news or one that students have read about in a book. That allows students to think somewhat dispassionately about the conflict, what has produced it, how it is being resolved, and how it might be resolved better.

A number of topics can be addressed in this manner—for example, situations involving anger and how to manage it, intimidation and how to deflect it, and hurt feelings and how to respond to them. Follow these steps:

1. Ask a question, such as "Why did you do that to me?" or "Have I offended you?"
2. Make a statement, such as "I feel really embarrassed when you do that" or "It makes me feel bad because I want to be friends with you."
3. Make a reasonable request of the other person, such as "Would you please, as a favor to me, not do that any more?" or "Knowing how it makes me feel, would you not call me that name again?"

The attitude conveyed by such responses promotes cooperation, compromise, and friendly problem resolution. Over time, with students' needs being met and with the teacher constantly modeling desirable behavior, an attitude of nonviolent cooperation will begin to permeate the class.

SPENCER KAGAN ON TEACHER–STUDENT COOPERATION IN DISCIPLINE

Many of the more recent approaches to discipline advocate strong levels of cooperation among class members and especially between teachers and students. One such program is described in a book by the same name, *Win–Win Discipline* (2004), written by Spencer Kagan, a psychologist, author, and publisher. (Kagan's concept of *misbehavior* was mentioned earlier in Chapter 2.)

Kagan makes same-side cooperation between teachers and students one of the so-called three pillars of his approach to discipline; the other two pillars are collaborative solutions to problems and learned responsibility. As Kagan puts it, quality discipline, where students manage themselves responsibly, is best achieved when teachers and students work together cooperatively from the same side to find a common ground in planning the class and resolving class problems. When teachers and students work together in this manner, they usually resolve problems with little difficulty.

Kagan's goal is to help students develop long-term, self-managed responsibility. He takes student needs strongly into account, treating their disruptive behavior as attempts to meet certain unfulfilled needs. He believes responsible behavior grows when teacher and student work together to meet those needs and to co-create effective solutions to behavior problems. Solutions involve tactics for (1) the moment of disruption, (2) later follow-up, and (3) long-term results. Through involvement in these solutions, students gradually develop self-management, responsibility, and other autonomous life skills.

To facilitate growth in self-management, Kagan advises teachers to create a "we" approach with students for working toward learning and positive behavior. Discipline tactics are kept harmonious with students' needs and states of mind and are applied tactfully and considerately to improve behavior in a positive manner.

Kagan does not view disruptive behavior as necessarily bad. The positive side is that it can be used as a starting point for helping students become more responsible and self-directing. Similarly, disruptive students should not be thought of as bad kids but rather as individuals who are attempting (albeit ineffectively) to meet their personal needs. In this light, to say a student is misbehaving is simply to say that he or she is making poor choices in meeting his or her needs.

PART 2. CLASS MEETINGS AS A REGULAR PART OF THE CURRICULUM

In 1969, William Glasser introduced the concept of class meetings and advocated their regular use in addressing class concerns. He suggested that such meetings offered many important benefits, including a forum for students to express their concerns and a venue where teachers and students could work in a collaborative manner to address issues that affect the class. He provided suggestions for organizing and conducting class meetings—ideas that have been expanded and explained in greater detail by others, such as Jane Nelsen and Lynn Lott, whose advice on class meetings follows.

Consultants

JANE NELSEN AND LYNN LOTT ON ORGANIZING AND USING CLASS MEETINGS

Jane Nelsen and Lynn Lott (2006) explain how classroom meetings can be used to help students learn to live harmoniously in the classroom and resolve problems together. These educators show how meetings can promote the social skills of listening, taking turns, hearing different points of view, negotiating, communicating, helping one another, and taking responsibility for personal behavior. Academic skills are strengthened in the process, as well, because as students participate, they must practice skills in language, attentiveness, critical thinking, decision making, and problem solving.

Class meetings also help students see that teachers and other adults need support as much as students do. When teachers involve themselves as partners with students in class meetings, a climate of mutual respect begins to grow. Teachers and students listen to one another, take each other seriously, and work together to solve problems for the benefit of all. Antagonisms typically seen in classrooms tend to fade away.

Building Blocks for Class Meetings

Nelsen and Lott advise teachers to consider eight "building blocks" for organizing class meetings, each of which focuses on a particular skill. It takes about two hours to introduce the eight building blocks to students. After that, approximately four additional class meetings are required to give adequate attention to what the building blocks entail. Nelsen and Lott provide the following suggestions:

1. Explain that you would like to begin holding class meetings in which class members can express concerns and use their power and skills to help make decisions. Elementary students are usually eager to try class meetings, but middle school and high school students may need some persuading. A way to introduce class meetings to older students is to initiate a discussion about power, how problems are usually handled in school, and how that method results in teachers and administrators telling students what to do.

2. Next, ask students, "Who has an example they would like to share about what happens when someone tries to control you? What do you feel? What do you do? What do you learn?" Students usually say that they feel angry or scared and manipulated and want to withdraw or rebel. Ask them also, "How do you try to control or manipulate others, including your teachers?"

3. Continue by asking students if they would like to be more involved in making decisions that affect their lives at school and if they would be willing to do the work to come up with solutions they like. Point out that some students actually prefer having adults boss them around, so that they can rebel or so they don't have to take responsibility themselves. Make it clear that you don't intend to waste time teaching and learning a respectful method if students prefer continuing with the usual way, where the teacher is in control and students' only options are to comply, rebel, and/or spend time in detention.

Once students indicate support, decide together when the classroom meetings will be held. You can point out that possibilities vary from weekly half-hour meetings to three shorter meetings per week. A meeting every day is advisable for the first week, as students learn the process.

Building Block 1: Form a Circle.   A circular seating arrangement serves best because it allows face-to-face contact. Ask students for suggestions about how to form the circle. Write their ideas on the board, and make a decision based on their suggestions.

Building Block 2: Practice Compliments and Appreciations.   Begin class meetings on a positive note, which can be done by having the students and teacher say complimentary things to each other. Many students have difficulty giving and receiving compliments. Practice helps. Ask them to recall when someone said something that made them feel good about themselves. Let them share their examples with the group. Then ask them to think about something they would like to thank others for, such as thanking a classmate for lending a pencil or eating lunch together. See if they can put their feelings into words.

Receiving compliments is often as difficult as giving them. The best response to a compliment is often a simple "thank-you." Giving and receiving compliments seems especially embarrassing to some middle school students. When that is the case, use the term *show appreciation* instead of *compliment*.

Building Block 3: Create an Agenda.   Each class meeting should begin with a specific agenda. Students and teachers who have concerns connected with the class can jot them down in a notebook designated for that purpose. This can be done at a designated time and place, such as when students leave the room. The class meeting will address only the concerns that appear in the notebook.

Building Block 4: Develop Communication Skills.   A number of activities help develop communication skills—for instance, taking turns speaking (begin by going around the circle and letting each person speak), listening attentively to what others say, learning to use I-statements (saying, without placing blame, what one is thinking or feeling), showing respect for others by never humiliating or speaking judgmentally about them, learning to seek and find mutually acceptable solutions to problems, and framing conclusions in the form of "We decided," showing it was a group effort and conclusion.

Building Block 5: Learn about Separate Realities.   Help students understand that not everyone is the same or thinks the same way. Nelsen and Lott (2006) describe an activity where participants divide into four groups, based on their choice of which animal they would like to be: turtles, lions, eagles, and chameleons. Each group makes a list of what they like about their animal and what they don't like about the other animals. This leads to a lively discussion of how people can focus on the positive or negative of any animal (or person). This can lead to helping students see that what some people see as faults, others see as virtues, and that we can all learn from each other and benefit from each other's strengths.

Building Block 6: Recognize the Reasons People Do What They Do.   Ask students if they have ever wondered why different students behave as they do. Acknowledge their thoughts and then ask if they have ever heard of the primary goal of belonging and the four mistaken goals of misbehavior: undue attention, power, revenge, and giving up. Proceed by using examples to illustrate the goal of belonging and the mistaken goals. (Nelsen and Lott use Rudolf Dreikurs's 1995 explanation of why students behave as they do. As discussed in Chapter 5, there are alternative explanations concerning student motivation and causes of misbehavior.)

Building Block 7: Practice Role Playing and Brainstorming.   By the third class meeting, students are usually ready to begin considering problems and solutions. Here are some suggestions for exploring problems tactfully:

1. Discuss the key elements of the problem situation.
2. Have students act out roles involved in the problem.
3. Brainstorm a number of possible solutions to the difficulty or problem, and allow students to select the solution they believe would be best.

Building Block 8: Focus on Nonpunitive Solutions.   Ask students the following questions, and write their answers on the board: "What do you feel like when someone bosses you? What do you want to do when someone calls you names or puts you down? When others do these things to you, does it help you behave better?" Then ask them how their behavior is affected when someone is kind to them, helps them, or provides stimulation and encouragement. Have them compare their answers, which you have written on the board. Use the comparison to draw attention to the value of encouragement versus punishment.

Tell the students that you intend never to punish or belittle them in any way and that when they do something wrong you will try to help them find a solution that will be respectful to everyone concerned. Explain that the solution will always be *related* to what they have done, *respectful* of them as persons, *reasonable,* and *helpful.* These are what Nelsen and Lott call the "three Rs and an H of solutions."

Standard Format for Class Meetings

Nelsen and Lott (2006) suggest the following format for a class meeting. The teacher normally initiates the meeting and makes sure everyone abides by the rules and has an equal opportunity to speak.

1. *Express compliments and appreciations.* Each session begins in this way as a means of setting a positive tone.
2. *Follow up on earlier solutions applied to problems.* Any suggested solution is to be tried only for a week, so it is important to determine if the solution has been working. If it hasn't, the class may wish to put the issue back on the agenda for future problem solving.
3. *Go through agenda items.* When an agenda item is read, ask the person (student or teacher) with the issue if he or she still wants help with it. If so, ask that person what a satisfactory solution could be. If he or she can't think of one, go around the circle, giving every student an opportunity to offer a suggestion. Ask the person with the issue to select the most helpful solution from the suggestions offered.
4. *Make future plans for class activities.* End the class meeting by discussing an enjoyable activity for the entire class at a future date. For example, the class might decide to set aside some time on Friday to discuss an upcoming event, view a video, or complete homework assignments with friends.

As students begin to acquire the skills of problem resolution, urge them to work out solutions on their own, when the need arises. If they persist in involving you, you might say something like this: "I can't help you right now. See if you can work things out, and I'll check with you in a few minutes." You might also say, "This same situation came up two days ago. Try to remember what we did then. Talk it over, and let me know what you have decided."

Even though you may make every effort possible, things will not always go smoothly. At times, students become heated and need a place to calm down. Classroom life is demanding; everyone needs a break now and then and a designated place to go. Calm-down places can be established in the classroom where students can go to relax or cool off. You might wish to place a "peace table" in the classroom, where students can go to quietly work out a dispute together. This space is not to be used for isolating students from the group as punishment; they will learn no coping skills when put into isolation.

Nelsen and Lott (2006) suggest having students help create provisions for taking a "positive time-out," so they are involved in the process and thus take ownership of it. The point of positive time-out is to allow distressed students to calm down until they feel better and become ready to focus on solutions. Students can decide what to call their positive time-out area. One class decided on "Space," with a cosmic theme. Another class decided on "Hawaii." Teachers have found that students do not misuse the opportunity to choose time-out when they need it, provided they have been respectfully involved in creating the area and the rules for its use.

PART 3. CONNECTING WITH STUDENTS AND CONDUCTING COOPERATIVE LEARNING

In order to achieve a sense of togetherness in the classroom, teachers must learn how to connect with students on a personal level. Excellent advice on this matter comes from William Glasser.

Consultant

WILLIAM GLASSER ON HOW TEACHERS CAN CONNECT WITH STUDENTS

William Glasser, a psychiatrist and educational consultant, has for many years written and spoken extensively on issues related to education and discipline. He achieved early acclaim for his 1965 book *Reality Therapy: A New Approach to Psychiatry,* which shifted the focus in treating personal problems in people's lives away from earlier events and onto dealing with realities of the present.

Not long afterward, Glasser applied his ideas to schooling. His work with juvenile offenders convinced him that teachers could help students make better personal choices that would result in improved behavior in the classroom. He explained those views in *Schools without Failure* (1969), honored as one of the twentieth century's most influential books in education. In 1986, Glasser added a new facet to school discipline with his contention that in order for students to learn properly in school, they must "believe that if they do some work, they will be able to satisfy their needs enough so that it makes sense to keep working" (1986, p. 15).

Since that time, Glasser has focused on meeting students' basic needs as the primary means of ensuring class participation and desirable behavior. His ideas on teaching and discipline are presented in his books *Choice Theory in the Classroom* (1998a), *The Quality School: Managing Students without Coercion* (1998b), *The Quality School Teacher* (1998c), and *Every Student Can Succeed* (2001). The Glasser website is www.wglasser.com.

Glasser strongly advocates close cooperation between teachers and students and has much to say concerning its feasibility and advantages. Glasser invites students into a cooperative partnership by telling them the following:

> We are in this class together. I want to help you become competent or go beyond. My job is to teach you and help you learn, not to find out what you don't know and punish you for not knowing it. If you have a question, ask me. If you need more time, I'll give it to you. If you have an idea how to do what we are trying to do better, tell me. I'll listen. (Glasser, 2001, p. 113)

Instead of telling students what they must do and not do, Glasser advises teachers to befriend their students and say to them the following:

> I think an important part of my job is to do all I can to make sure you have a good time learning. You have to come to school and no one's going to pay you for doing schoolwork. So the least I can do is make this class fun for both you and me. I think we can learn a lot and still have a very good time. (Glasser, 2001, p. 54)

From that point forward, Glasser advises teachers to utilize what he calls the "seven connecting habits" in working with students—caring, listening, supporting, contributing, encouraging, trusting, and befriending. In relating to students, the connecting habits should be used instead of what Glasser calls the "seven deadly habits," which are criticizing, blaming, complaining, nagging, threatening, punishing, and rewarding. He observes that teachers use the deadly habits when attempting to control students, but those habits do not produce desirable results. Instead, they tend to stifle the development of caring relationships between teachers and students. The connecting habits, on the other hand, help teachers establish good relationships with students and gain their cooperation.

As for rules in the classroom, Glasser maintains that only one basic class rule is needed—the "golden rule." He says to think of it simply as *courtesy,* a concept that should be discussed at length with students. Glasser would have teachers do away with traditional discipline (meaning applying external control) and replace it with talking and listening to students whenever trouble seems imminent. His advice: Listen carefully. Try to understand the students' points of view. Help as you can. And inject a degree of humor into the situation, if appropriate, without seeming to make light of students' concerns.

Assure your students that you will not ask them to learn anything that is not useful to them and that when there is a question about usefulness, you will explain clearly the benefits of the new learning. Advise them that you have a way of teaching that helps everyone do competent work and make good grades. It involves asking students to work at any given assignment until they have brought it to a competent level. There will be no memorizing just for the sake of remembering. Students can use any resources available to help them, including textbooks, parents, and other students. The primary objective is to do competent work.

Toward that end, tests should be used frequently. Glasser says to teach students using your best techniques; then use tests to enhance learning but not to evaluate it. Use short essay or multiple-choice tests. Promise students no one will fail or receive a bad grade. When they have completed the test, have them go back over it and correct any incorrect or incomplete answers. Ask them to explain why the correction is better. Give them the time and help needed to get everything right. Once information has been acquired or skills have been developed in this manner, have students use them when speaking, listening, reading, writing, and problem solving.

PART 4. FORMALIZED COOPERATIVE LEARNING

Students in school cooperate in many ways. They exchange ideas and opinions, play together, work on projects, ask each other questions, help each other, take turns, and so forth. That cooperation usually occurs informally, without any structure provided by the teacher. However, it is possible for teachers to structure learning activities in a formal manner that requires close student cooperation. This helps students learn several important skills that are difficult to acquire otherwise. This formalized cooperative learning has been developed, researched, and popularized by Roger T. Johnson and David W. Johnson.

ROGER JOHNSON AND DAVID JOHNSON ON COOPERATIVE LEARNING

For many years, Roger Johnson and David Johnson investigated student cooperation and disseminated information about its nature, value, and procedures. Co-directors of the Cooperative Learning Center at the University of Minnesota, Johnson and Johnson have authored or co-authored more than 40 books and 350 research articles and book chapters. They have been honored for their work nationally and internationally. Their best known book is probably *Circles of Learning: Cooperation in the Classroom* (1993, with Edythe Johnson Holubec). They reported in 2006, "We have reviewed more than 800 studies dating back to the late 1800's and have contributed more than 80 research studies of our own to clarify the issue of student-to-student interaction and learning."

Johnson and Johnson describe *cooperative learning* as a group approach to learning that requires (1) positive interdependence among group members—a sense of "sink or swim" together; (2) individual accountability to ensure each student contributes and learns; (3) good interpersonal skills, such as communication, trust, leadership, decision making, and conflict resolution; and (4) face-to-face interaction and processing, including reflecting on how well the team is functioning and how it can function even better.

What are the central concepts in cooperative learning? Johnson and Johnson (1994) explain that in the classroom, students can work and learn more or less on their own, or they can work cooperatively with others. Often, when they cooperate, they do so for their own benefit, not for the progress of the group as a whole. However, activities can be organized for students to work cooperatively and have a vested interest in the progress of other members of the group. This approach, characterized by *positive goal interdependence,* offers several benefits, such as greater productivity and improved relations in the classroom, provided the following conditions are met:

- There is a clearly perceived positive interdependence.
- There is considerable face-to-face interaction.
- Individual accountability and responsibility are maintained.

- Interpersonal relationship skills are practiced and used.
- There is frequent analysis of group functioning to ensure its effectiveness.

Positive interdependence involves two responsibilities for all group members: (1) to learn the material being studied and (2) to help make sure that all other group members learn it as well. Positive interdependence exists when students perceive that they cannot succeed individually unless all group members also succeed and that, for that reason, they must coordinate their efforts with those of their fellow group members, sharing resources and providing mutual help and encouragement.

In this style of teaching, teachers structure group activities in such a way that individual members perform tasks or acquire information that the entire group needs for success. With each group member having only a portion of the necessary resources, information, or materials, members must rely on each other in order to complete their work satisfactorily.

Teachers may also assign complementary responsibilities to members of groups, such as reader, recorder, checker of understanding, encourager of participation, and elaborator of knowledge—roles that help promote high-quality learning. To ensure that cooperative groups function as intended, teachers may have to help students with certain skills in personal relationships, such as getting to know and trust each other, communicating accurately, accepting and supporting each other, and resolving conflict constructively.

Evaluation of learning in cooperative groups can be done as follows: Students earn (1) a group grade for the overall production of their group, (2) an individual grade based on individual test results, and (3) bonus points if all members of the group reach a certain high level on their individual tests.

Finally, cooperative groups require ongoing monitoring to ensure they are functioning as intended. Typically, this calls on group members to identify members' acts and contributions that were most helpful, to clarify and improve individual roles, and to make decisions about changes that seem desirable. Teachers, meanwhile, observe the groups to see how well students understand the process and contribute to it.

Johnson, Johnson, and Holubec (2001) point out that in *competitive* classrooms, students try to do better than their peers. This competition causes them to be cautious about sharing information with others. Individuals hoard their ideas, which isolates them somewhat from other students in the class. In contrast, the *cooperative* setting promotes inclusion and caring about others, which is not only productive but important to human beings. We are a gregarious species. Most (but not all) of us are at our best in groups and do not do well when isolated from others for long.

A predominantly cooperative classroom is more productive in many kinds of learning and is seen as such by its members. It is healthy psychologically and promotes the values one needs to be a good family member, neighbor, and member of the community. Values stressed in cooperative learning include commitment to group members and shared goals; responsibility to oneself and others; appreciation for diverse talents, skills, and perspectives; and caring about and having compassion for others. Cooperative learning leads students naturally toward those prized outcomes.

In 2001, Johnson, Johnson, and Holubec described their "three Cs of safe and effective schools." The first C has to do with developing *cooperative* classrooms and schools. The second C has to do with resolving *conflicts* constructively. And the third C has to do with infusing *civic* values into classrooms and schools where the first two Cs have been installed successfully.

For additional information on these matters, along with mistakes people make in using cooperative learning and how to correct them, see the following website: www.co-operation.org/pages/newsletter2001.html.

IN SUMMARY

This chapter suggested that most classrooms function better when organized in a way that allows teachers and students to work together actively and with a high level of mutual support. Alfie Kohn's contentions about classrooms as communities were reviewed, as were Spencer Kagan's observations on the relationship of community to discipline. Jane Nelsen and Lynn Lott's suggestions for conducting successful class meetings were presented. William Glasser's advice on using the seven connecting habits to improve relations with and among students was emphasized, and Roger Johnson and David Johnson's suggestions on the use of formal cooperative learning were discussed.

REFERENCES

Bickart, T., Jablon, J., and Dodge, D. 2000. Building a classroom community. In *Building the primary classroom: A handbook for teacher educators* (Chapter 2). Beltsville, MD: Gryphon House.

Dreikurs, R., and Cassel, P. 1995. *Discipline without tears.* New York: Penguin-NAL. Originally published in 1972.

Glasser, W. 1965. *Reality therapy: A new approach to psychiatry.* New York: Harper & Row.

Glasser, W. 1969. *Schools without failure.* New York: Harper & Row.

Glasser, W. 1986. *Control theory in the classroom.* New York: HarperCollins.

Glasser, W. 1998a. *Choice theory in the classroom.* New York: HarperCollins.

Glasser, W. 1998b. *The quality school: Managing students without coercion.* New York: HarperCollins.

Glasser, W. 1998c. *The quality school teacher.* New York: HarperCollins.

Glasser, W. 2001. *Every student can succeed.* Chatsworth, CA: William Glasser.

Johnson, D., Johnson, R., and Holubec, E. 1993. *Circles of learning: Cooperation in the classroom* (4th edition). Edina, MN: Interaction Book.

Johnson, D., Johnson, R., and Holubec, E. 2001. Cooperative learning. *Cooperative Link: The Newsletter of the Cooperative Learning Institute, 16*(1). www.co-operation.org/pages/newsletter2001.html.

Johnson, R., and Johnson, D. 1994. An overview of cooperative learning. In J. Thousand, A. Villa, and A. Nevin (Eds.), *Creativity and collaborative learning.* Baltimore: Brookes Press.

Johnson, R., and Johnson, D. 2006. The Cooperative Learning Center at the University of Minnesota. www.co-operation.org.

Kagan, S., Kyle, P., and Scott, S. 2004. *Win–win discipline.* San Clemente, CA: Kagan Publishing.

Kohn, A. 1993. *Punished by rewards: The trouble with gold stars, incentive plans, A's, praise, and other bribes.* Boston: Houghton Mifflin.

Kohn, A. 1996. *Beyond discipline: From compliance to community.* Alexandria, VA: Association for Supervision and Curriculum Development.

Kohn, A. 1999. *The schools our children deserve: Moving beyond traditional classrooms and "tougher standards."* Boston: Houghton Mifflin.

Kohn, A. 2001. *Beyond discipline: From compliance to community.* Upper Saddle River, NJ: Merrill/Prentice-Hall.

Nelsen, J., and Lott, L. 2006. *Positive discipline in the classroom* (2nd edition). Rocklin, CA: Prima.

Solomon, D., Schaps, E., Watson, M., and Battistich, V. 1992. Creating caring school and classroom communities for all students. In R. A. Villa, J. S. Thousand, W. Stainback, and S. Stainback (Eds.), *Restructuring for caring and effective education: An administrative guide to creating heterogeneous schools.* Baltimore: Paul H. Brookes Publishing.

STRATEGY

8

Improving Relationships and Communication

Working toward Positive Relationships and Effective Communication among Teacher, Students, and Parents and Guardians

You can achieve this strategy by communicating well with students and teaching them the basic behaviors of good relations and communication, all the while emphasizing how those behaviors promote cooperation, enjoyment, and progress. Also be sure to relate and communicate well with parents and guardians.

Chapter Preview

This chapter addresses the roles that human relationships and communication play in classrooms, especially in those with high levels of interaction. Three important matters are explored: (1) enhancing personal relations, (2) enhancing communication, and (3) communicating with students' parents and guardians. The chapter presents suggested tactics for connecting with others, building relationships, listening empathetically, avoiding roadblocks to communication, and using congruent communication.

ENHANCING PERSONAL RELATIONS

In these days of declining respect for others, we can do well to teach students about people who are outstanding in sales and customer relations. Ask students to imagine how they would behave toward others who were potential but not necessarily enthusiastic customers, upon whose business their livelihood depended. (Such is more or less the position in which teachers find themselves.) Ask students if they understand why good salespersons smile and welcome customers in a friendly manner, put them at ease, convey a sense of appreciation for their presence, ask if they might be of help, and listen to what we say without allowing themselves to be distracted. Business owners want their sales staff to treat customers in that way for obvious reasons: It increases the likelihood the customer will buy something, and it helps the business maintain a good reputation, which is not to be taken lightly. Even if no sale is made, the customer will remember the good treatment and will be predisposed to returning later. Word does get around about businesses (and people) who treat others well. We never go wrong when we deal with each other pleasantly and respectfully.

You might feel that if we carry the notion too far, we'll look like hucksters who depend on fakery and flattery. Certainly, we want to be sincere in relations with others, but when it comes to effective human relations, most of us err by showing too little appreciation for each other. We promote a positive outlook when we wish somebody a good day or say how nice it is to see him or her. We only appear insincere when we are inconsistent or when we seem to be trying to get others to do something they don't want to do.

Fundamental Skills in Human Relations

The term *good human relations* refers to human interactions that people, in general, find satisfying and beneficial. Interactive classrooms cannot function adequately unless class members engage with each other respectfully and helpfully. One way to enhance interaction involves teachers and students learning and practicing the techniques of attracting the attention of others in a positive manner, giving undivided attention in return, and fostering the impression they are considerate and trustworthy people with whom to associate.

The following paragraphs present basic interrelational skills that are useful in the classroom and elsewhere. Consider discussing them with students. The basic paradigm for teaching these skills consists of modeling the desired behavior, providing directed practice, calling on students to display the new skills in a variety of situations, and asking for student appraisal and other feedback on the resultant effects.

• *Skill 1: Break the ice and make a good impression.* It is difficult for many students and adults to initiate interactions with others, especially strangers and people who are older. If that applies to your students, you might discuss and practice what to do when you meet someone new. Point out the importance of making a good first impression by smiling, introducing oneself, shaking hands, and using the other person's name. Ask students to reflect on what they have seen and heard people do that makes a good impression.

• *Skill 2: Open up communication.* Discuss with students how they can use "door openers" and empathetic listening to initiate and sustain a conversation. *Door openers* are comments or questions that encourage another person to talk, such as "That's interesting; tell me more about it" or "What do you think we'd have to do if we tried something like that? Would it be possible? How could we make it happen?" As the other person responds, we can use *empathetic listening* to grasp not only what that person is saying but what it means from his or her point of view. Take mental notes and, from time to time, repeat what the other person has said and ask if you have understood him or her correctly. (Later in this chapter, we will examine Stephen Covey's suggestions for empathetic listening.)

- *Skill 3: Confer dignity on others.* One of the most powerful techniques for influencing other people is to confer dignity on them, making them feel valued and respected. We help people feel valued when we remember and use their names and mention admirable things we have learned about them. We help them feel respected when we treat them courteously as equal human beings, ask their opinions, listen to them, and acknowledge their contributions. When we confer dignity in these ways, others become inclined to seek us out, cooperate, and show us respect in return.

- *Skill 4: Encourage others to cooperate with you.* At times, you may find yourself in a working relationship with someone who, for one reason or another, is not inclined to cooperate. Let's say you are a student and are going to do a project with a new boy named Dennis. The two of you are assigned to make an oral report on the moons of Saturn. From the ice-breaker conversation, you get the idea that Dennis likes you well enough but is not going to do his part of the assignment. He says he has to work after school and doesn't have time to practice any speeches. He says he will write his part out, and you or the teacher can read it. You listen to him carefully and get the impression that what is really bothering him is not the work itself but making the oral presentation. You say, "Dennis, I'm wondering if we can work out a deal. I'll make the report to the class if you'll help look up the information and get it in order. We could call you the consultant and me the reporter. During the presentation, I might ask you from time to time where you found the information and what you think about it. It might be fun. Want to try it?"

- *Skill 5: Show yourself to be a trustworthy person.* Earlier chapters have presented tactics that help build bonds of trust among teachers and students. It has been explained that ethical principles such as kindness, consideration, helpfulness, fairness, and honesty should be emphasized in all facets of class work and practiced until they become second nature. In Chapter 7, William Glasser's suggestions for replacing deadly habits with connecting habits were discussed. You might wish to refer back to them at this point.

Giving Students Personal Attention

One of the most effective things teachers can do to establish positive relations with students is to make them feel noticed, valued, and capable of success. Students who receive regular positive attention from teachers don't cause much trouble in the classroom. Some teachers engage personally with students as the students enter the room by smiling, saying "hello," and greeting as many as possible by name. Primary teachers sometimes touch students on the head and give them personal greetings.

Many teachers, while circulating among students at work, stop for a moment beside individual students and ask a question or make a positive comment. It is difficult to get around to each student every day, especially for secondary teachers, but you can connect personally with more students than you would imagine. As you do so, make sure to distribute your attention evenly among students.

Discussing Students' Opinions about the Class

You might consider making it routine to discuss class matters with students in an open forum by asking students to review their daily, weekly, or monthly activities, efforts, and progress. This procedure will help you (and the students) appraise their progress while reviewing the topics and activities students have enjoyed, as well as those they have found tedious. You can learn a great deal from this exercise that will help students while making you a better teacher.

If you teach elementary students, set aside a few minutes at the end of each day for students to discuss what they liked best and least in the activities you provided. If you teach secondary students, set aside 15 minutes twice a week for similar reviews. Drop your defenses and let students speak frankly, even if it makes you uncomfortable.

When engaging in this exercise, mention to students that you have feelings, just as they do, and while they should be completely honest, they should speak to you in ways that do not give personal offense. You may have to teach them how to do this by prefacing their remarks with "It might be just me, but . . ." or "I might be wrong, but . . ." or "I was not able to understand exactly why we were doing . . ." Ultimately you will be grateful for what your students teach you in this regard.

Jane Nelsen and Lynn Lott on the Use of Relationship Builders

Jane Nelsen and Lynn Lott, whose contributions on classroom meetings were explored in Chapter 7, have identified five pairs of teacher behaviors that they believe can either nurture or inhibit relationships between teacher and students, depending on how they are used. They call the positive aspect of each pair a *builder* and the negative aspect of each pair a *barrier*. Builders are respectful and encouraging, while barriers are disrespectful and discouraging. As Nelsen and Lott (2000) flatly state,

> We guarantee 100% improvement in student–teacher relationships when teachers simply learn to recognize barrier behaviors and stop demonstrating them. Where else can you get such a generous return for ceasing a behavior? And when the builders are added, the payoff is even greater. (p. 18)

Here are their builders, contrasted with barrier counterparts:

• *Builder 1: Checking.* Teachers can establish stronger relations with students if they check in advance to see how students think and feel about class expectations and other matters. The barrier counterpart of checking is teachers' *assuming* they know how students feel and then proceeding from that basis.

• *Builder 2: Exploring.* Students relate better to teachers who allow them to explore and perceive situations for themselves and proceed accordingly. The barrier counterpart to exploring is *rescuing/explaining*. Teachers erroneously think they are being helpful when they make lengthy explanations, rescue students from difficulties, or do some of students' work for them. What they should do instead is ask students "What do you need to remember, do, or have in order to take care of yourself?"

- *Builder 3: Inviting/encouraging.* To build strong relationships, teachers should invite and encourage students to cooperate, contribute, and be self-directing. For example, the teacher might say, "The bell will ring soon. I would appreciate anything you might do to help get the room straightened up for the next class." The barrier counterpart of inviting/encouraging is *directing*. Teachers do not realize they are being disrespectful when they tell students "Pick that up," "Put that away," or "Straighten up your desk before the bell rings." Such commands build dependence while suppressing initiative and cooperation.
- *Builder 4: Celebrating.* Teachers should hold high expectations of students and show they believe in students' potential. They should celebrate student progress that is made evident when students take the initiative, make an effort, persevere, and improve. The barrier counterpart of celebrating is *expecting*. Students become easily discouraged when judged negatively because they have fallen short of expectations, as when teachers say, "I really thought you could do that" or "I thought you were more responsible than that."
- *Builder 5: Respecting.* Respect does much to build teacher–student relationships. A teacher shows respect by speaking with students as social equals and without using terms that suggest what students should do. The negative counterpart of respecting is the use of *adultisms,* which are teacher statements that tell students what to do or that sound like parents speaking to naughty children, such as "How come you never . . . ?" or "Why can't you ever . . . ?" or "I can't believe you would do such a thing!" These adultisms produce dependency and guilt rather than initiative and encouragement. If students have not performed up to expectations, the teacher should not admonish them but ask, "What is your understanding of the requirements for this assignment?"

Introducing and Practicing Human Relations Skills

Human relations skills are best introduced and first practiced in class meetings. There, students have a safe venue in which to learn what to say, how to say it, how to use body language, and how to maintain positive feelings during disagreements. Matters concerning what to do when human relations go sour can be discussed and strategies for correcting mistakes can be explored. From class meetings, the new skills can be carried over into actual work sessions.

Periodically, students can discuss how well they were able to maintain a positive focus in class activities when relationships were put under stress. Some authorities such as Jean Piaget (2001) and Alfie Kohn (1996) believe that arguing and squabbling help students develop intellectually and socially. This may be true, but for the sake of educational progress in school, teachers should help students learn to get along without traumatizing themselves and everyone around them.

Human Relations in the Primary Grades

You might wonder if primary-grade children can learn the relational skills discussed so far. Be assured, they are able to comprehend and put into practice practically everything covered to this point. They easily understand the basic concepts in human relations, such as the "golden rule," taking turns, being nice to others, and getting along without fussing or fighting. Here are examples of how two primary teachers have given attention to personal relations in their classes.

Ruth, a Kindergarten Teacher

Teaching human relations at the early primary level is best done when teachers, students, and parents work together. Young children learn by imitating the behavior of adults in their lives. One parent told me, "I am glad I like the way you act, because Jenny tries to act just like you."

The principal at our school is very good at setting examples of courtesy and friendliness. He stands on the school steps every morning and greets parents, teachers, and students as they arrive. Everybody likes this, and it helps students learn to greet others with a smile and a cheery good morning. Children have said to me about the principal, "I like him; he knows my name."

The importance of relations we maintain with parents cannot be overemphasized. They have a great influence on how effective we can be with the children we teach. I try to cultivate the good will and cooperation of parents. I always follow the golden rule when interacting with them.

For children in my class, I do the following:

1. Talk about how we feel when others push, call us names, or don't play with us.
2. Discuss treating others as we like to be treated. I remind students of this every day.
3. Always speak with students in a tactfully honest and respectful manner, and never embarrass them in front of others.
4. Choose my words carefully. I never accuse them of doing something wrong. That only makes them defensive. I just politely ask, "What could you have done differently?"
5. When two students disagree, I try to help them find a solution that both find acceptable.

When working with parents, here is what I try to do:

1. Choose my words carefully when telling the parent of their child's misbehavior or inadequate performance. I never accuse the child or make the parent feel the situation is their fault. I remember that they see the child as an extension of themselves. Parents will not cooperate with me if I attack or blame their child. The approach I take is suggesting what the parent and I together can do to help the child be more successful.
2. I try to convince the parent that I want the same for their child as they do—a successful school experience.

I have noticed that most teachers exhibit good human relations, but a few do not. Those who do so seem to have better behaved classes and experience less stress.

Cynthia, a Second-Grade Teacher

I begin the class with a discussion about my expectations for the year. I tell the children that I consider them my school "family." I explain that just as in any family we might not always agree on everything; nonetheless, I will always care about them. I say that each and every one of them is very special and important to me and that I want them to have the best school year possible.

I explain that because they are so important to me, we cannot accept any cruelty or unkindness to each other in our class. I expect them to be the best behaved and well-mannered class in the entire school, both in the classroom and on the playground. I tell them that good behavior is really just good manners, because it shows respect for others, whether they are children or adults. I go over the golden rule and make a bulletin board on that theme. I refer to the golden rule as our class motto. That is the only rule we have in our class. I discuss with them that it is the best guide for getting along with others. I clarify this point further with advice such as "If you don't want to be called names, then don't call other people names," "If you want people to listen to you, then be sure to listen to others," and most important, "If you want to have friends, then be a friend."

The children understand and accept all of this very well. They see it as a fair and sensible way to behave, and I think it helps them know they have a teacher who cares about them.

ENHANCING COMMUNICATION

Earlier it was mentioned that teachers can model and teach to students certain techniques of listening well and communicating clearly, abilities that help stu- dents in school and serve them for a lifetime, yet typically we give these matters little attention. The sections that follow present ideas and advice from Haim Ginott, Stephen Covey, and Thomas Gordon, all renowned experts in the skills of communication.

Haim Ginott on Congruent Communication

Haim G. Ginott (1922–1973)—psychologist, child therapist, parent educator, and author—made contributions of lasting impact concerning how adults should speak with children. Ginott began his career as an elementary teacher in Israel in 1947. After immigrating to the United States, he earned a doctorate in clinical psychology at Columbia University and went on to hold professorships in psychology at Adelphi University and New York University Graduate School. He also served as an UNESCO consultant in Israel, was resident psychologist on the *Today* show, and wrote a weekly syndicated col-umn entitled "Between Us" that dealt with interpersonal communication. His books *Between Parent and Child* (1965), *Between Parent and Teenager* (1967), and *Teacher and Child* (1971) have been translated into over 30 languages and are still very popular.

Ginott's suggestions are unsurpassed for showing respect for children's feelings while setting limits on their behavior. In his book *Teacher and Child*, he illuminated the value of communication and provided tactics that have been incorporated into virtually all systems of discipline in use today. His suggestions relate to the power of teachers, which he described as follows (1971):

As a teacher I have come to the frightening conclusion that I am the decisive element in the classroom. It is my personal approach that creates the climate. It is my daily mood that makes the weather. As a teacher I possess tremendous power to make a child's life miserable or joyous. I can be a tool of torture or an instrument of inspiration. I can humiliate or humor, hurt or heal. In all situations it is my response that decides whether a crisis will be escalated or de-escalated, and a child humanized or dehumanized. (p. 13)

Ginott reminds us that learning always takes place in the present tense, meaning that teachers should not prejudge students or hold grudges. Learning is always a personal matter to students, so teachers of large classes must remember that each student–learner is an individual who must be treated as such. Good communication is the key to working effectively with students.

The style of communication most effective for teachers is *congruent communication,* which addresses situations rather than students' character and is harmonious with students' feelings about situations and themselves. Ginott says that teachers at their best do not preach, moralize, impose guilt, or demand promises. Instead, they confer dignity on their students by treating them as social equals capable of making decisions for themselves. Contrarily, teachers at their worst label students, belittle them, and denigrate their character, although they rarely do so with malicious intent.

Ginott urges teachers conscientiously to avoid comments that do the following:

- Label students by referring to them as *lazy, thoughtless, bad helper, inconsiderate, poor citizen,* and the like.
- Ask rhetorical *why* questions: "Why did you write this so poorly? Why are you two talking? Why am I having to tell you this again?"
- Give moralistic lectures: "You are not making an effort to get along with each other. You will never get anywhere in life if you can't get along with other people."
- Make caustic or sarcastic remarks to students: "I simply don't believe that. You are not telling the truth. I believe that's the fourth time you have 'lost' your assignment."
- Deny students' feelings: "You have no reason to be upset. There is absolutely nothing to worry about."
- Demand students' cooperation: "That's enough fooling around. Get back in your seats and get to work, right now!"
- Show you have lost your temper and self-control: "Don't you dare speak to me like that again! You will be out of this class once and for all!"

Ginott goes on to say that effective teachers do not demand cooperation from their students but rather invite cooperation by describing the situation and indicating what needs to be done: "The noise level has gotten much too high. Let's speak very quietly for the next 10 minutes." They do not dictate to students or boss them around, because those acts too often provoke resistance. Effective teachers have a hidden asset upon which they can always call, which is to ask themselves, How can I be most helpful to my students right now?

Ginott says that teachers should feel free to express anger and other emotions but when doing so should use I-messages rather than you-messages (also stressed by Thomas Gordon and others). Using an I-message, the teacher might say, "I find the noise distracting." Using a you-message, the teacher might say, "You are being too noisy." Ginott said it is also wise to use *laconic language* when responding to or redirecting student misbehavior, meaning language that is brief and to the point.

Ginott also had a great deal to say about praise, and his contentions came as a surprise to teachers who, in the 1970s, were using praise extensively in behavior modification. *Evaluative praise* is worse than none at all, he said, and should never be used. An example of evaluative praise is "Good boy for raising your hand." Instead of evaluative praise, which speaks to a student's character, teachers should use expressions of appreciation for effort, improvement, or accomplishment, without evaluating the student's character or talent. For example, the teacher might say, "I enjoyed your story very much" or "I can almost smell those pine trees in your drawing."

Ginott asked teachers always to respect students' privacy but to indicate that they are available, should students want to talk. As for correcting inappropriate behavior, Ginott simply advised that teachers stop the misbehavior and teach the student the correct way to behave. Ginott placed strong sanctions on sarcasm and punishment, saying that sarcasm is almost always dangerous and should not be used with students. Punishment should not be used at all, as it too often produces hostility, rancor, and vengefulness, while never making students really want to improve.

Teachers, meanwhile, should continually strive for self-discipline in their work. They must be very careful not to display the behaviors they are trying to eradicate in students, such as raising their voice to end noise, acting rude toward students who are being impolite, or berating students who have used inappropriate language.

Finally, Ginott explained that classroom discipline is not accomplished immediately but develops gradually as the teacher—through self-discipline, concern, and helpfulness—promotes students' humaneness and self-control.

Stephen Covey on Empathetic Listening

Stephen R. Covey (1989) provides important advice on how to listen sensitively to others. He believes that we learn to be better listeners when we identify our frame of reference while trying to grasp the frame of reference of the other person. He explains that for many years, he believed that when he spoke, others accurately received the message he was trying to convey to them, since he tried hard to make it very clear. Finally, he realized that what he was trying to convey was framed in his own point of view, not that of the listener, which was sometimes often quite different.

That was when Covey understood that in order to communicate well, you have to understand both your point of view and that of your listeners. The two, he says, are seldom the same. For teachers, that means understanding students' deeper hopes, fears, realities, and difficulties. Given that understanding, you can adjust what you wish to communicate in terms of the student's frame of reference as child or adolescent, rather than from your frame of reference as an adult teacher. What the student sees as reality often differs substantially from what you consider reality, and matters you consider important may be trivial in the student's view of the world. If teachers are to work well with students, they need to know not just students' thoughts but what those thoughts mean in students' personal existence.

Covey (1989) goes on to say that highly successful people try to understand their listeners *before* they try to make listeners understand them. He writes,

> If I were to summarize in one sentence the single most important principle I have learned in the field of interpersonal relations, it would be this: *Seek first to understand, then to be understood.* This principle is the key to effective interpersonal communication. (p. 237)

He further reminds us,

> Empathetic listening takes time, but it doesn't take anywhere near as much time as it takes to back up and correct misunderstandings when you're already miles down the road, to redo, to live with unexpressed and unsolved problems. . . . People want to be understood. And whatever investment of time it takes to do that will bring much greater returns of time as you work from an accurate understanding of [their] problems and issues. (p. 253)

Thomas Gordon on Removing Roadblocks to Communication

Psychologist Thomas Gordon (1918–2002), a Nobel Prize nominee and recipient of numerous awards, is author of the acclaimed *Parent Effectiveness Training* (1970), *Teacher Effectiveness Training* (1987), and *Discipline That Works* (1989). He pioneered the teaching of communication skills and conflict resolution to parents, teachers, youth, and managers of organizations worldwide. Over 2 million people have been trained by his organization.

One of Gordon's major contributions to communication is his identification of 12 types of comments teachers make that seem a reasonable part of teaching but that actually stifle communication with students. He calls the comments "roadblocks to communication." For example, imagine that student Dale is supposed to be writing a composition in class. Dale learned just last night his parents intend to separate. He didn't sleep much and now can't concentrate on the assignment. Dale could use some comfort and kindness, but Mr. Askew does not detect his need. Mr. Askew thinks Dale is procrastinating, which he sometimes does. Mr. Askew asks Dale what the problem is. Dale shrugs and says "Nothing." Then he adds that he doesn't understand how to do the assignment.

The following are examples of typical teacher comments that Mr. Askew might make to get Dale going but that will have the opposite effect. They will discourage Dale and make him unwilling to talk further. They are what Gordon means by "roadblocks to communication."

Giving orders. "Dale, you get busy. I think you know how to do that composition. No more wasting time. Get your name and date on your paper and get to work."

Warning. "Dale, I'm telling you for the last time to get to work. If you don't, you'll be taking that home with you tonight along with a note to your parents."

Preaching. "Dale, you know you are expected to complete all your work. We are not doing this for the fun of it. It's for your own good. Don't you see that? If you don't try to learn this, you're never going to write well at all. You will never look like an educated person."

Advising. "Dale, let me give you a piece of advice. When I was younger, I was much like you, never doing what I was capable of. A good teacher got me out of that. He told me to set some personal goals for myself and work toward them, step by step. I think you'd benefit from that. I'd like you to come up with a plan such as that and see if it doesn't help."

Criticizing. "Dale, I can't believe you are fooling around again. Didn't we just talk about this last week? You have ability but you are not using it. I'm really disappointed in you."

Questioning. "What's wrong, Dale? You have been sitting here 10 minutes and still have nothing on that paper. You aren't even trying. Do you think something bad is going to happen if you write a few lines? What's the matter with you, anyhow?"

Comments like the ones Mr. Askew makes to Dale are commonly heard in classrooms, but they rarely help. In cases such as Dale's, they are likely to make the student grow more distant, feel worse, and become less inclined to approach the teacher. What could Mr. Askew have said to Dale that would have been more helpful? Consider the following responses. Note how they provide encouragement, rather than find fault:

"Dale, we need to get this assignment completed by the end of the period."

"Writing is not easy, is it? Many people have a difficult time at first. Let's see if we can begin with a title. What would your composition be about?"

"Sometimes we feel like working, and sometimes we can't seem to do it. We might be tired or our minds might be very much bothered by something. Do you ever have feelings like that?"

"Dale, I can tell you are having difficulty getting started. Is there something about the assignment that bothers you? I'd like to help resolve it, if there is."

"Dale, I feel something is not right for you. I don't want to pry. If you feel like talking, I'll listen now, or I'll be here in this room right after school if you want to drop by."

You see the point Gordon was making. The following statements indicate further why "roadblock" comments are usually counterproductive:

"Dale, you are being inconsiderate of me and your classmates." (Labeling or calling names in this manner tends to make students withdraw.)

"Dale, why am I having to tell you all this again?" (Rhetorical questions usually come across as scolding.)

"Dale, you will never get anywhere if you don't improve your attitude." (Students interpret moralizing as degradation of their character.)

"How odd, Dale. This is the third time this month you haven't 'felt like' doing your work." (Sarcasm punishes students and questions their character.)

"Don't be silly, Dale. There is absolutely nothing difficult about this assignment." (Such reassurance denies the student's legitimate feelings.)

"That's enough fooling around, Dale. Pick up your pencil and get to work." (Demands never make students truly want to do their assignments.)

"Dale, you pay attention to what I'm saying! I am the teacher in this room, and you darned well better remember it! (Losing your temper and self-control presents a negative impression and makes students wary of you.)

Consider teaching your students about these roadblocks to communication, how they can be avoided, and how they can be replaced with comments that attract cooperation. Students should be helped to understand that when others are worried or have made a mistake, the best thing they can do is try to help them in a positive manner.

Why You Should Not Argue with Students

When students complain about assignments or make excuses, many teachers move from a helping mode to a confronting mode. They don't want to listen to student comments they consider ill mannered and untrue, and they don't want to accept the seemingly bogus explanations students sometimes make to avoid responsibility. Teachers' natural inclination is to dispute what students say—to argue with them, in other words. However, that is a trap teachers should assiduously avoid.

We are speaking of the kind of arguing in which one person tries to convince the other of a particular point of view by means of logic (or louder voice or fiercer demeanor). When teachers argue this way with students, they almost never bring students to their point of view or cause them to see the logic or purpose behind their belief. That is because when people argue, they put up defenses against the other person and dig in their heels. After expending much emotional energy, they usually end up more firmly convinced of their opinion than they were before. Meanwhile, the argumentation batters feelings and puts an end to willing cooperation. As Dale Carnegie (1981) said, "There is only one way under high heaven to get the best of an argument—and that is to avoid it. Avoid it as you would avoid rattlesnakes and earthquakes" (p. 116).

What, then, should you do when disagreements arise between you and your students or between students? The best course of action, which should be taught and practiced, is for each side honestly to consider the other's point of view. Calm and reason might lead one of the disputants to see he or she has made an error, and the matter can end there. More realistically, the resolution process can identify a working middle ground that allows cooperation to continue. Teachers can help students learn to seek the middle ground in disputes. This skill lends itself well to role-playing, and students have a lot of fun with it.

You might consider teaching students to do the following:

1. Take turns listening carefully to the other person. Keep calm. Hear the person out, and wait your turn. Don't interrupt to deny or contradict what he or she says.
2. Drop your defenses. If you are offended, resist the impulse to strike back. Try for understanding.
3. Don't tell the other person he or she is wrong. Doing so will be seen as an insult to the person's intelligence, perception, or reasoning ability.
4. After the other person has had a say, you can reply, "I have listened carefully, and believe I understand your point of view. I am often wrong, but . . ." Then briefly state your position. Tell the other person you would like to find a middle ground that makes sense to both sides. If that is not possible, set the matter aside and agree to disagree in a friendly manner.

This is not to say teachers should never try to change students' minds. One of teachers' main duties is to open up new ideas and help students see different points of view. They will change their interests and opinions if they see reasons to do so. Instead of arguing, make your points clear through modeling, examples, and anecdotes. Allow others to state their views. As Ben Franklin said, if you argue and rankle and contradict, you may achieve a victory sometimes, but it will be an empty victory because you will never get your opponent's goodwill.

A Brief Self-Appraisal Guide Concerning Student Involvement

When you work closely with students, you want to make sure you interact with all of them equally, as much as possible. Students who are reticent or timid often get left out of class discussions and question and answer activities.

To help involve everyone, consider using the following descriptors as a personal guide. You might wish to devote at least one classroom meeting to discussing these descriptors with your students. Tell students why the descriptor topics are important to you as a teacher, and explain the benefits they can provide to class members:

1. The teacher contacts and involves all students in the class and gives them time to respond.
2. All students have an equal opportunity to volunteer to answer teacher questions.
3. All students seem willing to express their opinions freely in class.
4. Students inform the teacher when they do not understand what is being said or taught, so the teacher can reteach or explain in another way.
5. Students listen quietly when the teacher and classmates speak and seem intent on understanding the speaker correctly.

6. Students are able to *paraphrase* what has been said, or put concepts and ideas into their own words.
7. Students do not seem afraid or embarrassed to misspeak or make mistakes.
8. The teacher often organizes paired discussions and small-group discussion sessions in which all students can participate.
9. The teacher uses effective body language in maintaining connections with all students in the classroom.
10. Students participate actively in communicating class activities to parents.
11. Students participate in classroom meetings where they voice concerns and suggestions about class matters.

Communicating with Students' Parents and Guardians

Maintaining considerate communication with your students' parents or guardians is not only a professional duty but also a tactic that can bring rich rewards. Parents have a need and a right to know about your program for their children, how their children are progressing, what their strengths are, what difficulties they may be experiencing, and how you intend to help. If you tactfully maintain communication with parents on these matters, they will usually give you considerable support and spread the word that you are a good teacher who cares.

There are several ways to communicate with parents. Use the telephone if you need to talk with them about private matters. For information about the class and its activities, send out a newsletter. Better yet, establish a class page on the Internet where you can post pictures, schedules, requirements, activities, and other information. Give the newsletter or webpage a professional appearance. From third grade on, students can provide much of the content, which you should edit and organize. The postings should show photos of students at work. Try to mention all your students by name over time. Parents like that, and so do students.

Doing these things takes time, but they are good for communication and provide an excellent activity for students. Setting up a website is easy. Most schools now encourage this practice and have personnel who can help you get the site going.

What Parents Need to Know from You.   Parents need to know a number of things about their child in school, but once the child progresses beyond the first two or three years, most parents shy away from close involvement with teachers. Many feel they shouldn't meddle. Others feel insecure about approaching the teacher. In any case, they have the need and the right to be informed about such things as the following:

- The educational program provided in your class—a summary of your curriculum and the subject-area standards, materials being used, and typical instructional activities
- The expectations you hold for their child, including classwork, behavior, homework, makeup work, and so forth

- How their child is doing in school, both generally ("Does good work"; "Is a good citizen") and specifically ("Has improved from 75 percent correct to 85 percent correct in math")
- Any specific problems their child is having
- Special activities in which their child will be involved

Parents who speak with you personally will usually want to know things that are specific only to their child:

- Does my child seem happy?
- How does my child get along with others?
- How does my child react to trying new things? To making mistakes?
- What is my child best at? What is my child weakest in?
- Does my child cause problems?
- What after-school opportunities are there for my child?

Be ready to supply this information when parents request it. Also, realize that it will be difficult for them to accept anything that might sound negative about their child. Be honest but tactful in your comments. Be ready to back them up with evidence, and have some potential solutions in mind. Parents will often make comments such as these:

"He never was that way before" (to which you say, "I hope I can count on your help, because I know you don't want him behaving this way.")

"She was well liked in her other school" (to which you say, "She will be well liked here, too, if together we encourage her to be more friendly to others. I'm sure with your help we can.")

"He is just like his father, who has never learned to pick up after himself" (to which you say, "Let's see if we can work on this. Can I count on your help?")

"Her mother is the same way—just loves to talk" (to which you say, "I really like her. It's just that her talking often disturbs the class and keeps her from getting her work done. I'm sure you want her to learn, just as I do.")

Conferencing with Parents or Guardians.   From time to time, you can expect to conference privately with parents or guardians, either as a scheduled event or in response to a particular need or situation. The following suggestions can help you prepare for such conferences:

- In advance, prepare a folder with the student's name written on it attractively. In the folder, include (1) a summary of work covered to date, (2) a profile of the student's performance in that work, (3) samples of the student's work, good and bad, (4) tests, grade book, and other evidence pertinent to the conference, and (5) notes to remind you of anecdotes that provide insight into the student's behavior and progress.

- When the parent/guardian arrives, greet him or her in a friendly, relaxed manner. Ask him or her to sit beside you at a table, rather than on the other side of a desk. This conveys a message of cooperation.
- Begin by chatting about the child as a worthwhile person. Mention good traits. This reassures the parent/guardian.
- Guide the parent/guardian through the student's folder, commenting on its contents.
- Encourage the parent/guardian to talk. Listen carefully. Be accepting. Don't argue or criticize. Don't expect the person to be completely objective about the child.
- Show that you want the best for the child, just as the parent/guardian does.
- If appropriate, work with the parent/guardian to create a home action plan that will benefit the child.
- End the conference by describing your plans for the student's future progress. Earnestly request the parent/guardian's support. Thank him or her for talking with you about the child.

IN SUMMARY

All classrooms function better when students and teachers relate and communicate well with each other. This chapter provided a number of tactics for improving relationships and communication skills in classrooms. Emphasized were general skills of human relations, habits that help people connect with each other, tactics that help build relationships, empathetic listening, avoiding "roadblocks" to communication, other skills in communicating with students, and points to consider in communicating with parents. Haim Ginott's colossal insights on congruent communication were featured.

REFERENCES

Carnegie, D. 1981. *How to win friends and influence people.* New York: Pocket Books.
Covey, S. 1989. *The seven habits of highly effective people.* New York: Simon & Schuster.
Ginott, H. 1965. *Between parent and child.* New York: Macmillan.
Ginott, H. 1967. *Between parent and teenager.* New York: Macmillan.
Ginott, H. 1971. *Teacher and child.* New York: Macmillan.
Glasser, W. 1998. *Choice theory in the classroom.* New York: HarperCollins.
Glasser, W. 2001. *Every student can succeed.* Chatsworth, CA: William Glasser.
Gordon, T. 1970. *Parent effectiveness training: A tested new way to raise responsible children.* New York: New American Library.
Gordon, T. 1987. *T.E.T.: Teacher effectiveness training* (2nd edition). New York: David McKay.
Gordon, T. 1989. *Discipline that works: Promoting self-discipline in children.* New York: Random House.
Kohn, A. 1996. *Beyond discipline: From compliance to community.* Alexandria, VA: Association for Supervision and Curriculum Development.
Nelsen, J., and Lott, L. 2000. *Positive discipline in the classroom* (2nd edition). Rocklin, CA: Prima.
Piaget, J. 2001. *The psychology of intelligence.* London, England: Routledge & Kegan Paul.

Developing Responsibility

Helping Students Develop an Internal Sense of Responsibility

This strategy can be accomplished by interacting with students in ways that cause them to reflect deeply about the kinds of people they want to be and the kinds of lives they want to lead. With a few exceptions, the young want to think of themselves as ethical, trustworthy, and in charge of their own lives. Help them create plans of action that lead to their goals. Remember that you can influence this process but cannot force it.

Chapter Preview

A sense of personal responsibility is necessary for optimal personal development and is a requisite counterbalance to the freedom of choice we enjoy. There is increasing concern about the lack of responsibility in society today. Schools are being urged to do what they can to engender this trait during students' formative years. Until recently, there was a dearth of systematic procedures for doing so, but in the last few years, some strong programs have appeared. This chapter describes the nature and tactics of two such programs—Ed Ford's Responsible Thinking Process and Marvin Marshall's Raise Responsibility System.

DEVELOPING RESPONSIBILITY IN SCHOOL

Most educators consider a genuine sense of responsibility to be among the half dozen most important things students can learn. Responsibility imposes constraints on behavior that enable us to maintain a lifestyle that is safe and orderly. In the past, the young learned responsibility at home, but all too often, that is no longer the case, and the schools are being asked to assume that duty.

Responsibility means being accountable for one's actions—being trustworthy, fulfilling obligations, being able to justify behavior on ethical grounds, and being willing to accept the consequences of behavior. It is bound up in doing one's duty and behaving ethically. Students of all ages understand the concept. They recognize that you are supposed to answer for your own actions, that it is not right to make excuses or blame others. Yet more and more often, our students, like all of us, seem oblivious to their poor behavior, consider licentious conduct acceptable, and blame anyone or anything outside themselves when things go wrong.

Teachers do try to tell students about responsibility and how they can show it, but merely talking about it has little effect. This chapter features two approaches for working toward responsibility as a life value: (1) the Responsible Thinking Process, created and popularized by Ed Ford, and (2) the Raise Responsibility System, created and popularized by Marvin Marshall. As you will see, both are designed to promote personal reflection about the kind of person one wants to be and to explore plans of action for moving in the desired direction.

ED FORD ON THE RESPONSIBLE THINKING PROCESS (RTP)

Ed Ford is president of Responsible Thinking Process, Inc. His organization trains educators and parents in using the Responsible Thinking Process (RTP) to assist the young in conducting themselves more effectively, relating better with others, and becoming more responsible people. The Responsible Thinking Process is based on Perceptual Control Theory (PCT), developed by William T. Powers, which holds that behavior is best understood in terms of how we *control our perceptions*. That means we are always comparing our current perceptions to how we want them to be, and we are continually attempting to act so as to have the perceptions we want. Ford (2006a) does not view behavior as being "caused" by environmental forces, nor does he believe it is possible for one person to control another. He feels it is unfair to expect teachers to change those things over which they have no control. Instead, he believes teachers should teach students how to understand what they want for themselves in life and how to develop plans for getting what they want while not infringing on the rights of others.

Mr. Ford served in the U.S. Navy, was a newspaper reporter, and later worked in the industrial relations department of a large steel factory. He taught high school for six years, then earned a master's degree in social work and went into private counseling. Not long afterward, he joined the faculty of the Institute for Reality Therapy and began teaching Reality Therapy and consulting in schools and other institutions in Ohio. For the past 30 years, he has taught and consulted in alcohol and drug rehabilitation centers, in mental heath centers for residential and outpatients, in approximately 70 school districts, and on the faculty of Arizona State University's School of Social Work. Mr. Ford, a founding member and past president of the Control Systems Group that researches and promotes perceptual control theory, has authored 13 books, including *Discipline for Home and School, Book One*

(3rd edition, 2003) and *Book Two* (revised edition, 1999). He recommends his most recently published book be read first: *Discipline for Home and School, Fundamentals* (2004). Currently, he consults and trains extensively with school districts that want to use the Responsible Thinking Process. His website is www.responsiblethinking.com, and he can be contacted at edford@responsiblethinking.com.

The Nature of the Responsible Thinking Process

The Responsible Thinking Process is designed to help students develop a sense of responsibility for their own lives and respect for everyone around them. Ford describes it as a school discipline process that does not involve coercion, punishment, or rewards. When students have difficulties getting along with others, or when they disrupt in class or other school settings, they are taught how to plan ways to get what they want *without infringing on the rights of others.* This is rarely seen in education, Ford says.

As noted, Ford's approach to discipline is based on Perceptual Control Theory (PCT), which teaches how we are designed to learn to deal with our environment in ways that bring a satisfying life. Each of us tries to understand our environment and uses that understanding to find contentment. Each of us, ultimately, wants to stand as our own person—to be, as Ford says, "Captain of our own ship." We create our understanding of the world through the three highest levels of perception, which we use to help us determine who we are and what we do. Those levels, defined by Powers in PCT, are called the systems concepts level, the principles level, and the program level.

At the *systems concepts level,* we establish our beliefs and values, creating for ourselves how we each want to be as a person. We progressively clarify how we want to see ourselves as persons, as well as the values and beliefs we believe will bring us happiness. The beliefs and values we establish guide how we treat others while trying to achieve our goals.

At the *principles level,* we set our priorities, standards, criteria, and other guidelines for how we want to live in accordance with our values and beliefs. In school, these include rules and procedures to help us function more efficiently.

At the *program level,* we structure our lives by organizing what we do through plan making. This, we believe, will lead to satisfaction. Experience teaches us that if we are to live in harmony, our plans must not violate the rights of others, meaning we must not disturb their legitimate attempts to get what they want. The structures that guide our behavior must work *for* us and not work *against* others, while respecting others' attempts to do the same thing.

In the classroom, students can behave in many ways for personal benefit. If those behaviors infringe on the rights of others, conflict and disruptions occur, which teachers see as "discipline problems." Traditionally, teachers then take steps to deal with these "problems" by focusing on what they see the students "do," their "behavior." When students settle down and resume work, teachers feel they are successful in managing behavior. But all they have done, in most cases, is temporarily squelch the disturbance, without helping the students become conscious of how their behavior was interfering with the rights of others.

Ford insists that "misbehavior" is never truly corrected by reprimands or punishment. It is only corrected when students connect their actions to get what they want with the effects of those actions on others. Students who don't understand this process continue to behave inappropriately, meaning their behavior disturbs others.

When students behave, they are trying to achieve particular goals. Examples of such goals might be getting to class on time, finding out if a friend wants to play basketball after school, or hurting another student who was rude. Students can *directly* experience their own goals, but teachers and other students are exposed *only indirectly* to those goals, by way of the students' actions (which for the above examples could be running in the hallway, talking in class, or punching a student in the nose). Disturbances or conflicts can be truly resolved only when students realize the adverse effects of their actions on others, commit to resolving the issues, and plan to act in ways that will get them what they want *without violating the rights of others*. As we will see, the teacher can play a strong role by opening up alternative views and possibilities for the student involved.

Ford strongly emphasizes that the Responsible Thinking Process is *not* designed to control behavior, "change" students, keep students "in line," or maintain an "orderly" class. Rather, it is to cultivate respect for oneself and others, combined with a pervasive sense of responsibility for one's actions. When these results occur, classrooms acquire a climate of respect, discipline problems decline, and academic learning and positive human relations improve.

The Teacher's Role in the Responsible Thinking Process

Teachers want students to learn to think for themselves and deal effectively with their own problems. They typically feel they must tell students what to do and "correct" them when they fail or do the wrong thing. But that effort does not produce the results teachers want. The Responsible Thinking Process, on the other hand, leads to desirable outcomes because it relies *not* on threatening, directing, and correcting, but on asking key questions that help students learn (when they are willing) to look within themselves and decide how they want to be (Ford, 2006b). This, in turn, helps them learn how to make more effective plans that will, in the future, provide for them the necessary understanding of how to deal with getting what they want without violating the rights of others. To illustrate this point, Ford provides the following scenario, which has been edited and abridged from the website www.responsiblethinking.com:

> Mathew, late for class, is running in the hallway. Mrs. Kuhn, a teacher adept in using the RTP questioning process, calls to Mathew in a nonthreatening tone, "Mathew, what are you doing?" She does not scold him or tell him to stop. Mathew looks at her, stops running, and replies, "I'm trying not to be late to class." (Notice Mathew explained his *goal—what he wanted to accomplish.*) Mrs. Kuhn might then ask, "What were you doing to try to get there?" Mathew would probably answer, "I was running." Mrs. Kuhn would then tie the action to the rule by asking, "What's the rule about running in the halls?" Again, the key to RTP is to teach students to think about how they are going to

accomplish getting what they want without in any way violating the rights of others. Punishment, rewards, criticism, yelling, constantly correcting—none of these things teach students to think for themselves.

Later, Mrs. Kuhn might ask Mathew if he has managed to figure out a way of getting to his classes on time. If he says "no," then she might ask him if he is interested in learning a way of getting to class on time without violating any rules. If instead he were to say "yes," then she might take an interest in what he has figured out.

Ford points out that Mrs. Kuhn's approach is nonmanipulative and nonpunitive. Her questions and comments lead to Mathew's thinking through what he is doing *in relation to the rules*. Further, it predisposes him toward an action plan that respects the rights of others and gives him personal accountability for his actions. Mrs. Kuhn knows that when she discusses behavior with students, she is far more effective when asking questions than when telling students what to do. She knows that when you tell students what to do, you are doing the thinking for them. When you ask questions (especially "What you are doing?"), and they have to connect their actions to the rules of wherever they are, then the students are encouraged to reflect on their own accountability and think things through. *They* are doing the thinking. Asking questions that encourage students to think and plan is the best way to help them learn responsibility.

Ford reiterates that RTP does *not* deal with behavior, although it sounds as though it does. The first question in RTP is "What are you doing?" But it is always asked in concert with the second RTP question: "What are the rules?" The questions don't merely ask students to pay attention to their actions. They go beyond that by prompting students to think about whether their actions are disturbing others, as defined by school or class rules. Rules act as guidelines to help us avoid interfering with others around us who are trying to satisfy their own goals, and by following established rules, we show responsibility for our behavior while respecting the rights of others.

The fundamental rule of every school, Ford says, should be this: "We do not violate the rights of others." When students are asked the first two RTP questions ("What are you doing?" "What's the rule?"), they must consult their values concerning how others ought to be treated. Ford says that people only begin to change their behavior when they seriously examine their belief systems, assess their own values and standards, and set priorities and standards. Teachers must ask the RTP questions in a calm, respectful, curious tone. When they do so, students usually spend a moment in quiet introspection. It is then that real, permanent change can occur.

Ford maintains that when the Responsible Thinking Process is used as he suggests, classroom discipline problems decline at all levels, from minor disruptions to violence. When disruptions *do* occur, as they occasionally will, RTP provides a means for resolving issues calmly and respectfully, with a minimum of anger or frustration.

How Respect Is Taught in the Responsible Thinking Process

Ed Ford and George Venetis (2006) explain that when you use RTP, you are modeling respect for students in three ways: (1) by listening to what they say, without trying to control their answers or being critical, (2) by helping students focus on how their actions are breaking rules or disturbing others, and (3) by accepting what students say, by asking questions that will help them resolve problems *when they are ready,* and by showing your willingness to struggle through dealing with their actions in the meantime, without showing anger or being upset toward them.

You display no anger, because students see anger as an attempt to control them. You do not try to control them, because doing so implies you do not believe they can resolve their problems or deal with conflict. You show respect by allowing students to live with consequences even when you disagree with their decisions concerning behavior. When we try to control the perceptions of others, we are doing so from the basis of our own perception of the world. We must not do that, if we are to be fully effective. Instead, we must show and teach respect for people and the way they are designed. Doing so helps them learn what respect looks like, feels like, and sounds like.

The Questioning Sequence in the Responsible Thinking Process

Below is the sequence of questions Ford recommends for the Responsible Thinking Process. These descriptions are highly condensed. For more complete explanations, refer to the RTP website postings or to Ford's books for teachers.

- *Question 1. "What are you doing?"* This question should be asked first, but always in conjunction with question 2. When students hear this question, they look within themselves and identify their behavior. Telling them what they are doing wrong doesn't help them develop the skill of self-reflection. Neither do you ask them why they are behaving as they are—that only encourages students to make excuses.
- *Question 2. "What are the rules?"* When asked this question, students quickly tie the rules to what they are currently doing and assess their actions in terms of the rights of others. Questions 3, 4, and 5 follow, but as students grow in their understanding of the process, these three questions are no longer needed.
- *Question 3. "What happens when you break the rules?"* This simply gets students to reflect on the consequences that follow when they break rules and draws attention to how their behavior is affecting others.
- *Question 4. "Is this what you want to happen?"* Now you are asking students to look within themselves and decide how they want to see themselves as persons and how they want to live their lives.
- *Question 5. "Where do you want to be?"* or *"What do you want to do now?"* These questions help students come to closure concerning a plan of action that will resolve the conflict between their behavior and the rights of others.
- *Question 6. "What will happen if you disrupt again?"* This question should always be asked, even if students have already reflected and decided to change how they want to be. The reason for asking this question is to make sure students have a clear understanding of school procedures for those who continually disrupt, such as being sent to the Responsible Thinking Classroom where they are helped to make effective plans for resolving their problems.

The foregoing questions should never sound like warnings to students. Warnings imply possible punishment. All they should do is lead students to think about what they are doing in relation to the rules wherever they are and consider, without being prompted, whether there might be a better course of action available to them.

MARVIN MARSHALL ON RAISING STUDENT RESPONSIBILITY

Marvin Marshall believes desirable classroom behavior is best achieved by doing two things: (1) promoting responsibility in students rather than obedience and (2) articulating expectations and then empowering students to reach those expectations. These two elements provide the foundation for his *Raise Responsibility System,* which he believes is the best approach available for promoting positive behavior in the classroom. Marshall is an international consultant and former teacher, counselor, and administrator, with experience at all levels of public education. His suggestions concerning classroom discipline can be accessed in Phi Delta Kappa's *Fostering Social Responsibility* (1998), his book entitled *Discipline without Stress, Punishments, or Rewards: How Teachers and Parents Promote Responsibility and Learning* (2001a), and his monthly electronic newsletter, entitled *Promoting Responsibility and Learning* (2001b), which is available free of charge via e-mail from the following sites: www.MarvinMarshall .com, www.AboutDiscipline.com, and www.DisciplineWithoutStress.com.

The Nature of the Raise Responsibility System

Marvin Marshall describes his Raise Responsibility System as follows:

- Promotes responsibility, rather than obedience
- Relies on internal motivation, rather than external motivation
- Proactive, rather than reactive
- Noncoercive, rather than coercive
- Empowering, rather than overpowering
- Positive, rather than negative
- Reflective, rather than impulsive
- Establishes positivity, choice, and reflection as life-long practices

The system calls on teachers to do three main things: (1) *Teach* students about four levels of social development and relate the levels to behavior and learning, (2) *check for understanding* of the levels when students behave inappropriately, and (3) *provide guided choices* for acceptable behavior when disruptions continue. A major tactic in Marshall's approach is called *elicitation,* which he refers to as "authority without punishment." Elicitation calls on students to suggest ways in which they might conduct themselves more responsibly.

Moving toward Responsible Behavior

In explaining his approach, Marshall refers to Douglas McGregor's Theory X and Theory Y, which are common and contrasting views on how to manage people (McGregor, 1960). *Theory X* holds that people dislike work, try to avoid it, and must be directed, controlled, or threatened with punishment to do their work. *Theory Y* holds that people will work gladly if their tasks bring satisfaction and they can exercise self-direction, self-control, and personal responsibility in doing them.

Marshall's Raise Responsibility System is aligned with Theory Y. He believes most students are naturally inclined to behave responsibly. When they fail to do so, it is because they don't know how or because peer pressure or lack of self-control overrides their better judgment. For teachers to help strengthen students' ability to behave responsibility, Marshall (2005e) suggests weaving three simple practices into the daily school program—positivity, choice, and reflection, which together have the power to make school a place where students and teachers like to be.

Positivity is an emotion of optimism that seeks the upside of things. Being around optimistic people makes us feel better. When someone treats us nicely or says something complimentary to us, we tend to feel good. Negativity has the opposite effect. Unfortunately, students often perceive teachers and schools in a negative light. Marshall says that happens because teachers unwittingly set themselves up as enforcers of rules, rather than as encouragers, mentors, and role models. They aim at promoting obedience without realizing that obedience has no energizing effect on students but only distances them into apathy, resistance, and even defiance. Marshall advises teachers to strive for positivity in their outlook and ways of speaking and to encourage students to do the same.

Choice empowers students by offering them options. Marshall (2005b) illustrates the power of choice in the following comments he received from a school administrator:

> I began to experiment with giving choices to students. When speaking to students about their behavior at recess, in the lunchroom, or on the bus, I would try to elicit from them what choices they had and how they could make better choices. If a consequence were needed, we would talk together about some of the choices. I would usually start with "What do you think we should do about the situation?" When I was satisfied with the student's choice, I would say, "I can live with that." The process worked every time, and I would wonder at its simplicity.

Reflection on one's own behavior is necessary if genuine behavioral change is to occur. We cannot directly change people's attitudes or motivations. Although we can control others by imposing some activity or consequence, we cannot change how they think, want to behave, or will behave after our presence is no longer felt. Usually, teachers try to change students' inappropriate behavior by requesting obedience or coercively making demands. What they should do instead is establish expectations and then influence students in a noncoercive manner by empowering them to reach the expectations.

One of the best ways to do this is to ask students questions that prompt them to think about how they are behaving. This reflection often sets in motion a positive change in their behavior. Teachers should encourage students to ask themselves questions such as "If I wanted to be successful in this class right now, what would I be doing?" In most cases, the answer will be apparent to them, and they will move toward that behavior.

The Hierarchy of Social Development, Its Value, and How It Is Used

Marshall (2001) has articulated a *hierarchy of social development*, which consists of four levels that are used to help students conduct themselves more responsibly:

- *Level A (Anarchy)*. When functioning at this lowest level, students give no thought to expectations or standards. They have no sense of order or purpose, and they seldom accomplish anything worthwhile.
- *Level B (Bossing/Bullying/Bothering)*. When functioning at this level, students are bossing, bullying, or bothering others without concern for the harmful effects of their actions. Here, students only obey the teacher or others when authority is used. In effect, they are saying to the teacher, "We are unable to control ourselves. We need you to boss us." Marshall says sharing this concept with students has a strong effect on improving their behavior.
- *Level C (Cooperation/Conformity)*. When functioning at this level, students conform to expectations set by the teacher or others and are willing to cooperate with them. Their motivation comes mainly from *external* influences, imposed by the teacher or peer pressure. Being able to articulate and reflect on the concept of external motivation helps students understand and resist such influences.
- *Level D (Democracy and taking the initiative to do the right thing)*. Democracy and responsibility are inseparable. When functioning at this level, students take the initiative and do what is right and proper—that is, they behave responsibly without having to be told to do so. They do this because of *internal motivation* associated with the desire to take the initiative to do what they feel is the right thing in any given circumstance. Marshall suggests explaining to students that democracy requires citizens to make decisions for themselves, rather than have decisions made for them, as in dictatorships. Democracy requires that people do the right thing because they believe it is best for society and themselves. Marshall says that Level C behavior is acceptable in school, but he advises teachers and students to aim for Level D.

To illustrate the hierarchy in action, suppose two boys are talking together audibly while another student is making a class report. The teacher quietly asks the disruptive boys, "At what level is that behavior?" They think for a moment and answer, "Level B." Students' misbehavior will typically cease at this point, and their minds will turn toward behavior at a higher level.

Value of the Hierarchy.   Marshall (2001) says that once students understand the hierarchy, their attention turns to self-control and then to social responsibility. He describes a number of outcomes that he believes makes the hierarchy valuable.

To begin, it enables teachers to separate the act from the actor, the deed from the doer. Without that separation, students naturally become defensive when questioned about their behavior. The hierarchy also helps students realize they are constantly making choices, both consciously and nonconsciously. It helps them understand and deal with peer pressure. It fosters internal motivation to behave responsibly. It promotes good character development without calling attention to personal values, ethics, or morals. It serves as a vehicle for communication that uses the same conceptual vocabulary for youths and adults. It encourages students to help keep their classroom environment conducive to learning, rather than always relying on the teacher to do so. It raises awareness of individual responsibility. It empowers students by helping them analyze and correct their own behavior. It serves as an inspiration to improve. It encourages mature decision making. It fosters understanding about the source and effects of internal and external motivation. And it promotes self-management and doing the right thing, even when no adult is around or when no one else is watching.

Teaching the Hierarchy to Students.   Marshall (2001a, pp. 70–80) describes several activities that are useful in teaching students about the names and characteristics of the four levels. Some examples are visualizing each level and then drawing a picture of it, describing it in writing, describing it orally to others, and listening to others' examples of applying the levels to schools. Marshall explains that by using these various modalities and illustrations, the four levels become pictures in students' minds. He argues that it is the pictures in our minds that drive behavior. We move toward activities we believe will bring pleasure and success and away from those we believe will bring displeasure or failure.

Marshall urges teachers to emphasize that the major difference between the acceptable levels of C and D is *motivation.* Level C is behaving responsibly because of adult directions. Classroom procedures, for example, are at Level C. Level D is being responsible without being asked or told and resisting irresponsible peer influence. At Level D, students take the initiative to do the right thing because they believe it is best for the class, the school, and themselves.

You might wonder how well students can understand these levels and relate them to real life. Brief excerpts from "A Letter Worth Reading" provide commentary on that question. The letter (abridged here) was sent to Marvin Marshall by a teacher using the Raise Responsibility System (Marshall, 2005a):

> Just this week we had a discussion with our students about how they could use their understanding of the four levels of development to help themselves become better readers. We talked about our 30-minute "Whole School Read" time that we participate in each morning. We had the children come up with scenarios of what it would look like if someone were operating at each of the four levels.
>
> Students said persons at Level D would be using reading time each morning to really practice reading. They wouldn't have to have an adult directly with them at all times; they would keep on task simply because they know what is expected of them. They would read and re-read sections of their book because they know that by doing so they will become better readers. The motivation would be internal. They wouldn't be wasting any time watching the teacher in hopes of being specially noticed as "someone

who was reading," and they wouldn't rely on an adult to keep then on task. Instead they would be reading in an effort to become the best reader that they could be.

The children discussed further that Level D is where people take the initiative to do things that are truly going to pay off for them. At this level, people *motivate themselves* to work and achieve. People at this level feel good about themselves because they experience improvement, which they understand is a result of choices they have consciously made.

It is amazing to see the results of discussions such as these. That night, without any suggestion or prompting on my part, our poorest reader in the class went home and read his reader over and over again. Although his parents are kind people, they haven't understood the importance of nightly reading for their child despite many conversations with us. That night they watched as their little boy independently read and re-read his reader. Both the parents and little boy could see the dramatic improvement in his ability to read. They experienced the powerful impact that internal desire, coupled with one night of true effort, could have on someone's skill at reading. He came back to school the next day bursting with pride and determination to practice more and more so that he could move on to a new, more difficult reader.

For additional cases of how the hierarchy promotes learning in reading, mathematics, spelling, physical education, and other areas, see "Samples of Hierarchies for Promoting Learning" (Marshall, 2005g).

Focus on Internal Motivation

Marshall maintains that although humans are influenced by many factors, all true motivation emanates from within a person. We hear an outstanding speaker, are motivated to take action, and then refer to the person who prompted our action as a great motivator. Technically speaking, however, the person only stimulated or influenced us. In both thought and speech, our language is such that we simply do not refer to people as "stimulators." We call them "motivators" and refer to what they do as "motivation."

Stimulators can be very influential, however. Few people are born with an innate desire to consider the effect of their actions on others, but they learn to do so when stimulated by role models who prompt them to reflect on their own behavior. In that manner, they learn to share and show consideration for others.

External motivation is in effect when we behave to avoid discomfort or gain the approval of others. In the past, external motivation was dominant in classrooms, as evident in teachers' directing, cajoling, admonishing, criticizing, and using rewards and punishment. Marshall believes those external approaches do not produce the results intended but only lead to stress and poor relations in the classroom.

Twenty-Five Tactics to Stimulate Students to Behave Responsibly

To help students increase their reliance on internal motivation, Marshall suggests a number of tactics teachers can use to stimulate students to behave responsibly and put forth effort to learn. Here are 25 of them:

1. *Think and speak in a positive manner.* If we behave in a positive manner, we reduce stress, improve relationships, and help our students become more successful.

2. *Use the power of choice.* By calling on students to make choices, we help them move away from seeing themselves as victims of life events. This promotes self-control and responsibility. Consider offering your students a number of choices in school activities, including homework. Doing so promotes positive changes in behavior.

3. *Emphasize the reflective process.* Encourage students to ask themselves questions about the behavior they are choosing at a particular time. Reflective questioning jump-starts the thinking process. When students ask themselves "what?" and "how?" their alertness and interest increase.

4. *Control the conversation by asking questions.* One way for the teacher to control and direct conversations is to ask questions. (In this case, *control* refers to the conversation, not the student's behavior.) When someone asks you a question, there is a natural inclination to answer it. The person who does the asking controls the conversation or situation. If you find yourself in a reactive mode, you can regain control by asking a question of your own. For example, suppose a student asks you, "Why do we have to do this assignment?" Instead of answering, redirect the conversation by simply asking "Do you feel there is another way we can learn this information more easily?" When students complain, you will likely get good results by asking "What can I do to improve the situation, and what can you do?"

5. *Create curiosity.* Much of the learning we do on our own occurs because of curiosity, a very powerful motivator. Marshall suggests presenting a problem or a challenge to students and allowing them to grapple with it at the beginning of a lesson. Their involvement in attempting to figure something out will engender curiosity and internal motivation.

6. *Create desire to know.* Allow some time at the beginning of each lesson to talk about what the lesson offers. Students always want to know what's in it for them. Point out how new knowledge, skills, and insights can make life more enjoyable. Also show students how the new knowledge can help them solve problems, make better decisions, get along better with others, and live life more effectively.

7. *Use acknowledgment and recognition.* Acknowledgment and recognition help students feel affirmed and validated. Such a simple comment as "I see you did well on that" fosters reflection and feelings of competence, as does a comment such as "Evelyn raises an interesting question, one that applies to what we've been exploring."

8. *Encourage students.* Let students know that you believe they can accomplish the task before them, especially when they make mistakes. A word of encouragement following a mistake is worth more than a great deal of praise after a success. Emphasize that learning is a process and no one can learn something and be perfect at the same time. Doing something in a particular way and not being successful is a valuable way of learning. It should be seen as a learning experience, not as a failure. (For more, see Marshall, 2005f, "Reducing Perfectionism.")

9. *Use collaboration.* Generally speaking, collaborative learning is a better teaching tactic than is competition, which is a great motivator for improving performance

but not for learning. Competing with others is not effective for youngsters who never reach the "winner's circle." Consider allowing students to work together, preferably in pairs, which works well for shy students. (See Marshall, 2005d, "Collaboration for Quality Learning.")

   10. *Get yourself excited.* You can't expect others to get excited about what you are teaching if you are not excited about it yourself. Select worthwhile topics, and show enthusiasm for them. When you lecture or lead directed lessons, use a little more animation than when you are conversing, facilitating, or reviewing.

   11. *Foster interpersonal relationships.* Connecting with your students on a one-on-one basis is extremely valuable, as is helping them connect with each other one on one. Relationships are extremely important to young people. One good method for improving relationships is to have students work in pairs at an activity called Think, Pair, and Share concerning what they have learned in the lesson. The pairs are changed frequently to allow all students to interact personally with the other students in the class.

   12. *Use variety.* Variety spices up segments of the curriculum that students might otherwise find tedious. A myriad of visual, auditory, and manipulative techniques can be employed in teaching: showing charts, cartoons, models, selected parts of films, videos, DVDs, PowerPoint creations, and overhead transparencies; listening to music, recording music, rapping, creating verse, creating rhythms, and doing physical movements; enacting the roles of characters in stories or events; and participating in large-group discussions, case studies, and projects with small groups or buddies.

   13. *Stress responsibility rather than rules.* For behaviors you expect in class, consider calling them "responsibilities," not "rules." If you find that any of the responsibilities you expect of students are actually a procedure rather than a matter of personal conduct, teach the appropriate procedure and have students practice until they can do it correctly. When you write and post rules or responsibilities, state them in positive terms.

   14. *See situations as challenges, not problems.* By helping students view situations as challenges, rather than problems, we help them learn to deal better with what life brings. Discuss how adversity can serve as a catalyst to help us become better, stronger, wiser, and more capable in all life matters.

   15. *Use listening to influence others.* The more we listen to other people, the more influence we seem to have on them. Teach students how to listen attentively to each other. One activity Marshall suggests is to have students listen to each other in pairs and then pretend they are doing the talking for the other person.

   16. *Use caution in challenging students' ideas.* Very few people like to have their ideas and beliefs challenged. It tends to put them on the defensive. Instead of challenging, ask students questions such as "How did you come to that interesting conclusion?" and "An alternative point of view is (such and such). Have you ever considered that viewpoint?"

   17. *Avoid telling.* Seldom do students like being told what to do, which they perceive as criticism or an attempt to control. If Josh states an opinion you consider questionable, rather than tell him he is mistaken, you might use a reflective question stated as if you were curious, such as "What would be the long-term effect of doing that?" or "Is there any other way this could be handled? What would a responsible action look like?"

18. *Raise your likability level.* Most teachers want students to like them. They will do so if you relate to them in a friendly manner as social equals and provide them attention, encouragement, empowerment, positivity, and choice.

19. *Empower by building on successes.* The road to success for students moves them ahead based on their assets, not their shortcomings. The more they are successful, the more they are willing to put effort into areas needing improvement. This is especially true for students at risk, who have negative perceptions of their achievement and therefore of the value of school in general.

20. *Nurture students' brains.* Marian Diamond and Janet Hopson, specialists in mammalian brains and authors of *Magic Trees of the Mind: How to Nurture Your Child's Intelligence, Creativity, and Healthy Emotions from Birth through Adolescence* (1998), offer important advice to teachers. They assert that students learn better when teachers do the following: Provide a steady source of positive emotional support, stimulate all the senses (though not necessarily all at the same time), maintain an atmosphere free of undue pressure and stress but suffused with a degree of pleasurable intensity, present a series of novel challenges that are neither too easy nor too difficult, allow students to select many of their instructional activities (as each brain is unique), offer opportunities for students to assess the results of their learning and modify it as they think best, provide an enjoyable atmosphere that promotes exploration and fun of learning, and allow time for students to reflect and let their brains assimilate new information.

21. *Emphasize the four classical virtues.* The four classical virtues are prudence, temperance, justice, and fortitude. *Prudence* is making proper choices without doing anything too rash. *Temperance* is remaining moderate in all things, including human passions and emotions. *Justice* refers to ensuring fair outcomes, based on honesty. *Fortitude* is showing courage in pursuit of the right path, despite the risks, with strength of conviction.

22. *Tutor a few students every day.* Marshall says tutoring students one on one is the easiest, quickest, and most effective way of establishing personal relationships with them.

23. *Hold frequent classroom meetings.* Classroom meetings provide excellent opportunities for all members of the class to work together. These meetings are useful in resolving challenges that involve the whole class and in helping individual students deal with certain problems. (See Marshall, 2005c, "Classroom Meetings.")

24. *Resolve conflict in a constructivist manner.* When people are involved in conflict, ask each of them what they are willing to do to resolve the situation. Get across the notion that we can't force other people to change. We can only influence them to change through what we do and through changes we are willing to make in ourselves.

25. *Establish trust.* Relationships with others are extremely important to most students. Relationships with trusted teachers motivate students and provide emotional security. To establish optimal trust, employ the three principles of positivity, choice, and reflection.

How to Intervene When Misbehavior Occurs

Although we can control student behavior temporarily, we cannot control how or what students think or the way they want to behave. We must recognize that teachers very rarely bring about genuine behavior change through force. But when teachers *empower* students with better ways of conducting themselves, classroom behavior becomes more self-directed and considerate.

You have seen how Marshall's hierarchy of social development provides a meaningful reference for students to identify their level of behavior, reflect on it, and move toward a more responsible level. Let's suppose a student behaves inappropriately and the teacher needs to intervene. How should the intervention be done? The following process comes from Marshall's suggestions, which assume students understand the hierarchy and its relevance in the classroom. The three intervention steps are normally employed in the following order:

1. *Use an unobtrusive tactic.* Suppose Syong is annoying Neri. Before saying anything to Syong, prompt her to stop by using an unobtrusive technique, such as facial expression, eye contact, hand signal, moving near to Syong, changing voice tone, thanking students for working, saying "Excuse me," or asking students for help. Marshall (2001a, pp. 90–93) offers 22 unobtrusive visual, verbal, and kinetic techniques that are useful at this juncture.

2. *Check for understanding.* If the unobtrusive tactic doesn't stop Syong's misbehavior, check to see if she understands the level of her chosen behavior. Use a neutral, unemotional tone of voice and phrase the question as "Syong, which level are you choosing?" or "Syong, reflect on the level you have chosen." No mention is made of the nature of the behavior or what Syong is doing but only the level of chosen behavior. This helps prevent the natural self-defensiveness that often leads to confrontation. Without the hierarchy—which separates the student from the student's inappropriate behavior—a teacher may ask, "What are you doing?" This too often leads to a confrontational situation, especially if Syong responds "Nothing." However, asking "On what level is that behavior?" prompts not only acknowledgment but also self-evaluation. You are not attacking Syong; you are separating her as a person from inappropriate behavior, something educators often talk about but find difficult to do.

3. *Use guided choice.* This procedure can stop the disruption, provide the student a responsibility-producing activity to encourage self-reflection, and allow the teacher to return promptly to the lesson. When you provide choices, do so by asking students which of two or three choices they prefer, rather than by telling them they must select one of the choices you offer.

Marshall (2001a, pp. 102–104) suggests several other options for various grade levels. In the example just explored, Syong has probably stopped misbehaving and has selected a more responsible way of behaving. However, if her behavior continues to be unacceptable, move to *authority without punishment* by eliciting (rather than imposing) a procedure for Syong to help herself. The conversation with Syong would be something like the following:

> You realize that every time you choose to act on an inappropriate level, you are allowing yourself to be a victim of your impulses. Do you really want to be a victim? If not, see if you can come up with some procedure so that when you get that impulse again you will be able to redirect it. When you have a procedure to rely on, you are in control and not a victim of your impulses.

Working with Syong individually during a lesson will take time away from the lesson. For that reason, you might plan to work with her at a more convenient time. For now, place an essay form on Syong's desk while quietly offering three choices, such as "Do you prefer to complete the form in your seat, in the rear of the room, or in the office?" The prepared form is one on which Syong writes about the following:

What did I do? (acknowledgment)

What can I do to prevent its happening again? (choice)

What will I do? (commitment)

Guided choice options should be adjusted in accordance with the grade level, the individual student, and the class. Before leaving the classroom, the student is asked two questions: (1) "Do you know the reason the form was given to you?" and (2) "Do you feel it is personal?" Students understand that the form is given because when they behave on an unacceptable level, the teacher needs to quickly resolve the disruption and return to the lesson. Teacher authority is used in a nonpunitive way.

After the student responds to the second question, the teacher (of grades six and above), asks, "What would you like me to do with the form?" Students generally respond, "Throw it away." Marshall's approach is to tear the form up and place it in the wastepaper basket in front of the student as a means of allowing the student to leave the class without any negative feelings.

It is very unlikely that after having completed the essay form, Syong will continue to bother others. Even so, teachers always want to know what to do in case a student continues to misbehave. Marshall suggests the following:

4. *Make a self-diagnostic referral.* Before moving to a more in-depth reflective form, Syong is given a second essay form. However, if and when the essay form loses its effectiveness, then a self-diagnostic referral is given. This form contains items such as the following:

- Describe the problem that led to writing this.
- Identify the level of behavior.

- Explain why this level of behavior is not acceptable.
- On what level should a person act in order to be socially responsible?
- If you had acted on an acceptable level, what would have happened?
- List three solutions that would help you act more responsibly.

Marshall advises keeping the completed referrals on file for the entire year, as they might be used in discussions with parents or administrators.

5. *Give an additional self-diagnostic referral.* If Syong continues to bother other students, assign an additional referral to complete, in the same manner as the first. Then mail a copy of the first and second referrals to Syong's parents or guardian, together with a brief note explaining the problem.

6. *Give a final self-diagnostic referral.* If Syong continues to behave on an unacceptable level, assign a third and final self-diagnostic referral. Mail a copy along with copies of the first two referrals and both notes to parents. The final note indicates to the parents that you have exhausted all positive means of fostering social responsibility and will refer future disruptions to the administration. Marshall points out that in all these cases, it is the student who has identified the problem and proposed positive solutions. All the teacher does is write brief notes to parents and mail them copies of the student's self-diagnostic referrals. The student has done most of the thinking and planning, which gives ownership to the student—a necessary ingredient for lasting change. Marshall notes that the last few steps rarely, if ever, need to be used.

IN SUMMARY

Two approaches were presented for helping students develop a greater sense of personal responsibility for their behavior in school and elsewhere. Ed Ford's Responsible Thinking Process emphasizes helping students to make plans for getting what they want in life without infringing on the rights of others. Marvin Marshall's Raise Responsibility System directs student attention to four levels of social development and encourages them to strive for Level D, in which they take the initiative to behave in ways they know are correct and proper. Both approaches assume that students have an inherent desire to be seen as ethical, trustworthy, and in charge of their lives. Both make it clear that teachers cannot force responsibility but can influence student thinking so students clarify responsible goals for themselves and create personal plans for their achievement.

REFERENCES

Diamond, M., and Hopson, J. 1998. *Magic trees of the mind: How to nurture your child's intelligence, creativity, and healthy emotions from birth through adolescence.* New York: Dutton.

Ford, E. 1999. *Discipline for home and school, Book Two* (revised and expanded). Scottsdale, AZ: Brandt.

Ford, E. 2003. *Discipline for home and school, Book One* (3rd edition). Scottsdale, AZ: Brandt.

Ford, E. 2004. *Discipline for home and school, fundamentals.* Scottsdale, AZ: Brandt.

Ford, E. 2006a. A school discipline program that is radically different from other classroom management programs, traditional classroom discipline programs, or any school behavior management program. www.responsiblethinking.com.

Ford, E. 2006b. How the Responsible Thinking Process works. www.responsiblethinking.com.

Ford, E., and Venetis, G. 2006. Teaching respect using RTP. www.responsiblethinking.com.

Marshall, M. 1998. *Fostering social responsibility.* Bloomington, IN: Phi Delta Kappa.

Marshall, M. 2001a. *Discipline without stress, punishments, or rewards: How teachers and parents promote responsibility and learning.* Los Alamitos, CA: Piper Press.

Marshall, M. 2001b. *Promoting Responsibility and Learning: The Monthly Newsletter.* www.MarvinMarshall.com.

Marshall, M. 2005a. A letter worth reading. www.marvinmarshall.com/aletterworthreading.html.

Marshall, M. 2005b. A principal's experience. www.marvinmarshall.com/principal.htm.

Marshall, M. 2005c. Classroom meetings. www.disciplinewithoutstress.com/sample_chapters.html.

Marshall, M. 2005d. Collaboration for quality learning. www.disciplinewithoutstress.com/sample_chapters.html.

Marshall, M. 2005e. Promoting positivity, choice, and reflection. www.MarvinMarshall.com/promoting_positivity.htm.

Marshall, M. 2005f. Reducing perfectionism. www.disciplinewithoutstress.com/sample_chapters.html.

Marshall, M. 2005g. Samples of hierarchies for promoting learning. www.marvinmarshall.com/hierarchy.htm.

McGregor, D. 1960. *The human side of enterprise.* New York: McGraw-Hill.

Using Special Tactics

Using Special Discipline Tactics to Help Students with Neurological-Based Behavior

A special set of tactics is needed for helping students with neurological-based behavior (NBB) conduct themselves in an advantageous manner. Due to differences in the way their brains work, these students behave in somewhat unpredictable ways and do not respond well to many of the discipline tactics that are successful with other students. A number of effective tactics are known, however, and using them can help make classroom life happier and more productive for everyone.

Chapter Preview

This chapter reviews the nature of neurological-based behavior (NBB) and presents tactics for helping students with various mental health diagnoses make behavior choices that lead to greater school success. The tactics involve understanding those students and their behavior, relating to them on a personal level, using the power of positive images, and teaching self-control. Emphasis is placed on working with students with attention-deficit hyperactivity disorder (ADHD) and those who have sensory processing disorders.

THE MEANING, EFFECTS, AND INCIDENCE OF NEUROLOGICAL-BASED BEHAVIOR

Virtually all students behave inappropriately at times, especially when tired, bored, provoked, threatened, or in a boisterous mood. Misbehavior associated with these causes can be managed effectively with the strategies and tactics presented in earlier chapters.

Collaboration by Paula Cook

This chapter has been organized and presented in close collaboration with Paula Cook, who teaches in a highly specialized program for students with behavioral, emotional, and psychiatric disorders with mild to moderate cognitive impairment. Her responsibilities include curriculum modifications and adaptations, individualized educational planning, advocacy, behavior management, social skills, and life skills education. She also teaches at Red River Community College and the University of Manitoba. She has made numerous presentations at regional, national, and international conferences and was a 2003 recipient of the Council for Exceptional Children's Outstanding Educator of the Year award.

Cook urges teachers to keep in mind the acronym ART when working with students who learn differently and behave unusually. ART refers to Attitude, Relationships, and Time—an *attitude* of helpfulness, determination, and acceptance; *relationships* that result from connecting with students personally; and *time* sufficient for students to assimilate information and skills they are learning and to let the teacher–student relationship develop and grow.

Cook is author of *Sensory Integration Dysfunction: A Layperson's Guide* (2004b); *Behaviour, Learning and Teaching: Applied Studies in FAS/FAE* (2004a); *Rage: A Layperson's Guide to What to Do When Someone Begins to Rage* (2005); and contributing author of "NBB: The Special Challenges of Neurological-Based Behavior," Chapter 3 in *Building Classroom Discipline* (Charles, 2008).

However, not all misbehavior originates from familiar causes. In some cases, students behave erratically or inconsistently because of the way their brains function—differences caused by factors such as chemical imbalances, congenital brain differences, brain injuries, and brain diseases. These students are identified as having *neurological-based behavior (NBB),* and they typically show greater than average levels of inattention, hyperactivity, impulsivity, emotionality, anxiety, mood swings, inconsistency of responses, withdrawal, and episodes of rage (Cook, 2004a; Hall and Hall, 2003; Papolos and Papolos, 2002). Because neurological differences are often difficult to detect, many students are not properly diagnosed with NBB for several years after the onset of symptoms (Papolos and Papolos, 2002). Even then, however, teachers know something is producing behavior that is erratic and unpredictable and that students cannot control themselves in a normal manner (Kranowitz, 1998).

The incidence of NBB is greater than most educators imagine. About one in five students exhibits one or more mental health conditions that affect behavior in school (DeAngelis, 2004). As many as one in ten may suffer from a serious emotional disturbance (National Institute of Mental Health, 2005). *Attention-deficit hyperactivity disorder (ADHD)* is the most commonly diagnosed mental health disorder in children, affecting 3 to 5 percent of school-age children (National Institute of Mental Health, 2005). Diagnosis of a single individual often reveals a constellation of mental health symptoms (Feldman, 2004).

Mental health disorders are biological in nature. They cannot be overcome through willpower and are not related to a person's character or intelligence. Most can be treated effectively through a combination of pharmacological and psychosocial support (National Institute of Mental Health, 2005). Types of disorders that teachers are likely to encounter include learning disabilities (LD), attention-deficit hyperactivity disorder (ADHD), sensory processing disabilities (SPD), and fetal alcohol spectrum disorder (FASD).

Occasionally, teachers will have contact with students with other neurological conditions, such as generalized anxiety disorder, autism, explosive behavior disorder, paranoia, obsessive-compulsive disorder, substance dependence, phobias, eating disorders, and Tourette's syndrome. Treatment for these disorders varies. Appropriate medication is of great help in many cases, but it is also likely at times to have adverse effects on students' attention, memory, abstract thinking, and organizational skills (Davidson, 2002). (If you wish to learn more about any of these diagnoses, you can find them discussed at length on the Internet.)

TACTICS FOR TEACHERS

This chapter presents advice from selected authorities whose work is related to or has implications for NBB. Included are the following: (1) Dave Hingsburger's concerns about the improper use of power in relating to students with NBB; (2) Marvin Marshall's advice on the use of positive images; (3) Joyce Pickering's commentaries on teaching proper behavior to students who are experiencing delays in developing self-control; (4) Tom Daly's advice on working with students with ADHD; (5) Michele Mitchell's advice on working with students who have sensory processing disorders; and (6) Paula Cook's suggestions on how to deal with episodes of rage.

Dave Hingsburger on Power and Mindset

Dave Hingsburger, a Canadian psychologist and therapist, provides direct services to people with disabilities and consults with schools, parents, practitioners, and agencies on problematic behavior. He lectures extensively and has given keynote addresses at national and international conferences. He also operates Diverse City Press, a publishing house that specializes in materials for working with people who are developmentally disabled. He offers important observations concerning the use of power by teachers of students with NBB. Most of his suggestions have implications for teachers and students in the mainstream as well.

Hingsburger believes that teachers who work with students who are developmentally disabled should seriously analyze the attitudes they (like most others) hold toward people with disabilities and how to help them. He is very uncomfortable with the use of power and the effects it has in interpersonal relations. He says those who work in human care have enormous power over the people they are trying to help, although they may not be fully aware of it. The problem lies in how they use that power. All too often, they try to force students to behave in certain so-called normal ways. Sometimes, they are successful in doing so, but not often; in many cases, the use of power sets up unnecessary barriers between teachers and students.

In his book *Power Tools* (2000a), Hingsburger explains that most teachers don't realize or take into account the power they have, how they exercise it, and the effects it has on children. He stresses that teachers are responsible for the results of power usage even when they mean well. He says, "This little book is aimed at getting you to think about what you do on a daily basis with those within your care" (p. 5). He urges teachers and caregivers to understand that people with disabilities have their own perspectives on life and the world and that it is self-defeating to try continually to get them to see what may be perceived as the right way of doing things. He says it is important for teachers to help students with disabilities learn how to disagree with others respectfully. Listen to their arguments. Give them time to formulate their points of view. Remember that the matters they are involved in concern their lives.

Teachers do best when they accept students as they are. Hingsburger insists it is not teachers' job to make people over in their image. Trying to do so will only produce frustration and battles of will, leading to more use of force. It is best to recognize that people with disabilities need to discover their own way in the world. A major role of teachers is to help with that discovery.

In his book *First Contact* (2000b), Hingsburger advises teachers to see students who seem different from the norm as simply having another unique perspective on life, frequently not the same as teachers' unique perspectives. This difference doesn't prevent teachers and students from sharing emotions, points of view, thoughts, ideas, and ideals. Such sharing becomes much easier when teachers truly realize it is all right for students to be different.

Marvin Marshall on the Value of Positive Images

Marvin Marshall is the creator of the Raise Responsibility System, featured in Chapter 9. (To review his many credentials and accomplishments, please refer to his biographical sketch there.) One of the things Marshall emphasizes in working with students is making heavy use of positive images as concerns personalities, capabilities, and behavior. This practice is powerful and especially useful for teachers who work with students with NBB.

Marshall (2003) maintains that body, mind, and emotions fully intermingle and that each is understood in terms of the others. Feelings, learning, and physical behavior all work in conjunction and are inseparable. A change in behavior is as much emotion based as it is cognition based—that is, it has as much to do with feelings as with knowledge. The human mind thinks not so much through the use of simple language but through the heavy use of pictures, images, and visions. One of the best ways to influence behavior for the better is to empower students with positive images, a view set forth in the teachings of Douglas McGregor (1960), William Glasser (1998), and Stephen Covey (2004). In teaching students to conduct themselves appropriately, we should make use of positive images of what responsible people do, as opposed to images of punishment for irresponsible behavior.

Joyce Pickering on Teaching Self-Control

Joyce S. Pickering is executive director of the Shelton School, a Montessori school located in Dallas, Texas. The following material is adapted from her article entitled "Discipline—Developing Self-Control," published in the Summer 2003 issue of *Montessori Life.*

Pickering points out that it is not until the age of 3 that our neurological systems mature sufficiently to permit us to be cooperative and wait for what we want, both of which are necessary for self-control. At age 3, parents and caregivers can begin to establish reasonable boundaries on behavior. As students accept those boundaries, they undertake the process of developing self-control.

Unfortunately, not all children progress in this normative manner. Some of them experience delays in the development of motor, language, and speech skills. Some experience difficulties with attention, inhibition, temper, and oppositional behavior. These difficulties can last for many years and often lead to disruptive behavior in school.

Children with delayed development can be helped toward self-control by directly teaching them what self-control involves. This teaching must be done with love and support for the child. The following suggestions, useful with all students, are especially appropriate for students with behavioral issues:

- Make expectations very clear to students, and ensure that teaching is consistent with ample repetition.
- Direct teaching is used to teach specific target behaviors, such as how to greet visitors, make way for someone to pass, ask one's pardon, walk in line, ask for something, and say "please" and "thank-you." The behavior is explained and modeled by the teacher, with students replicating what they see the teacher do and say.
- Following direct teaching, students are given work to do under the direction of the teacher, who observes student work closely.
- During this time, the teacher stops doing anything for students that they can do for themselves. Students are allowed to settle their own differences if they can; otherwise the teacher helps them.
- Specific correction is provided when students fail to do any of the expected tasks correctly. They are shown how to do them once more and are asked to perform them in the correct way.
- Should students continue to behave inappropriately despite knowing what they are supposed to do—such as repeating the misbehavior or yelling or throwing tantrums—they may be sent to a "quiet chair" for a time and given an explanation for what is being done: "Johnny, we do not yell out in class. Please sit in this chair and get control. You may come rejoin us when you can talk nicely in your own voice." If Johnny gets out of the chair, take him back and explain again that he must stay there until he is in control. You may have to sit with him at this point. If he stays too long, you can ask in a friendly manner, "Are you ready to join us now?"

Pickering advises that certain kinds of misbehavior are best corrected through having students do *repetitive behavior*. For example, when students slam doors, they can be asked to repeat the behavior properly. The teaching procedure is as follows:

- Show the student the correct behavior you expect.
- Tell him or her reason for the repetition, such as "We open and close doors quietly so we won't disturb others."
- Indicate how many times the repetition must be done. You might say, for example, "Do it correctly three times." Doing repetitions helps the child feel the expected behavior.
- Finally, ask the student, "Why did I have you close the door properly three times?"

Other types of corrections include reminders, removal of privileges, and behavior modification through reinforcement. In all cases, the teacher must provide the following, as necessary:

- Teacher presence and support in the learning environment
- Structure for behavior—clear expectations, modeling, reenactment, reteaching
- Direct assistance on attention, focus, and concentration
- Modification in instruction as needed by students who have sensory or learning disabilities

Attention-Deficit Hyperactivity Disorder (ADHD): Nature and Incidence

ADHD appears in three subtypes, with the characteristics shown in the following list (Finstad, 2006). The symptoms of this condition usually appear before age 7, although they may occur later in association with brain injuries, and typically last for years or even a lifetime.

ADHD-1: *Primarily Inattentive*

- Does not appear to listen or has difficulty sustaining attention
- Is easily distracted and forgetful in daily activities
- Makes many careless mistakes
- Struggles to comply with instructions
- Has difficulty with organization
- Avoids or dislikes tasks requiring sustained mental effort

ADHD-H1: *Primarily Hyperactive and Impulsive*

- Fidgets with hands or feet or squirms in chair
- Has difficulty remaining seated; runs about or climbs excessively
- Talks excessively

- Has difficulty waiting or taking turns
- Interrupts or intrudes upon others
- Blurts out answers before questions have been completed

ADHD-C: Combined
- Meets both sets of attention and hyperactive/impulsive criteria

Tom Daly on Discipline for Students with ADHD

Tom Daly is a teacher and adjunct professor in San Diego, California, who has worked for many years on a daily basis with students who have serious ADHD issues. He has developed and refined a number of tactics for helping his students enjoy greater success. He has shared those ideas with thousands of beginning and experienced teachers in more than 10 countries. His ideas and suggestions are set forth in his book *The ADHD Solution for Teachers: How to Turn Any Disruptive Child into Your Best Student* (2004), also available in condensed version on CD. Mr. Daly's website is www.adhdsolutions.com.

Daly says that teachers who experience behavioral issues with students with ADHD must first realize that the solution to the problem lies within themselves, not in their students. Once they accept that fact, they are ready to begin learning how to work more effectively with students to improve behavior, increase success, promote respect for authority figures, and confirm for students that education is their ticket to success in life.

Daly says that when students with ADHD misbehave, they are actually sending coded messages to the teacher. Usually, that message is "Reach me," meaning they are asking for a personal connection. Daly states that if you can reach your students in a likeable way while holding their respect, you will eliminate 90 percent of behavior problems.

To reach out effectively, he says, teachers must stop thinking in terms of confronting or controlling students' behavior and turn their attention to replacing unacceptable behavior with acceptable behavior. That is best done in a manner akin to coaching or personal training. You first establish a personal connection with students and then progressively coach them in how to behave appropriately. The "connect, then coach" approach should be used any time you see students displaying annoying little behaviors, such as pencil-tapping and blurting out. That is not a time to ignore behavior but a time to move closer to the student, literally and figuratively. Daly points out that people become good, responsible adults not because someone rewards them for being good but because they have made a real connection with a teacher or another responsible adult. Making that connection, he says, is the key to transforming students' lives.

Teachers' ability to make good connections with their students increases as they endeavor to know the students' world, including with whom students associate, their chief concerns, and their personal likes and dislikes. This knowledge gives teachers a foothold into the students' world, which plays a pivotal role in student success. Daly suggests a number of tactics for teachers to use in forging better connections with students:

1. *Walk and talk with your ADHD students as frequently as you can.* Walk along with them casually and talk about anything at all. The topic doesn't matter. When students go on casual walks with you, they act differently than they do in a class situation. For one thing, they stop seeing you as an adversary. If you don't try to pry information from them, they will open up and divulge more and will often tell you why they act out in class.

2. *Find ways to get your students to follow your directions quickly and quietly the first time they are given.* Daly devotes an entire section of his book to explaining how this can be done. Students' following directions eliminates headaches, prevents battles, and makes your job much more enjoyable. More important, it has a major impact on students' futures. Nowadays, says Daly, you see kids everywhere, in all walks of life, refusing to follow directions—a habit that predisposes them to failure in school. Teachers have to take up that burden and teach students to follow directions the first time they are given.

3. *Get physically closer to your students—even if you are afraid to or don't feel like it.* No matter how inappropriately particular students are behaving, your physical proximity can work wonders. You may not need to do anything more than sit beside them from time to time in a relaxed manner. Daly tells us to think of physical proximity in the proactive sense, rather than the reactive. If Jason knows he can get you to react in a dramatic way by acting out, he can take control of you and the class. Students with ADHD have histories of behaving in certain ways. They are experienced with ADHD behaviors, while you are inexperienced in dealing with them, so they have the upper hand. They will often try to play your for all they can. But if you can *act* instead of *react,* they will never get the chance. Daly claims that 95 percent of teachers' success in managing students with ADHD has to do with what they do before a problem manifests itself. Getting closer to students is an easy step to take and the best place to begin.

Daly assures teachers that the foregoing suggestions will work, but this way of relating with students won't happen by itself. Teachers have to make it happen. A good way to begin is by showing enthusiasm for teaching and for the students you are helping. Daly says to think back to your own school days and see if you can remember a teacher who scowled at you and another teacher who seemed happy to see you each day. You can probably remember how much happier you were around the teacher who was friendly toward you.

If students with ADHD are to succeed in life, they must also learn how to be more likeable and show respect and appreciation for authority figures. Students need to like authority figures, and they need to be liked by authority figures. This liking and being liked is essential to students' success because students will follow the lead of teachers they like and respect. We should make it clear to students that we want to like and respect them, as well, and that it is human nature to try to help those we like.

Finally, Daly emphasizes that teacher attitude is the key to turning disruptive students into models of cooperation, productivity, and good behavior. While a positive outlook does not instantaneously change the personality of a difficult student, it does affect the student's innate desire to do well, and most will do so naturally.

Most underachieving kids want to be successful in school, even if their behavior doesn't indicate it. Send the message to students, administrators, parents, and (most importantly) yourself that "I care enough about these kids and my own happiness to roll up my sleeves and find a better way of helping them." When others sense this message emanating from you, they will give you the immediate respect that comes to those willing to go the extra mile. But you need to know what you want to achieve, make a plan for getting it, and resolve to make it happen in your classroom.

In summary, Daly emphasizes the following:

- Make real connections with your students and help them forge life-changing relationships with other mentors and authority figures like yourself. (Do this, and you will eliminate most of the disruptive behavior in your classroom.)
- Listen to your students and watch their misbehavior so you can decipher what they are trying to convey to you.
- Get your students to follow your directions quickly and quietly, the first time given.
- Divert and redirect the energy of students with ADHD. (Failure to do so, Daly says, is like standing in front of a runaway train.)
- Work toward getting all your students, even the worst behaved, to see that success in school is their ticket to success in life.

Sensory Processing Disorder: Nature and Incidence

Sensory processing disorder (also referred to as *sensory integration dysfunction*) is an inability to accurately receive and organize information taken in by the senses. Imagine that we are sitting in a classroom where our ears bring in a multitude of different sounds; our eyes note faces, physical ambience, and movement; our noses take in various odors; our skin experiences pressure and textures; our bodies sense their positions in space; and our internal organs provide information from inside us. From that bombardment of information, our brains selectively organize images that are pertinent at any given time and try to make sense of them.

But for some people—those with sensory processing disorder—the normal noises of a classroom may sound like a freight train blasting past. The clamor is so great that the teacher cannot be heard or understood. It is impossible for the student to focus attention and concentrate, and his or her coordination and body control may be affected (Morris, 2002). In these situations, the brain does not make efficient or correct use of the information. Sometimes it perceives too much, and sometimes too little. Some people with this disorder can function normally in most circumstances, but others find that their disorder interferes substantially with normal living and learning.

One does not grow out of this condition, which affects learning and the ability to have normal relationships, nor does it go away on its own. However, there are certain accommodations teachers can make in the classroom, as noted in the following information from Michele Mitchell. In addition, treatment by an occupational therapist can help the individual function more effectively.

Michele Mitchell on Discipline for Students with Sensory Processing Disorder

Michele Mitchell, an occupational therapist, maintains a website that provides comprehensive information about sensory processing disorder (SPD) along with suggested materials and activities for working with students with SPD. Much of the following information is adapted from Mitchell's (2006) article "Problem Behavior in the Classroom: Dealing with Children and Sensory Processing Disorders at School." The article is posted on her website: www.sensory-processing-disorder.com.

For many years, Mitchell has worked with children and adults in group homes, day rehabilitation centers, sensory integration clinics, preschools, school systems, and psychiatric hospitals. She reaffirms that problem behavior in the classroom is one of the most difficult aspects of teachers' jobs. Many teachers deal unknowingly with students who have sensory processing disorder and who are usually disruptive. Among the inabilities that afflict those students are the following:

- Inability to focus
- Inability to take in, organize, and sequence information properly
- Inability to read social and environmental clues
- Inability to sit or stand still long enough to benefit from class activities
- Inability to handle a day at school without excessive fatigue
- Inability to perform or stay on tasks

Teachers should consider chronic student misbehavior to be a "red flag," warning that something might be going wrong, neurologically, for a particular student. If you experience misbehavior that seems outside the norm, look for these indications that your student might need further assessment:

- Avoidance of certain activities, such as messy play, movement experiences, playground equipment, and of certain sounds, smells, or tastes
- Clumsiness, lack of coordination, crashing and banging into objects
- Difficulty with transitions, stopping one activity and starting another
- Difficulties with social interactions and relating to peers
- Inability to adjust to and meet challenges that arise, such as asking for help in solving problems
- Difficulty in maintaining an optimal arousal level for activities; energy level is too high or too low

Mitchell points out a number of things teachers can do to help children function better in the classroom. Most of these suggestions involve arrangements that can be made in advance. (For a more complete list, see Mitchell's article, cited earlier.)

Space Adjustments

- Adjust chairs, desks, and tables so students can sit with feet flat on the floor and hips bent at a 90 degree angle.

- Seat easily distracted students away from doorways and windows.
- Allow students to work in a variety of positions—lying on the floor, propped on elbows, standing at a table or easel, or lying on the side and using a clipboard.
- Use a soft, plush rug when possible to help muffle noise.
- Use a small tent or play hut with soft pillows and/or a bean bag chair for a student to use when overaroused.

Visual Adjustments

- Post a daily schedule that includes pictures.
- Use visual cues, such as words and pictures, for organizing personal belongings, containers, and shelves.
- Keep visual distractions to a minimum. Hang art projects on the wall in the hallway or on the wall behind the overhead screen so you can use the screen to cover the visual clutter when it is not needed. Keep bulletin boards simple and uncluttered, and limit the number of decorations in the room.
- Cover areas of the page the student is not currently working on to help with focus.
- Use study carrels to decrease outside stimulation.
- Use dim lighting and pastel colors. Turn off lights during quiet breaks.
- Keep memos and informational posters away from the front of the classroom so children can focus on the teacher.

Auditory Adjustments

- Use earplugs or sound-blocking headphones for students who are sensitive to or distracted by environmental noises.
- Ask the student to repeat directions back to you and demonstrate he or she understands what you say.
- Establish eye contact with the child before speaking to him or her.
- Break directions down into steps, and allow extra time for students to process them if needed.
- Warn students of any loud noises, such as bells and alarms, before they occur.

Sensory Adjustments for Lethargic Students

- Allow the students to sip on ice water in a water bottle throughout the day.
- Use bright lighting.
- Have students pat cool water on their faces as needed.
- Organize frequent breaks for students to use their big muscles—jump, hop, march in place, do sit-ups.
- Have students chew strong or flavorful sugar-free gum or suck on sugar-free candies.

Calming Adjustments for Overly Active Students

- Use low level, nonfluorescent lights.
- Allow students to listen to calming music with headphones.
- Use a soft voice, and slow down your speech and movements.

- Allow students to lie on the floor in a secluded area with weighted blankets, heavy pillows, or bean bag chairs on top of them during written work or reading.
- Push down heavily on the student's shoulders, with equal and constant pressure.
- Avoid rushing the student.
- Use students as assistants to carry books to the library, deliver notes to the office, pass out papers, sharpen pencils, and so forth.
- Allow students to use quiet fidget toys and squeeze stress balls while sitting and listening or during deskwork.
- Have students do chair push-ups (raising their body off the chair with hands next to them on their seat).

Instructional Adjustments

- Give simple step-by-step directions. Have students verbalize the steps needed to accomplish the task. Use a peer or yourself to demonstrate the task first; then ask the student to try it.
- Use a consistent approach, and allow time to practice and master the new skill.
- Model, demonstrate, and repeat as needed. Monitor progress.
- Help the student plan for each task by asking questions such as "What materials will you need?" "What will you do first?" and "What do you need to do when you are finished?"
- Help students prepare for transitions with an orderly clean-up and a consistent musical selection that indicates it is time to move on to the next activity.
- Provide a consistent, organized place to store materials when finished.

When Students Misbehave. The suggestions just mentioned make the learning environment better and reduce disruptive behavior from students with sensory processing disabilities. The following are suggestions for what the teacher should do when the student misbehaves or seems about to misbehave:

- Establish firm, clear rules. Teach students how to abide with them. When students break a rule, have them tell you what they should have done and then have them repeat the action correctly.
- Teach students about personal space. Help them learn to stay within their boundaries and out of the boundaries of others.
- Be aware of signs that indicate a student is beginning to lose control. Talk through a task or problem if the student is struggling.
- Be specific with suggestions. Make positive statements about what the student *did* accomplish, and then make suggestions for improving. Be clear and concise.
- Elicit suggestions from the student on how he or she can improve behavior in the future.

Mitchell explains that misbehavior alerts teachers to the possibility of sensory processing disorders, sometimes before parents notice anything at home. She advises teachers to analyze problem behaviors in terms of the environmental stimuli present at the time the student misbehaved, asking questions such as "What was going on? How did the student react? Did the student seem to be seeking or avoiding something in particular?" If you suspect the student might be experiencing a sensory processing disorder, talk with the head of special education, your school occupational therapist, or your site administrator, who will help you find additional resources for assisting the student. It is possible to help students learn what their bodies need, how to avoid or seek needed sensory stimuli, how to feel more in control, how to focus and learn better, and how to stop disrupting the class.

PAULA COOK ON DEALING WITH STUDENT RAGE

The Nature of Rage

Rage is manifested as an outburst of temper that occurs suddenly, with no real warning and may turn violent. Paula Cook (2005) explains that rage is not a type of neurological disorder but rather is a neurological event in which students display extreme behavior. It is often exhibited by students with NBB. The process is traumatic for everyone, and it should be understood that the student has little control over his or her behavior during an episode.

Rage is not goal oriented; rather, it is a release of built-up tension or frustration. It differs from a *tantrum*, which is goal directed with the purpose of getting something or getting somebody to do something. (Tantrums sometimes evolve into rage.) Once a rage episode has begun, there is little that can be done to stop it. The episode may only last for a few minutes, or it may continue for hours. Usually, it must run its full course, although it can be softened and controlled somewhat by teachers and other adults.

The Rage Cycle and Its Phases

The *rage cycle* is considered to consist of five phases—pre-rage, triggering, escalation, rage, and post-rage. These phases, their characteristics, and how you can help students in each of them are described in the sections that follow:

- *Phase 1. Pre-Rage.* This is the time preceding the rage, just before something triggers the rage event and sets it in motion.
- *Phase 2. Triggering.* Triggers are precipitating events that provoke episodes of rage, apparently by stimulating neurochemical changes in the brain that greatly heighten the fight/flight/freeze reactions (self-protective responses). Triggering conditions seem to appear most often in association with work transitions, sensory overload, being told "no," fatigue, frustration, confusion, hunger, central nervous system executive dysfunction, anxiety, and mood swings. For children with ADHD, triggers tend to be related to sensory and/or emotional overstimulation. For children with bipolar disorder, triggers are often related to having limits set on their behavior. In the triggering phase students may appear angry, confused, frustrated, dazed, tense, or flushed, and they may swear and use other rude language.

> *What you can do to help at this point in the rage cycle*

- Recognize that a rage episode may be forthcoming and you may not be able to prevent it.

- Understand that this is a neurological event. The student's flight/fight/freeze responses are strongly activated.
- Understand that the rage is not intentional or aimed at you personally.
- Stay calm. Use a quiet tone of voice. Do not become adversarial.
- Use short, direct phrases and nonemotional language.
- Do not question, scold, or become verbose.
- Use nonthreatening body language. Stand on an angle, off center to the student and at least a long stride away. Make sure the student can see your hands.
- Use empathetic verbal support ("It sounds like you're upset." "That would upset me too.").
- Deflect control elsewhere ("The clock says it's time to clean up." "The big rule book in the office says . . .").
- Calmly, quietly, and succinctly use logical persuasion to provide the student an alternative behavior.

- *Phase 3. Escalation.* Following the triggering, the rage may escalate mildly or rapidly. In *mild escalations,* the student may begin to get angry, call names, swear, exhibit startled verbal or physical responses, talk rapidly, increase the volume and cadence of speech, and show tension in arms, hands, and body. *Rapid escalations* are characterized by violent temper, hostility, aggressive comments ("Leave me alone! I'm going to kill you!"), profanity, flushed face, and clammy body. The student may show fists and throw objects or furniture.

What you can do to help during this phase of the rage cycle

- Stay calm.
- Ensure the safety of others by clearing them from the room or supporting them to ignore the escalation.
- If the student threatens you, walk away (but stay close enough to supervise the student).
- Calmly direct the student to a safe place (e.g., quiet room or designated area) to allow the energy to dissipate.
- When speaking to the student, use short, direct phrases and nonemotional language.
- Use body language that is nonthreatening and nonconfrontational.
- Use supportive empathy to acknowledge the student's feelings.
- Calmly, quietly and succinctly use logical persuasion to provide the student an alternative.
- Praise the student as soon as he or she begins to respond to your direction.
- Do not mention the student's inappropriate language, threats, or other behavior at this time, because he or she cannot process the information and may only become further inflamed. These matters can be addressed during a debriefing process after the student has calmed.

- *Phase 4. Rage or Meltdown.* Here, the student is caught up in the rage.

  What you can do to help during this phase of the cycle
  - Allow the student to go through the physical manifestations.
  - Do not restrain the student unless there is an immediate threat to physical safety.
  - Do not bully, question, make sarcastic comments, yell, scream, or try to talk the student out of the rage.
  - Do not try to make the student understand instructions.
  - While the student is going through the cycle of reactions, support others in the room and help ensure that their interpretations of the rage event are correct.

- *Phase 5. Post-Rage or Post-Meltdown.* After a rage event, the student may or may not remember the behavior or the triggering causes. This is a low point for the student because he or she has expended a great amount of energy and is left confused and often embarrassed. The student will now be tired, passive, headachy, and sometimes remorseful and apologetic. The student may be in need of sleep or may be ready to continue the day.

  What you can do to help during this phase of the cycle
  - Reassure the student that he or she is all right now.
  - Do not talk about consequences or punishments; they are not appropriate.
  - When the student is ready, help him or her put language to the event.
  - Help him or her plan what to do the next time a rage occurs, such as finding a sensory-friendly refuge (a safe place or room in which to rage), using words to get what he or she needs, and timing himself or herself out (that is, remaining in a safe place until able to calm down).
  - After the rage event has ended and the student is calm, take care of yourself. Relax, drink water, and remind yourself that it was not personal and that you did the best you could. Meanwhile, document your observations, hold debriefing conversations with a colleague, and listen to reflections made by anyone involved. Take note of any evident triggers, sensory influences, or other environmental characteristics that may be implicated in the rage. It is perfectly acceptable for you *not* to talk during the rage, but just be there with the student, without crowding.

IN SUMMARY

This chapter reviewed some of the special tactics that are effective in managing the behavior of students with neurological-based behavior (NBB). Emphasis was placed on understanding the affected students' worlds, accepting the students as fellow human beings struggling to meet personal needs, relating to those individuals on a personal basis, using positive mental images when teaching students, teaching self-control to students whose development is delayed, understanding the nature of

ADHD and managing its associated behaviors, understanding sensory processing disorder and managing its associated behaviors, and understanding rage and its cycles and what you can do to help during episodes of rage.

REFERENCES

Cook, P. 2004a. Behaviour, learning and teaching: Applied studies in FAS/FAE (Distance Education Curricula). Red River College, Winnipeg, MB, Canada.

Cook, P. 2004b. *Sensory integration dysfunction: A layperson's guide.* Booklet available from Paula Cook: pcook59@shaw.ca.

Cook, P. 2005. *Rage: A layperson's guide to what to do when someone begins to rage.* Booklet available from Paula Cook: pcook59@shaw.ca.

Cook, P., and Charles, C. 2008. NBB: The special challenges of neurological based behavior. In C. Charles, *Building classroom discipline* (9th edition, Chapter 3). Boston: Allyn & Bacon.

Covey, S. 2004. *The seven habits of highly effective people.* New York: Free Press.

Daly, T. 2004. *The ADHD solution for teachers: How to turn any disruptive child into your best student.* San Diego, CA: Smarty Pants Publications. (A CD is available [2006] that contains this material in abbreviated form.)

Davidson, H. 2002. *Just ask! A handbook for instructors of students being treated for mental disorders.* Calgary, AB, Canada: Detselig Enterprises.

DeAngelis, T. 2004. Children's mental health problems seen as "epidemic." *APA Monitor on Psychology, 35*(11), 38.

Finstad, M. 2006. ADD and ADHD coaching. www.spectrumcoaching.com/ADHD-coaching.html.

Glasser, W. 1998. *Choice theory in the classroom.* New York: HarperCollins.

Hall, P., and Hall, N. 2003. *Educating oppositional and defiant children.* Alexandria, VA: Association for Supervision and Curriculum Development.

Hingsburger, D. 2000. *First contact.* Eastman, Quebec: Diverse City Press.

Hingsburger, D. 2000. *Power tools.* Eastman, Quebec: Diverse City Press.

Kranowitz, C. 1998. *The out-of-sync child.* New York: Skylight Press.

McGregor, D. 1960. *The human side of enterprise.* New York: McGraw-Hill.

Mitchell, M. 2006. Problem behavior in the classroom: Dealing with children and sensory processing disorders at school. www.sensory-processing-disorder.com.

Morris, M. 2002. Just what is sensory integration? www.ideallives.com.

National Institute of Mental Health. 1999. Mental Health: A Report of the Surgeon General. www.surgeongeneral.gov/library/mentalhealth.

National Institute of Mental Health. 2005. Health Information Quick Links. www.nimh.nih.gov.

Papolos, D., and Papolos, J. 2002. *The bipolar child.* New York: Broadway Books.

Pickering, J. 2003, Summer. Discipline—Developing self-control. *Montessori Life.* (This article can be reviewed at the following website: www.shelton.org/montessori/discipline.html.)

Bibliography

Albert, L. 1996. *Cooperative discipline* (2nd edition). Circle Pines, MN: American Guidance Service.

Albert, L. 2003. *A teacher's guide to cooperative discipline.* Circle Pines, MN: American Guidance Service.

Ascher, C. 1991. School programs for African American males. ERIC Digests. ED334340. www.ericdigests.org.

Baldwin, R. 1998. Academic civility begins in the classroom. *Essays on Teaching Excellence,* 9(8). Professional and Organizational Development Network in Higher Education. www.clemson.edu/OTEI/newspdf/f986.pdf.

Baruth, L., and Manning, M. 1992. *Multicultural education of children and adolescents.* Boston: Allyn & Bacon.

Beegle, D. 2004. Quoted in *Breaking barriers: Poverty—The elephant in the room.* www.osba .org/hotopics/gap/poverty.htm.

Bempechat, J. 1992. Fostering high achievement in African American children: Home, school, and public policy influences. ERIC Document ED348464. www.eric.ed.gov.

Benard, B. 1997. Drawing forth resilience in all our youth. *Reclaiming Children and Youth,* 6(1), 29–32.

Bickart, T., Jablon, J., and Dodge, D. 2000. Building a classroom community. In *Building the primary classroom: A handbook for teacher educators* (Chapter 2). Beltsville, MD: Gryphon House.

Borba, M. 1999. *Parents do make a difference: How to raise kids with solid character, strong minds, and caring hearts.* San Francisco: Jossey-Bass.

Borba, M. 2001. *Building moral intelligence.* San Francisco: Jossey-Bass.

Borba, M. 2003. *No more misbehavin': 38 difficult behaviors and how to stop them.* San Francisco: Jossey-Bass.

Borba, M. 2004. *Don't give me that attitude! 24 rude, selfish, insensitive things kids do and how to stop them.* San Francisco: Jossey-Bass.

Borba, M. 2005. *Nobody likes me! Everybody hates me! The top 25 friendship problems and how to solve them.* San Francisco: Jossey-Bass.

Burgess, G., and Burgess, H. 1997. *The meaning of civility.* Conflict Research Consortium, University of Colorado, Boulder. www.colorado.edu/conflict/civility.htm.

Butterfield, R. 1994. Blueprints for Indian education: Improving mainstream schooling. ERIC Digests. ED372898. www.ericdigests.org.

Cajete, G. 1986. Science: A Native American perspective (A culturally-based science education curriculum). Ph.D. dissertation, International College/William Lyon University, San Diego, CA.

Canter, L., and Canter, M. 1976. *Assertive discipline: A take-charge approach for today's educator.* Seal Beach, CA: Lee Canter & Associates.

Carnegie, D. 1981. *How to win friends and influence people.* New York: Pocket Books.

Charles, C. 1974. *Teachers' petit Piaget.* Belmont, CA: Fearon.

Charles, C. 2000. *The synergetic classroom.* Boston: Allyn & Bacon.

Charles, C. 2008. *Building classroom discipline* (9th edition). Boston: Allyn & Bacon.

Chavkin, N., and Gonzalez, J. 2000. Mexican immigrant youth and resiliency: Research and promising programs. ERIC Digests. ED447990. www.ericdigests.org.

Cheng, L. 1996. Enhancing communication: Toward optimal language learning for limited English proficient students. *Language, Speech and Hearing Services in Schools, 28*(2), 347–354.

Coker, D. 1988. Asian students in the classroom. *Education and Society, 1*(3), 19–20.

Coloroso, B. 2002. *Kids are worth it! Giving your child the gift of inner discipline* (2nd edition). New York: Quill.

Coloroso, B. 2003. *The bully, the bullied, and the bystander: How parents and teachers can break the cycle of violence.* New York: HarperCollins.

Cook, P. 2004a. Behaviour, learning and teaching: Applied studies in FAS/FAE. Distance Education Curricula, Red River College, Winnipeg, MB, Canada.

Cook, P. 2004b. *Sensory integration dysfunction: A layperson's guide.* Booklet available from Paula Cook: pcook59@shaw.ca.

Cook, P. 2005. *Rage: A layperson's guide to what to do when someone begins to rage.* Booklet available from Paula Cook: pcook59@shaw.ca.

Cook, P., and Charles, C. 2008. NBB: The special challenges of neurological based behavior. In C. Charles, *Building classroom discipline* (9th edition, Chapter 3). Boston: Allyn & Bacon.

Cornett, C. 1983. What you should know about teaching and learning styles (Fastback no. 191). Bloomington, IN: Phi Delta Kappa Foundation.

Covey, S. 1989. *The seven habits of highly effective people.* New York: Simon & Schuster.

Cox, B., and Ramirez, M. 1981. Cognitive styles: Implications for multiethnic education. In J. Banks (ed.), *Education in the 80s: Multiethnic education* (pp. 61–71). Washington, DC: National Education Association.

Curwin, R. 1992. *Rediscovering hope: Our greatest teaching strategy.* Bloomington, IN: National Educational Service.

Curwin, R., and Mendler, A. 1988. *Discipline with dignity.* Alexandria, VA: Association for Supervision and Curriculum Development.

Curwin, R., and Mendler, A. 1997. *As tough as necessary. Countering violence, aggression, and hostility in our schools.* Alexandria, VA: Association for Supervision and Curriculum Development.

Curwin, R., and Mendler, A. 1999. *Discipline with dignity.* Alexandria, VA: Association for Supervision and Curriculum Development.

Daly, T. 2004. *The ADHD solution for teachers: How to turn any disruptive child into your best student.* San Diego, CA: Smarty Pants.

Davidson, H. 2002. *Just ask! A handbook for instructors of students being treated for mental disorders.* Calgary, AB, Canada: Detselig Enterprises.

DeAngelis, T. 2004. Children's mental health problems seen as "epidemic." *APA Monitor on Psychology, 35*(11), 38.

Diamond, M., and Hopson, J. 1998. *Magic trees of the mind: How to nurture your child's intelligence, creativity, and healthy emotions from birth through adolescence.* New York: Dutton.

Diller, D. 1999. Opening the dialogue: Using culture as a tool in teaching young African American children. *Reading Teacher, 52*(8), 820–858.

Dreikurs, R., and Cassel, P. 1995. *Discipline without tears* (2nd edition). New York: Penguin–NAL.

Dunn, R., Griggs, S., and Price, G. 1993. Learning styles of Mexican-American and Anglo-American elementary-school students. *Journal of Multicultural Counseling and Development, 21*(4), 237–247.

Education Trust. 2003. African American achievement. Washington, DC. www.edtrust.org.

Faircloth, S., and Tippeconnic, J. 2000. Issues in the education of American Indian and Alaska Native students with disabilities. ERIC Digests. EDO-RC-00-3. www .ericdigests.org.

Feng, J. 1994. Asian-American children: What teachers should know. ERIC Digests. EDO-PS-94-4. www.ericdigests.org.

Finstad, M. 2006. ADD and ADHD Coaching. www.spectrumcoaching.com/ADHD-coaching .html.

Ford, E. 1999. *Discipline for home and school, Book Two* (revised and expanded). Scottsdale, AZ: Brandt.

Ford, E. 2003. *Discipline for home and school, Book One* (3rd edition). Scottsdale, AZ: Brandt.

Ford, E. 2004. *Discipline for home and school, fundamentals.* Scottsdale, AZ: Brandt.

Ford, E. 2006a. A school discipline program that is radically different from other classroom management programs, traditional classroom discipline programs, or any school behavior management program. www.responsiblethinking.com.

Ford, E. 2006b. How the Responsible Thinking Process works. www.responsiblethinking.com.

Ford, E., and Venetis, G. 2006. Teaching respect using RTP. www.responsiblethinking.com.

Forni, P. 2002. *Choosing civility: The twenty-five rules of considerate conduct.* New York: St. Martin's Press.

Forni, P. 2006. The other side of civility. www.jhu.edu.

Foster, M. 1999. Teaching and learning in the contexts of African American English and culture. *Education and Urban Society, 31*(2), 177ff.

Ginott, H. 1965. *Between parent and child.* New York: Macmillan.

Ginott, H. 1967. *Between parent and teenager.* New York: Macmillan.

Ginott, H. 1971. *Teacher and child.* New York: Macmillan.

Glasser, W. 1965. *Reality therapy: A new approach to psychiatry.* New York: Harper & Row.

Glasser, W. 1969. *Schools without failure.* New York: Harper and Row.

Glasser, W. 1986. *Control theory in the classroom.* New York: HarperCollins.

Glasser, W. 1990. *The quality school: Managing students without coercion.* New York: Perennial Library.

Glasser, W. 1992. The quality school curriculum. *Phi Delta Kappan, 73*(9), 690–694.

Glasser, W. 1993. *The quality school teacher.* New York: Harper Perennial.

Glasser, W. 1998a. *Choice theory in the classroom.* New York: HarperCollins.

Glasser, W. 1998b. *The quality school: Managing students without coercion.* New York: HarperCollins.

Glasser, W. 1998c. *The quality school teacher.* New York: HarperCollins.

Glasser, W. 2001. *Every student can succeed.* Chatsworth, CA: William Glasser.

Glavac, M., 2005. Summary of major concepts covered by Harry K. Wong. *The Busy Educator's Newsletter.* www.glavac.com.

Goorian, B., and Brown, K. 2002. Trends and issues: School law. ERIC Clearinghouse on Educational Management. http://eric.uoregon.edu/trends_issues/law/index.html.

Gordon, T. 1970. *Parent effectiveness training: A tested new way to raise responsible children.* New York: New American Library.

Gordon, T. 1987. *T.E.T.: Teacher Effectiveness Training* (2nd edition). New York: David McKay.

Gordon, T. 1989. *Discipline that works: Promoting self-discipline in children.* New York: Random House.

Goularte, R. 2006. Creating Class Rules: A Beginning to Creating Community. www .readwritethink.org/lessons/lesson_view.asp?id=136.

Griggs, S., and Dunn, R. 1996. Hispanic-American students and learning style. ERIC Digests. ED393607. ERIC Clearinghouse on Elementary and Early Childhood Education, Urbana, IL.

Hall, P., and Hall, N. 2003. *Educating oppositional and defiant children*. Alexandria, VA: Association for Supervision and Curriculum Development.

Hargan, L. 2003. Teaching students of poverty. NCL Brief. www.ctlonline.org/ESEA/newsletter.html.

Hingsburger, D. 2000. *First contact*. Eastman, Quebec: Diverse City Press.

Hingsburger, D. 2000. *Power tools*. Eastman, Quebec: Diverse City Press.

Huang, G. 1993. Beyond culture: Communicating with Asian American children and families. ERIC Digests. ED366673. www.ericdigests.org.

Irvine, J., and Fraser, J. 1998. Warm demanders. *Education Week on the WEB*. www.edweek.org/ew/1998/35irvine.h17.

Johnson, D., Johnson, R., and Holubec, E. 1993. *Circles of learning: Cooperation in the classroom* (4th edition). Edina, MN: Interaction Book.

Johnson, D., Johnson, R., and Holubec, E. 2001. Cooperative learning. *The Cooperative Link: The Newsletter of The Cooperative Learning Institute, 16*(1).

Johnson, R., and Johnson, D. 1994. An overview of cooperative learning. In J. Thousand, A. Villa, and A. Nevin (Eds.), *Creativity and collaborative learning*. Baltimore: Brookes Press.

Johnson, R., and Johnson, D. 2006. The Cooperative Learning Center at the University of Minnesota. www.co-operation.org.

Jones, F. 1987. *Positive classroom discipline*. New York: McGraw-Hill.

Jones, F. 2001. *Fred Jones's tools for teaching*. Santa Cruz, CA: Fredric H. Jones & Associates.

Jones, F. 2003. Weaning the helpless handraisers: Part 3. Teaching to the physical modality. *Education World*. www.educationworld.com/a_curr/columnists/jones/jones005.shtml.

Jones, F. 2004. Beyond Say, See, Do teaching: Exploiting structured practice. *Education World*. www.educationworld.com/a_curr/columnists/jones/jones006.shtml.

Joyce, B., Weil, M., and Calhoun, E. 2003. *Models of teaching* (7th edition). Boston: Allyn & Bacon.

Kagan, S. 2002. What is win–win discipline? *Kagan Online Magazine, 1*(15). www.KaganOnline.com.

Kagan, S., Kyle, P., and Scott, S. 2004. *Win–win discipline*. San Clemente, CA: Kagan.

Kim, B. (Ed.). 1985. *Literacy and languages. The second yearbook of literacy and languages in Asia*. International Reading Associations special interest group. International Conference on Literacy and Languages, Seoul, South Korea, August 12–14, 1985.

Kohn, A. 1993. *Punished by rewards: The trouble with gold stars, incentive plans, A's, praise, and other bribes*. Boston: Houghton Mifflin.

Kohn, A. 1996. *Beyond discipline: From compliance to community*. Alexandria, VA: Association for Supervision and Curriculum Development.

Kohn, A. 1999. *The schools our children deserve: Moving beyond traditional classrooms and "tougher standards."* Boston: Houghton Mifflin.

Kohn, A. 2001. *Beyond discipline: From compliance to community*. Upper Saddle River, NJ: Merrill/Prentice-Hall.

Kounin, J. 1971. *Discipline and group management in classrooms*. New York: Holt, Rinehart & Winston. Reissued in 1977.

Kranowitz, C. 1998. *The out-of-sync child*. New York: Skylight Press.

Krovetz, M. 1999. *Fostering resiliency: Expecting all students to use their minds and hearts well*. Thousand Oaks, CA: Corwin Press.

Ladson-Billings, G. 2000. Fighting for our lives: Preparing teachers to teach African American students. *Journal of Teacher Education, 51*(3), 206–214.

Latinos in school: Some facts and findings. 2001. ERIC Digests. www.ericdigests.org.

Levine, M. 2002. *A mind at a time*. New York: Simon & Schuster.

Lockwood, A., and Secada, W. 2000. Transforming education for Hispanic youth: Exemplary practices, programs, and schools. U.S. Department of Education. www.ncela.gwu.edu/pubs/resource/hispanicyouth/ch6.htm.

Lucas, T., Henze, R., and Donato, R. 1990. Promoting the success of Latino language minority students. An exploratory study of six high schools. *Harvard Educational Review, 60,* 315–340.

Marshall, M. 1998. *Fostering social responsibility.* Bloomington, IN: Phi Delta Kappa.

Marshall, M. 2001a. *Discipline without stress, punishments, or rewards: How teachers and parents promote responsibility and learning.* Los Alamitos, CA: Piper Press.

Marshall, M. 2001b. *Promoting Responsibility & Learning: The Monthly Newsletter.* www.MarvinMarshall.com.

Marshall, M. 2003, July. Descartes' error. http://teachers.net/gazette/JUL03/marshall.html.

Marshall, M. 2005a. A letter worth reading. www.marvinmarshall.com/aletterworthreading.html.

Marshall, M. 2005b. A principal's experience. www.marvinmarshall.com/principal.htm.

Marshall, M. 2005c. Classroom meetings. www.disciplinewithoutstress.com/sample_chapters.html.

Marshall, M. 2005d. Collaboration for quality learning. www.disciplinewithoutstress.com/sample_chapters.html.

Marshall, M. 2005e. Promoting positivity, choice, and reflection. www.MarvinMarshall.com/promoting_positivity.htm.

Marshall, M. 2005f. Reducing perfectionism. www.disciplinewithoutstress.com/sample_chapters.html.

Marshall, M. 2005g. Samples of hierarchies for promoting learning. www.marvinmarshall.com/hierarchy.htm.

Marshall, M. 2006, June. *Promoting Learning and Responsibility,* 6(6). www.DisciplineWithoutStress.com.

Maslow, A. 1954. *Motivation and personality.* New York: Harper.

Matsuda, M. 1989. Working with Asian family members: Some communication strategies. *Topics in Language Disorders, 9*(3), 45–53.

McCollough, S. 2000. Teaching African American students. *Clearing House, 74*(1), 5–6.

McKinley, J. 2003. Leveling the playing field and raising African American students' achievement in twenty-nine urban classrooms. New Horizons for Learning. www.newhorizons.org.

McMillan, D., and Chavis, D. 1986. Sense of community: A definition and theory. *Journal of Community Psychology, 14*(1), 6–23.

Mendler, A., and Curwin, R. 1999. *Discipline with dignity for challenging youth.* Bloomington, IN: National Education Service.

Mitchell, M. 2005. Problem behavior in the classroom: Dealing with children and sensory processing disorders at school. www.sensory-processing-disorder.com/problem-behavior-in-the-classroom.html.

Morris, M. 2002. Just what is sensory integration? www.ideallives.com.

Morrish, R. 1997. *Secrets of discipline: 12 keys for raising responsible children.* Fonthill, Ontario, Canada: Woodstream.

Morrish, R. 2000. *With all due respect: Keys for building effective school discipline.* Fonthill, Ontario, Canada: Woodstream.

Morrish, R. 2003. *FlipTips.* Fonthill, Ontario, Canada: Woodstream.

National Center for Education Statistics. 2001a. Overview of public elementary and secondary schools and districts: School year 2001–02. http://nces.ed.gov/programs/quarterly/vol_5/5_2/q3_5.asp#top.

National Coalition of Advocates for Students. 1994. *Delivering on the promise: Positive practices for immigrant students.* Boston: Author.

National Education Association. 1975. Code of ethics of the education profession. www.nea.org/aboutnea/code.html.

National Institute of Mental Health. 1999. Mental Health: A Report of the Surgeon General. www.surgeongeneral.gov/library/mentalhealth.

National Institute of Mental Health. 2005. Health Information Quick Links. www.nimh.nih.gov.

Nelsen, J., and Lott, L. 2006. *Positive discipline in the classroom* (3rd edition). Rocklin, CA: Prima.

Papolos, D., and Papolos, J. 2002. *The bipolar child.* New York: Broadway Books.

Payne, R. 2001. *A framework for understanding poverty.* Highlands, TX: Aha! Process.

Payne, R. 2003. Quoted in D. Claitor (2003), Breaking through: Interview of Ruby Payne. www.hopemag.com/issues/2003/septOct/breakingThrough.pdf.

Payne, R. 2005. Making the transition out of generational poverty. The aha! Process. www.ahaprocess.com.

Pellegrino, K. 2005. The effects of poverty on teaching and learning. www.teachnology.com/tutorials/ teaching/poverty.

Philips, S. 1983. *The invisible culture.* New York: Longman.

Piaget, J. 1951. *Judgment and reasoning in the child.* London, England: Routledge & Kegan Paul.

Piaget, J. 2001. *The psychology of intelligence.* London, England: Routledge & Kegan Paul.

Pickering, J. 2003, Summer. Discipline—Developing self-control. *Montessori Life.* www.shelton.org/montessori/discipline.html.

Portland Public Schools. 2003. Supporting American Indian/Alaska Native Students in School. Title IX Indian Education Project Staff and Parent Board. http://comped.salkeiz.k12.or.us/indian-ed/ai-an.htm.

Poverty in America. 2006. U.S. Census Bureau. www.educationcoffeehouse.com/K12/poverty.htm.

Qualities of effective programs for immigrant adolescents with limited schooling. 1998. ERIC Digests. ED423667. www.ericdigests.org.

Raasch, C. 2003, August 25. Teachers, parents, outside world are key to classroom civility. *USA Today.* www.usatoday.com/news/opinion/columnist/raasch/2003-08-25-raasch_x.htm.

Redl, F., and Wattenberg, W. 1951. *Mental hygiene in teaching.* New York: Harcourt, Brace & World.

Schwartz, W. 2000. New trends in language education for Hispanic students. ERIC Digests. ED442913. www.ericdigests.org.

Schwartz, W. 2002. School practices for equitable discipline of African American students. ERIC Digests. ED455343. www.ericdigests.org.

Skinner, B. 1954. The science of learning and the art of teaching. *Harvard Educational Review, 24,* 86–97.

Solomon, D., Schaps, E., Watson, M., and Battistich, V. 1992. Creating caring school and classroom communities for all students. In R. A. Villa, J. S. Thousand, W. Stainback, and S. Stainback (Eds.), *Restructuring for caring and effective education: An administrative guide to creating heterogeneous schools.* Baltimore: Paul H. Brookes.

St. Germaine, R. 1995. Drop-out rates among American Indian and Alaska Native Students: Beyond cultural discontinuity. ERIC Digests. ED 388 492. www.ericdigests.org.

Storti, C. 1999. *Figuring foreigners out: A practical guide.* Yarmouth, ME: Intercultural Press.

Strategies for Teaching Minorities. 2004. www.as.wvu.edu/~equity/general.html.

Strategies for Teaching Science to African American Students. 2005. www.as.wvu.edu/~equity/african.html.

Swisher, K. 1991. American Indian/Alaskan Native learning styles: Research and practice. ERIC Digest. ED335175. www.ericdigests.org.

Traynor, P. 2005. *Got discipline? Research-based practices for managing student behavior.* Mansfield, OH: Bookmasters.

Trueba, H., and Cheng, L. 1993. *Myth or reality: Adaptive strategies of Asian Americans in California.* Bristol, PA: Falmer Press.

U.S. Department of Education. 1998. *Preventing bullying: A manual for schools and communities.* www.cde.ca.gov/spbranch/ssp/bullymanual.htm.

Walsh, C. 1991. Literacy and school success: Considerations for programming and instruction. In C. Walsh and H. Prashker (Eds.), *Literacy development for bilingual students.* Boston: New England Multifunctional Resource Center for Language and Culture Education.

Wierzbicka, A. 1991. Japanese key words and core cultural values. *Language in Society, 20*(3), 333–385.

Wong, H. 2001. Selection of tips for teachers. www.glavac.com/harrywong.htm.

Wong, H., and Wong, R. 2000a. The first five minutes are critical. *Gazette Article.* Teachers.net. http://teachers.net/gazette/NOV00/wong.html.

Wong, H., and Wong, R. 2000b. The problem is not discipline. *Gazette Article.* Teachers.net. http://teachers.net/gazette/SEP00/wong.html.

Wong, H., and Wong, R. 2000c. Your first day. *Gazette Article.* Teachers.net. http://teachers.net/gazette/JUN00/covera.html.

Wong, H., and Wong, R. 2002. How to start school successfully. *Gazette Article.* Teachers.net. http://teachers.net/gazette/AUG02/wong.html.

Wong, H., and Wong, R. 2004a. A well-oiled learning machine. *Gazette Article.* Teachers.net. http://teachers.net/wong/MAR04.

Wong, H., and Wong, R. 2004b. *The first days of school: How to be an effective teacher.* Mountain View, CA: Harry K. Wong.

Wong, H., and Wong, R. 2005. The first ten days of school. *Gazette Article.* Teachers.net. http://teachers.net/wong/JAN05.

Yong, F., and Ewing, N. 1992. A comparative study of the learning-style preferences among gifted African-American, Mexican-American and American born Chinese middle-grade students. *Roeper Review, 14*(3), 120–123.

Index